Cooking Light

FIVE ★ STAR

R E C I P E S

The Best of 10 Years

Cooking Light.

FIVE ★ STAR
RECIPES

The Best of 10 Years

Oxmoor
House®

COVER:

BLACKENED CHICKEN SALAD, *page 132*

PAGE 2:

SOUTHWESTERN TURKEY AND
BLACK BEAN SALAD, *page 131*

BACK COVER (*top to bottom*):

ITALIAN CREAM CAKE, *page 206*

HUCKLEBERRY COFFEE CAKE, *page 33*

CREAMY POTATO SALAD, *page 125*

GREEK SPAGHETTI WITH TOMATOES
AND FETA, *page 92*

MOCHA FUDGE PIE, *page 212*

Cooking Light®
Editor: Doug Crichton
Managing Editor: Nathalie Dearing
Senior Food Editor: Jill G. Melton, M.S., R.D.
Senior Editor: John Stark
Senior Editor, Projects: Ellen Templeton Carroll, M.S., R.D.
Food Editor: Mary S. Creel, M.S., R.D.
Assistant Food Editors: Cynthia Nicholson LaGrone,
    L. Alyson Moreland
Test Kitchens Director: Rebecca J. Pate
Test Kitchens Staff: Leigh Fran Jones, M. Kathleen Kanen,
    Kellie Gerber Kelley, John Kirkpatrick, Karen Mitchell Wilcher
Editorial Assistant: Michele Mann
Art Director: Susan Waldrip Dendy
Assistant Art Director: D. Austin Davis, Jr.
Senior Photographer: Howard L. Puckett
Photo Stylists: Cindy Manning Barr, Ashley Wyatt
Copy Chief: Tim W. Jackson
Copy Editors: Ritchey Halphen, Sherry S. Stokes
Production Coordinators: Hazel R. Eddins, Polly Pabor Linthicum

Oxmoor House, Inc.
Editor-in-Chief: Nancy Fitzpatrick Wyatt
Senior Foods Editor: Katherine M. Eakin
Senior Editor, Editorial Services: Olivia Kindig Wells
Art Director: James Boone

Cooking Light® **Five-Star Recipes**
Editor: Deborah Garrison Lowery
Assistant Foods Editor: Kathryn Matuszak, R.D.
Copy Editor: Keri Bradford Anderson
Associate Art Director: Cynthia R. Cooper
Senior Designer: Melissa Jones Clark
Editorial Assistant: Alison Rich Lewis
Director, Test Kitchens: Kathleen Royal Phillips
Assistant Director, Test Kitchens: Gayle Hays Sadler
Test Kitchens Home Economists: Susan Hall Bellows, Julie Christopher,
    Michele Brown Fuller, Natalie E. King, Elizabeth Tyler Luckett,
    Jan Moon, Iris Crawley O'Brien, Jan A. Smith
Senior Photographer: Jim Bathie
Photographer: Ralph Anderson
Senior Photo Stylist: Kay E. Clarke
Photo Stylist: Virginia R. Cravens
Additional Photography/Styling: Donna Creel, Tina Evans,
    Connie Formby, Bob Gager, Brit Huckabay, Lee Isaacs,
    Darryl L. Moland
Publishing Systems Administrator: Rick Tucker
Production and Distribution Director: Phillip Lee
Associate Production Manager: Theresa L. Beste
Production Assistant: Valerie Heard

CONTENTS

INTRODUCTION

Cooking Light RECIPES

APPENDIXES, GLOSSARY & INDEXES

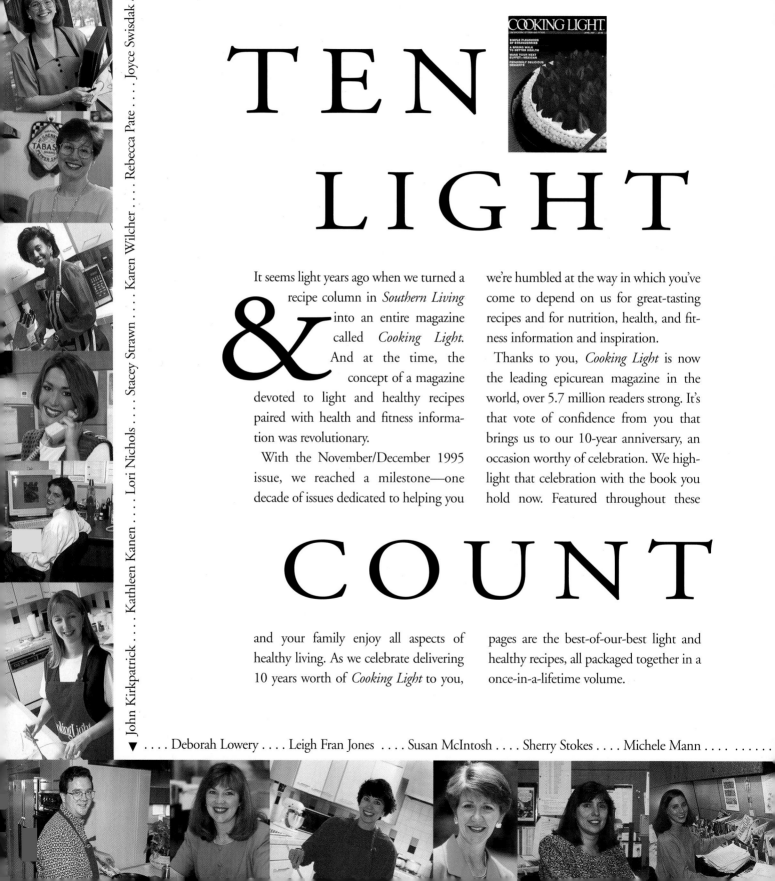

Melissa Aspell . . . . Alyson Moreland . . . . Austin Davis . . . . Doug Crichton . . . . Cynthia LaGrone . . . . John Stark . . .

Joyce Swisdak ▲ . . . . Rebecca Pate . . . . Karen Wilcher . . . . Stacey Strawn . . . . Lori Nichols . . . . Kathleen Kanen . . . . John Kirkpatrick . . . .

TEN

LIGHT

It seems light years ago when we turned a recipe column in *Southern Living* into an entire magazine called *Cooking Light.* And at the time, the concept of a magazine devoted to light and healthy recipes paired with health and fitness information was revolutionary.

With the November/December 1995 issue, we reached a milestone—one decade of issues dedicated to helping you

we're humbled at the way in which you've come to depend on us for great-tasting recipes and for nutrition, health, and fitness information and inspiration.

Thanks to you, *Cooking Light* is now the leading epicurean magazine in the world, over 5.7 million readers strong. It's that vote of confidence from you that brings us to our 10-year anniversary, an occasion worthy of celebration. We highlight that celebration with the book you hold now. Featured throughout these

COUNT

and your family enjoy all aspects of healthy living. As we celebrate delivering 10 years worth of *Cooking Light* to you,

pages are the best-of-our-best light and healthy recipes, all packaged together in a once-in-a-lifetime volume.

▼ . . . . Deborah Lowery . . . . Leigh Fran Jones . . . . Susan McIntosh . . . . Sherry Stokes . . . . Michele Mann . . . .

.. Nathalie Dearing .... Tim Jackson .... Elizabeth Taliaferro ....Katherine Eakin .... Carol Noe .... Mary Creel ▲

Lee Puckett .... Kellie Kelley .... Polly Linthicum .... Ritchey Halphen .... Telia Johnson .... John Davis .... Maya Metz ....

We're considering it a sort of scrapbook of great recipes, the building blocks that have made *Cooking Light* what it is today. As you cook your way through the book,

reference—inside the back cover. Our **Easy Menus chapter, step-by-step photographs** with recipes, **vegetable cooking chart**, and **pictorial glossary** will assist

YEARS

we hope you'll enjoy getting to know our staff, both present and past, and the recipes they love most. (Look for the staff favorites labeled **Editor's Choice**.)

And because we know that you're busier now than you were 10 years ago, we've built in some bonus features that will make your life easier. Look for our **95 quick and easy recipes** throughout the book. All are labeled and even printed in red in our **bonus index** for easy reference. And, as always, you'll find a **complete**

you, too. And don't forget to see **How to Lighten Up** on page 222. Here, we reveal our secrets for making any recipe healthier for you.

From all of us who've helped to shape *Cooking Light* into the celebration of healthy living it portrays today, we say thanks for a wonderful first 10 years.

ING

nutritional analysis of every recipe. Check out our **handy substitution charts** where they're easiest to find for quick

To subscribe to *Cooking Light*, call 1-800-336-0125.

.... Jill Melton .... Hazel Eddins .... Vanessa Johnson .... Ellen Carroll .... Cindy Barr .... Susan Dendy ▶

THE WINNER:
ITALIAN CREAM CAKE, page 206

THIRD PLACE *(a tie)*:
Huckleberry Coffee Cake, page 33,
and Creamy Potato Salad, page 125

FOURTH PLACE:
Greek Spaghetti With
Tomatoes and Feta, page 92

SECOND PLACE:
Mocha Fudge Pie,
page 212

Cooking Light's staff met for the taste-off.

THE ENVELOPE, PLEASE. . .

For years, we kept the names of our best recipes a secret. Not on purpose, of course. It's just that we found ourselves making mental notes of our favorite recipes in taste-testing sessions, or writing them on scraps of paper at our desks so we'd be sure to remember which were the best for our own personal use. We never thought of compiling a list—or of voting for our top five favorites—until now.

THE ULTIMATE CONTEST

Actually, someone came up with the idea in a meeting.

"Why don't we make each food staff member's favorite recipe and vote to see which ones are our top five?"

It was a challenge we couldn't resist. And when it was over, we all agreed that, indeed, we had singled out the cream of the crop.

"It's a good mix of our favorites," said Senior Food Editor Jill Melton. Represented among the 19 recipes were beef, poultry, meatless entrées, breads, sides, salads, and, naturally, desserts. We've noted each of these staff favorites throughout the book as an Editor's Choice recipe. Along with each recipe, you'll find a photograph of the staff member who selected it and a few  words about why it's his or her favorite—and maybe a tip or two. Or, if you don't want to search through the book, you can find a complete list of Editor's Choice recipes in the index on page 240.

AND THE WINNER IS...

Before we voted, we wondered, is it fair to compare potato salad with a decadent chocolate dessert? Just what parameters should we use to judge spaghetti against a three-layer cake? So we marked our ballots with these criteria in mind:

1. Does the recipe taste terrific in comparison to any similar recipe, light or not?

2. Would we make this recipe again and again in our own kitchens?

When our impartial tabulators announced the results, it was really no surprise. Italian Cream Cake...the winner by a landslide.

"You know, the issue with the Italian Cream Cake on the cover was our best seller of all time. People loved it," said Editor Doug Crichton. So it seems the staff and readers of *Cooking Light* agree.

We hope you will, too.

Tex-Mex Black Bean Dip,
page 12

APPETIZERS

Oh, go ahead and shock them. Even if your guests are into naughty noshing, the surprise will do them—and their health—some good. But maybe it's best if you don't say a word. They'll never know that the decadent cream puffs (filled with Chicken Salad) are really low-fat pastries. Or

& BEVERAGES

That, thanks to low-fat and nonfat sour cream, yogurt, mayo, and cream cheese, a spread of healthy appetizers can be more than celery sticks and seltzer. Even cool, creamy beverages get the green light again when you use nonfat frozen yogurt.

So which one to try first? We suggest Roasted Red Pepper Dip. Bet you'll make more than one trip to this dip.

ROASTED RED PEPPER DIP

To mix this dip in a matter of minutes, use a jar of roasted peppers instead of roasting your own. The commercial version isn't as flavorful, but it'll save you time.

3   large sweet red peppers
1   small clove garlic
½   cup nonfat sour cream
2   tablespoons chopped fresh basil
1   teaspoon anchovy paste
½   teaspoon lemon juice
¼   teaspoon freshly ground pepper

Cut peppers in half lengthwise; remove and discard seeds and membranes. Place peppers, skin side up, on a baking sheet; flatten with palm of hand. Broil 5½ inches from heat (with electric oven door partially opened) 15 to 20 minutes or until charred. Place peppers in ice water until cool; peel and discard skins.

Position knife blade in food processor bowl. Drop garlic through food chute with processor running; process 3 seconds or until garlic is minced. Add roasted pepper, sour cream, and remaining ingredients. Process until smooth. Serve with raw vegetables or toasted baguette slices. Yield: 1½ cups (serving size: 1 tablespoon).

Calories 10 (9% from fat) **Protein** 0.6g **Fat** 0.1g (sat 0.0g) **Carbohydrate** 1.7g **Fiber** 0.4g **Cholesterol** 0mg **Iron** 0.3mg **Sodium** 33mg **Calcium** 4mg

TEX-MEX BLACK BEAN DIP

QUICK & EASY

1   (15-ounce) can black beans, drained
1   teaspoon vegetable oil
½   cup chopped onion
2   cloves garlic, minced
½   cup diced tomato
⅓   cup mild picante sauce
½   teaspoon ground cumin
½   teaspoon chili powder
¼   cup (1 ounce) shredded reduced-fat Monterey Jack cheese
¼   cup chopped fresh cilantro
1   tablespoon fresh lime juice
Cilantro sprigs (optional)

Place beans in a bowl; partially mash until chunky. Set aside.

Heat oil in a medium nonstick skillet over medium heat. Add onion and garlic; sauté 4 minutes or until tender. Add beans, tomato, and next 3 ingredients; cook, stirring constantly, 5 minutes or until thickened. Remove from heat; add cheese, cilantro, and lime juice, stirring until cheese melts.

Garnish with cilantro sprigs, if desired. Serve warm or at room temperature with fat-free corn chips or flour tortilla chips. Yield: 1⅔ cups (serving size: 1 tablespoon).

Calories 21 (21% from fat) **Protein** 1.3g **Fat** 0.5g (sat 0.2g) **Carbohydrate** 3.1g **Fiber** 0.5g **Cholesterol** 1mg **Iron** 0.3mg **Sodium** 68mg **Calcium** 15mg

GULF COAST SHRIMP SPREAD

2   quarts water
1¼   pounds unpeeled medium-size fresh shrimp
1   large shallot, peeled and quartered
1¼   cups low-fat sour cream
1   tablespoon fresh lemon juice
½   teaspoon salt
½   teaspoon pepper
½   teaspoon grated lemon rind
¼   teaspoon hot sauce

Bring water to a boil in a large saucepan; add shrimp, and cook 3 to 5 minutes. Drain well; rinse with cold water, and let cool. Peel and devein shrimp; set aside.

Position knife blade in food processor bowl. Drop shallot through food chute with processor running; process 3 seconds or until shallot is finely chopped. Add shrimp to processor; pulse 10 times or until shrimp is finely chopped.

Combine shrimp mixture, sour cream, and remaining ingredients in a bowl; stir well. Cover and chill. Serve with bread or crackers. Yield: 3 cups (serving size: 1 tablespoon).

Calories 18 (45% from fat) **Protein** 1.4g **Fat** 0.9g (sat 0.5g) **Carbohydrate** 0.5g **Fiber** 0.0g **Cholesterol** 11mg **Iron** 0.2mg **Sodium** 36mg **Calcium** 10mg

SMOKY BABA GHANOUSH (EGGPLANT DIP)

QUICK & EASY

In the Mediterranean, it's tradition to dip pitas in this puree of eggplant and tahini. Tahini is a thick paste of ground sesame seeds and tastes a bit like peanut butter. Find it in large supermarkets or health food stores.

6   (6-inch) pita bread rounds, split in half horizontally
Vegetable cooking spray
2   (1-pound) eggplants, cut in half lengthwise
1   clove garlic
¼   cup tahini (sesame seed paste)
3   tablespoons fresh lemon juice
½   teaspoon salt
Dash of paprika

Cut each pita round into 4 wedges. Place wedges in a single layer on a baking sheet. Bake at 400° for 5 minutes or until crisp. Set aside.

Coat grill rack with cooking spray; place on grill over medium-hot coals (350° to 400°). Place eggplant, cut side up, on rack; grill, covered, 20 minutes or until very tender. Remove eggplant from grill; let cool slightly. Peel eggplant; set aside.

Position knife blade in food processor bowl. Drop garlic through food chute with processor running. Process 4 seconds or until garlic is finely chopped. Add grilled eggplant, tahini, lemon juice, and salt; process until smooth. Cover and chill; sprinkle with paprika. Serve with toasted pita chips. Yield: 12 appetizer servings (serving size: ¼ cup dip and 4 pita chips).

Calories 108 (29% from fat) **Protein** 3.5g **Fat** 3.5g (sat 0.5g) **Carbohydrate** 17.0g **Fiber** 2.0g **Cholesterol** 1mg **Iron** 1.4mg **Sodium** 214mg **Calcium** 65mg

CALIFORNIA QUESADILLAS

Fat-free flour tortillas help make this appetizer low in fat and calories. Find them in the refrigerated section of most supermarkets.

1½   cups peeled, seeded, and diced papaya
¼   cup chopped fresh cilantro
3   tablespoons diced purple onion
3   tablespoons fresh lime juice
1   cup (4 ounces) goat cheese, crumbled
¼   cup jarred roasted red peppers, drained and chopped
¼   cup nonfat cream cheese, softened
1   teaspoon seeded, minced jalapeño pepper
6   (8-inch) fat-free flour tortillas
Vegetable cooking spray

Combine first 4 ingredients; stir well. Cover and chill.

Combine goat cheese and next 3 ingredients in a bowl, and stir mixture well. Spread 2 tablespoons cheese mixture over each tortilla, and fold in half.

Coat a large nonstick skillet with cooking spray; place over medium heat until hot. Add 2 quesadillas, and cook 1 minute on each side or until browned. Remove quesadillas from skillet. Place on a baking sheet, and keep warm. Repeat procedure with remaining quesadillas. Cut each quesadilla in half crosswise; arrange halves and papaya mixture evenly on 6 plates. Serve warm. Yield: 6 appetizer servings (serving size: 2 quesadilla halves and ¼ cup papaya mixture).

Calories 183 (21% from fat) **Protein** 6.5g **Fat** 4.2g (sat 2.9g) **Carbohydrate** 30.1g **Fiber** 0.9g **Cholesterol** 18mg **Iron** 0.4mg **Sodium** 690mg **Calcium** 136mg

DIP STICKS

Try these crispy fat-free dippers.
Pita chips: Split pita rounds; cut each into 8 wedges. Place on a baking sheet; bake at 400° for 5 minutes.
Bagel chips: Cut bagels in half; cut each half horizontally into thin slices. Place on a baking sheet; bake at 350° for 5 minutes.
Tortilla chips: Cut each corn or flour tortilla into 8 wedges. Place on a baking sheet; bake at 350° for 10 minutes.

1. Fold each piece of phyllo in half lengthwise to form strips. Working with 1 strip at a time, spoon 1 tablespoon of the mushroom mixture at the base of strip.

2. Fold the right bottom corner of phyllo over mushroom mixture to form a triangle.

3. Keep folding phyllo strip back and forth into a triangle to the end of the strip.

CURRIED MUSHROOM TURNOVERS

Layers of phyllo crust help the savory filling in these turnovers stay hot longer than most appetizer fillings would—so you can save the warming tray for another appetizer.

Butter-flavored vegetable cooking spray

3½	cups minced fresh mushrooms
¾	cup minced shallots
2	tablespoons all-purpose flour
½	teaspoon curry powder
½	teaspoon salt
¼	teaspoon ground cumin
¼	teaspoon pepper
½	cup plain low-fat yogurt
2	tablespoons chopped fresh cilantro
14	sheets frozen phyllo pastry, thawed

Coat a large nonstick skillet with cooking spray; place over medium-high heat until hot. Add mushrooms and shallots; cook, stirring constantly, 11 minutes or until mixture appears dry. Combine flour and next 4 ingredients; add to mushroom mixture in skillet. Cook, stirring constantly, 3 minutes or until thickened. Remove from heat; stir in yogurt and cilantro.

Cut 1 phyllo sheet in half lengthwise (keeping remaining phyllo sheets covered). Lightly coat phyllo halves with cooking spray, and fold halves in half lengthwise to form strips. Working with 1 strip at a time, spoon 1 tablespoon mushroom mixture onto base of strip. Fold right bottom corner over mixture to form a triangle; keep folding back and forth into a triangle to end of strip. Repeat entire procedure with remaining phyllo sheets and mushroom mixture.

Place triangles, seam side down, on baking sheets. Lightly coat tops with cooking spray. Bake at 400° for 15 minutes or until golden. Serve immediately. Yield: 28 appetizers (serving size: 1 turnover).

Calories 43 (19% from fat) Protein 1.4g Fat 0.9g (sat 0.1g) Carbohydrate 7.3g Fiber 0.3g Cholesterol 0mg Iron 0.6mg Sodium 92mg Calcium 12mg

POTATO SKINS WITH CHEESE AND BACON

4	medium baking potatoes (about 2 pounds)

Vegetable cooking spray

4	slices turkey bacon
¾	cup (3 ounces) shredded reduced-fat sharp Cheddar cheese
¼	cup nonfat sour cream
1	tablespoon minced fresh chives

Bake potatoes at 425° for 1 hour or until done. Cool slightly. Cut each potato in half lengthwise, and scoop out potato pulp, leaving a ¼-inch-thick shell. Reserve pulp for another use.

Place potato shells on a baking sheet. Spray inside of shells with cooking spray. Bake at 425° for 8 minutes or until crisp; set aside.

Cook bacon in microwave according to package directions; cool slightly. Chop cooked bacon into small pieces, and set aside.

Sprinkle cheese evenly in potato shells. Bake at 425° for 5 minutes or until cheese melts. Sprinkle evenly with bacon. Dollop sour cream on potatoes; sprinkle with chives. Yield: 8 appetizer servings (serving size: 1 stuffed potato skin and 1½ teaspoons sour cream).

Calories 106 (29% from fat) **Protein** 6.4g
Fat 3.4g (sat 1.6g) **Carbohydrate** 12.7g
Fiber 1.1g **Cholesterol** 12mg **Iron** 0.9mg
Sodium 182mg **Calcium** 104mg

Potato Skins With Cheese and Bacon

STEP BY STEP

Cream Puff Pastry for
Chicken Salad-Filled Cream Puffs

1. Bring water and margarine to a boil. Add flour, salt, and pepper. Cook 1 minute, stirring until the mixture is smooth and pulls away from sides of the saucepan to form a ball.

2. Add egg whites and egg, one at a time, beating vigorously after each addition. The dough will separate slightly as the eggs are added. It will become smooth during beating and will hold its shape when it is lifted with a spoon.

3. Spoon the pastry into a pastry bag fitted with a ½-inch round tip. Pipe 30 (1½-inch) mounds onto a baking sheet coated with cooking spray.

4. Cool baked cream puffs on a wire rack. Then cut off the cream puff tops, and spoon in the desired filling.

CHICKEN SALAD-FILLED CREAM PUFFS

To save time, make the chicken salad in advance. It makes a good spread for sandwiches and a good filling for stuffed tomatoes, too.

Chicken Salad
1 cup all-purpose flour
¼ teaspoon salt
⅛ teaspoon ground red pepper
1 cup water
2 tablespoons margarine
2 egg whites
1 egg
Vegetable cooking spray

Prepare Chicken Salad, and chill.
Combine flour, salt, and pepper; set aside.

Combine water and margarine in a medium saucepan, and bring to a boil. Reduce heat to low; stir in flour mixture, and cook 1 minute, stirring well until mixture is smooth and pulls away from sides of pan. Remove from heat, and let cool 5 minutes.

Add egg whites and egg, one at a time, beating vigorously with a wooden spoon until smooth. Spoon mixture into a pastry bag fitted with a ½-inch round tip, and pipe 30 (1½-inch) mounds onto a baking sheet coated with cooking spray. Bake at 425° for 10 minutes. Reduce oven temperature to 350°, and bake 10 additional minutes; cool completely on a wire rack.

Cut tops off cream puffs; fill each cream puff with 1 tablespoon

Chicken Salad. Serve immediately.
Yield: 30 appetizers (serving size: 1
filled cream puff).

Calories 47 (33% from fat) Protein 3.6g
Fat 1.7g (sat 0.4g) Carbohydrate 4.0g
Fiber 0.2g Cholesterol 15mg Iron 0.4mg
Sodium 103mg Calcium 8mg

CHICKEN SALAD:

⅓   cup diced celery
¼   cup finely chopped green
    onions
¼   cup reduced-fat mayonnaise
3   tablespoons chopped fresh
    parsley
2   tablespoons plain nonfat
    yogurt
1   tablespoon fresh lemon juice
½   teaspoon salt
½   teaspoon dried basil
¼   teaspoon pepper
1   (2-ounce) jar diced
    pimiento, drained
1¾ cups chopped cooked
    chicken breasts (skinned
    before cooking and cooked
    without salt)

Combine all ingredients, stirring
well. Cover and chill. Yield: 2 cups
(serving size: 1 tablespoon).

Calories 20 (32% from fat) Protein 2.6g
Fat 0.7g (sat 0.2g) Carbohydrate 0.7g
Fiber 0.1g Cholesterol 7mg Iron 0.2mg
Sodium 65mg Calcium 5mg

SPICY CHICKEN BITES WITH CUCUMBER DIP

Cucumber Dip

1   pound skinned, boned
    chicken breasts, cut into
    1-inch pieces
¼   cup minced onion
1   large clove garlic, minced
1   egg, lightly beaten
⅓   cup fine, dry breadcrumbs
1   teaspoon ground ginger
½   teaspoon ground cumin
½   teaspoon curry powder
½   teaspoon salt
½   teaspoon ground red pepper
¼   teaspoon black pepper
3   tablespoons all-purpose
    flour
2   teaspoons vegetable oil,
    divided
¼   teaspoon paprika, divided

Prepare Cucumber Dip, and chill.
Position knife blade in food
processor bowl. Add half of chicken
pieces, and pulse 6 times or until
chicken is smooth. Spoon chicken
into a large bowl. Repeat procedure
with remaining half of chicken
pieces, and add to pureed chicken in
bowl. Stir in onion, garlic, and egg.
Combine breadcrumbs and next 6
ingredients; add to chicken mixture,
stirring well. Shape mixture into 40
(1-inch) balls.
Dredge chicken balls in flour.
Place half of chicken balls in an
11- x 7- x 1½-inch baking dish.
Microwave at MEDIUM-HIGH
(70% power) 6 minutes, stirring
every 2 minutes. Repeat with

remaining chicken balls. (Micro-
waving the chicken balls before
sautéing helps the soft chicken mixture hold its shape when cooked in
the skillet.)
Combine 1 teaspoon oil and ⅛
teaspoon paprika in a large skillet;
place over medium heat until hot.
Add 20 chicken balls, and cook 10
minutes or until done, stirring occasionally. Remove from skillet; set
aside, and keep warm. Repeat procedure with remaining oil, paprika,
and chicken balls. Serve warm with
Cucumber Dip. Yield: 40 appetizer
servings (serving size: 1 chicken ball
and 1½ teaspoons dip).

Calories 27 (23% from fat) Protein 3.3g
Fat 0.7g (sat 0.2g) Carbohydrate 1.8g
Fiber 0.1g Cholesterol 12mg Iron 0.2mg
Sodium 50mg Calcium 16mg

CUCUMBER DIP:

1   cup peeled, seeded, and
    shredded cucumber
1   cup plain low-fat yogurt
1   teaspoon dried dillweed
½   teaspoon lemon juice

Press shredded cucumber between
paper towels to remove excess moisture. Let stand 15 minutes, pressing
paper towels down occasionally.
Combine cucumber, yogurt, dillweed, and lemon juice in a small
bowl. Cover and chill. Yield: 1⅓
cups (serving size: 1 tablespoon).

Calories 9 (30% from fat) Protein 0.6g
Fat 0.3g (sat 0.1g) Carbohydrate 0.9g
Fiber 0.0g Cholesterol 0mg Iron 0.0mg
Sodium 9mg Calcium 21mg

SHRIMP-STUFFED ENDIVE

Back in 1990, we featured an Atlanta host who packs a picnic basket to serve friends at a pops concert in the park. This recipe was a favorite of hers because it's easy to make ahead and then carry along. It's even easier if you buy the shrimp cooked and peeled. You'll need only ¼ pound.

3	cups water
½	pound unpeeled medium-size fresh shrimp
⅓	cup light process cream cheese
1	tablespoon chili sauce
½	teaspoon sugar
½	teaspoon lemon juice
¼	teaspoon salt
2	drops hot sauce
⅓	cup seeded, diced cucumber
1	tablespoon thinly sliced green onions
1	(8-ounce) can water chestnuts, drained and finely chopped
32	Belgian endive leaves (about 4 large heads)

Bring water to a boil in a medium saucepan; add shrimp. Cook 3 to 5 minutes or until shrimp turn pink. Drain well, and rinse with cold water. Peel, devein, and chop shrimp. Set aside.

Combine cream cheese and next 5 ingredients in a medium bowl; beat at medium speed of an electric mixer until smooth. Add shrimp, cucumber, green onions, and water chestnuts; stir. Cover and chill.

To serve, spoon 1 tablespoon shrimp mixture into each endive leaf. Yield: 32 appetizers (serving size: 1 shrimp-stuffed endive leaf).

Calories 13 (28% from fat) Protein 1.1g Fat 0.4g (sat 0.3g) Carbohydrate 1.2g Fiber 0.0g Cholesterol 8mg Iron 0.2mg Sodium 47mg Calcium 5mg

HONEY MUSTARD-GLAZED MEATBALLS

¼	cup honey
2	tablespoons low-sodium soy sauce
1	tablespoon Dijon mustard
½	teaspoon grated lemon rind
1	tablespoon fresh lemon juice
	Vegetable cooking spray
2	teaspoons vegetable oil
1	cup finely chopped onion
1	cup finely chopped green pepper
2	cloves garlic, minced
1½	pounds freshly ground raw chicken thighs
¾	cup fine, dry breadcrumbs
½	cup coarsely shredded zucchini
½	teaspoon salt
½	teaspoon grated lemon rind
¼	teaspoon pepper
2	teaspoons fresh lemon juice
2	teaspoons Dijon mustard
1	teaspoon low-sodium soy sauce

Combine honey, 2 tablespoons soy sauce, 1 tablespoon mustard, ½ teaspoon lemon rind, and 1 tablespoon lemon juice. Stir mixture well with a wire whisk, and set aside.

Coat a large nonstick skillet with cooking spray; add oil. Place over medium heat until hot. Add onion, green pepper, and garlic; sauté 3 minutes or until vegetables are tender. Let cool.

Combine onion mixture, chicken, and remaining 8 ingredients in a bowl; stir well. Shape into 48 (1¼-inch) balls.

Coat skillet with cooking spray; place over medium heat until hot. Add half of meatballs; cook 20 minutes or until browned, stirring often. Remove from skillet, and keep warm. Repeat procedure with remaining meatballs. Return cooked meatballs to skillet. Pour reserved honey mixture over meatballs; cook, stirring constantly, 3 minutes or until thickened. Yield: 4 dozen (serving size: 1 meatball).

Calories 35 (26% from fat) Protein 3.2g Fat 1.0g (sat 0.2g) Carbohydrate 3.3g Fiber 0.2g Cholesterol 11mg Iron 0.3mg Sodium 86mg Calcium 7mg

CARAMBOLA COOLER

QUICK & EASY

A carambola is a tropical star-shaped fruit that's in season from September to March. The sweetest varieties have thick fleshy ribs.

1	pound carambola, quartered
⅓	cup sugar
¾	cup club soda, chilled
2	(¼-inch-thick) slices carambola (optional)

Position knife blade in food processor bowl; place carambola and sugar in processor bowl, and process 1 minute or until mixture is smooth. Strain mixture through a sieve into a bowl, reserving 1¼ cups juice; cover and chill. Discard solids.

Add club soda to carambola juice; stir gently. Pour over ice. Garnish with carambola slices, if desired. Serve immediately. Yield: 2 cups (serving size: ⅔ cup).

Calories 136 (3% from fat) **Protein** 0.8g **Fat** 0.5g (sat 0.0g) **Carbohydrate** 34.0g **Fiber** 1.7g **Cholesterol** 0mg **Iron** 0.4mg **Sodium** 15mg **Calcium** 9mg

Sparkling Cranberry Blush

SPARKLING CRANBERRY BLUSH

QUICK & EASY

Remember this recipe from the wedding reception story we ran in April 1995? It's too easy and delicious to save for just weddings.

3	cups cold water
2	(48-ounce) bottles cranberry juice cocktail, chilled
2	(6-ounce) cans frozen lemonade concentrate, thawed and undiluted
2	(750-milliliter) bottles brut champagne, chilled

Combine first 3 ingredients in a punch bowl, and stir well. Add chilled champagne; stir gently. Serve immediately. Yield: 6 quarts (serving size: ¾ cup).

Calories 104 (0% from fat) **Protein** 0.2g **Fat** 0.1g (sat 0.0g) **Carbohydrate** 18.2g **Fiber** 0.0g **Cholesterol** 0mg **Iron** 0.4mg **Sodium** 6mg **Calcium** 5mg

POINSETTIA SIPPER

2	cups cranberry juice cocktail
2	cups apple juice
½	cup sugar
2	tablespoons unsweetened orange juice
3	whole cloves
2	(3-inch) cinnamon sticks
2	cups water

Orange rind curls (optional)

Combine first 7 ingredients in a saucepan, stirring until sugar dissolves. Bring to a simmer; cover and cook 30 minutes. Remove cloves and cinnamon sticks from pan with a slotted spoon. Serve warm or chilled. Garnish with orange rind curls, if desired. Yield: 6 cups (serving size: ¾ cup).

Calories 117 (1% from fat) Protein 0.1g
Fat 0.1g (sat 0.0g) Carbohydrate 29.8g
Fiber 0.1g Cholesterol 0mg Iron 0.3mg
Sodium 5mg Calcium 7mg

OLD-FASHIONED LEMONADE

To make decorative lemon ice cubes, place a lemon twist inside each ice cube before freezing.

1¼	cups fresh lemon juice
¾	cup sugar
4¼	cups cold water

Lemon slices

Combine lemon juice and sugar in a large pitcher; stir until sugar dissolves. Add water and lemon slices; stir well, and chill. Serve lemonade over ice. Yield: 1½ quarts (serving size: 1 cup).

Calories 109 (0% from fat) Protein 0.2g
Fat 0.0g (sat 0.0g) Carbohydrate 29.4g
Fiber 0.0g Cholesterol 0mg Iron 0.0mg
Sodium 1mg Calcium 4mg

MOCK SANGRÍA

For an icy refresher, freeze the sangría; then let it stand at room temperature about an hour or until it's slushy.

1	(¾-pound) bunch seedless green grapes, separated into small clusters
2	limes, each cut into 8 wedges
1	medium-size orange, cut into 8 wedges
5	cups unsweetened white grape juice, chilled
½	cup lime juice, chilled
1	(33.8-ounce) bottle club soda, chilled
1	(32-ounce) bottle apple-cherry juice, chilled

Arrange first 3 ingredients in a single layer in a shallow pan; cover and freeze at least 3 hours.

Combine white grape juice and remaining 3 ingredients in a large punch bowl; stir well. Add frozen fruit. Serve immediately. Yield: 3½ quarts (serving size: 1 cup).

Calories 87 (1% from fat) Protein 0.2g
Fat 0.1g (sat 0.1g) Carbohydrate 22.4g
Fiber 0.4g Cholesterol 0mg Iron 0.3mg
Sodium 19mg Calcium 19mg

CITRUS SUNSHINE SODAS

3	cups Citrus Ice Milk
¼	cup frozen orange juice concentrate, thawed and undiluted
1	(8-ounce) can unsweetened crushed pineapple, undrained
4	cups lemon-lime carbonated beverage, chilled and divided

Prepare Citrus Ice Milk; freeze. Combine juice concentrate and pineapple in container of an electric blender; cover and process until smooth. To serve, spoon 3 tablespoons juice mixture into each of 6 tall glasses. Spoon ½ cup Citrus Ice Milk into each glass. Add ⅔ cup carbonated beverage to each glass. Serve immediately. Yield: 6 servings.

Calories 212 (2% from fat) Protein 37.1g
Fat 0.4g (sat 0.2g) Carbohydrate 39.7g
Fiber 0.5g Cholesterol 2mg Iron 0.6mg
Sodium 72mg Calcium 113mg

CITRUS ICE MILK:

¾	cup sugar
1	(4-ounce) carton fat-free egg substitute
2	teaspoons grated orange rind
1	teaspoon grated lemon rind
1¼	cups orange juice
¼	cup fresh lemon juice
1	cup evaporated skimmed milk
½	cup 2% low-fat milk

Combine sugar and egg substitute in a large bowl. Beat at medium speed of an electric mixer 3 minutes or until sugar is dissolved. Add orange rind, lemon rind, orange juice, and lemon juice; beat until blended. Stir in milks.

Pour mixture into freezer container of a 2-quart hand-turned or electric freezer; freeze according to manufacturer's instructions. Spoon into a freezer-safe container; cover mixture, and freeze at least 1 hour. Yield: 5 cups (serving size: ½ cup).

Calories 105 (3% from fat) **Protein** 3.7g **Fat** 0.3g (sat 0.2g) **Carbohydrate** 22.7g **Fiber** 0.1g **Cholesterol** 2mg **Iron** 0.3mg **Sodium** 53mg **Calcium** 97mg

FRESH CITRUS COOLER

1	cup fresh orange juice
½	cup fresh lemon juice
½	cup fresh lime juice
⅓	cup sugar
1	cup lime-flavored sparkling water, chilled

Lime wedges (optional)

Combine orange juice, lemon juice, lime juice, and sugar in a pitcher; stir mixture until sugar dissolves. Add chilled sparkling water, and stir well. Serve immediately over ice. Garnish with lime wedges, if desired. Yield: 3 cups (serving size: 1 cup).

Calories 144 (1% from fat) **Protein** 0.9g **Fat** 0.1g (sat 0.0g) **Carbohydrate** 38.1g **Fiber** 0.2g **Cholesterol** 0mg **Iron** 0.1mg **Sodium** 18mg **Calcium** 18mg

GINGERED WATERMELON SPRITZER

Grenadine, a red syrup made with pomegranates, adds sweetness and color to this fruity spritzer. Check the label to select an alcoholic or non-alcoholic syrup.

¼	cup peeled, grated gingerroot
2	cups seeded, cubed watermelon (about 1¼ pounds)
3	tablespoons frozen orange juice concentrate, thawed and undiluted
1	tablespoon fresh lemon juice
1	tablespoon grenadine syrup
2	cups ginger ale, chilled

Watermelon wedges (optional)

Place gingerroot on an 8-inch cheesecloth square. Bring cheesecloth edges together at top; hold securely. Squeeze cheesecloth bag by hand over a small bowl to extract juice; reserve 1 tablespoon juice. Discard grated gingerroot.

Combine reserved 1 tablespoon gingerroot juice, cubed watermelon, juice concentrate, lemon juice, and grenadine in container of an electric blender; cover and process until smooth. Pour into a pitcher; stir in ginger ale. Serve over ice; garnish with watermelon wedges, if desired. Yield: 4 cups (serving size: 1 cup).

Calories 102 (4% from fat) **Protein** 1.1g **Fat** 0.5g (sat 0.2g) **Carbohydrate** 25.3g **Fiber** 0.7g **Cholesterol** 0mg **Iron** 0.3mg **Sodium** 11mg **Calcium** 14mg

TECHNIQUE

For Grating Gingerroot

1. Carefully peel away skin from the knobby root. Then shred the peeled root, using a sharp grater.

2. Place grated gingerroot in the center of an 8-inch cheesecloth square, and bring all the edges together.

3. Squeeze grated gingerroot over a small bowl to extract juice. Discard the shredded gingerroot pulp.

Banana-Orange Daiquiri

BANANA-ORANGE DAIQUIRI

QUICK & EASY

1½ cups sliced banana
½ cup light rum
½ cup bottled sweet-and-sour cocktail mix
¼ cup frozen orange juice concentrate, thawed and undiluted
30 ice cubes
Orange slices (optional)

Combine banana, rum, cocktail mix, and orange juice concentrate in container of an electric blender; cover and process until smooth. With blender running, add ice cubes, one at a time, and process until smooth. Serve immediately. Garnish each serving with an orange slice, if desired. Yield: 5 cups (serving size: 1 cup).

Calories 154 (1% from fat) **Protein** 0.8g **Fat** 0.2g (sat 0.1g) **Carbohydrate** 20.6g **Fiber** 1.4g **Cholesterol** 0mg **Iron** 0.2mg **Sodium** 11mg **Calcium** 7mg

PIÑA COLADA

QUICK & EASY

1½ cups unsweetened pineapple juice, chilled
¼ cup powdered sugar
1 tablespoon lime juice
¾ teaspoon coconut flavoring
½ teaspoon rum flavoring
1 (20-ounce) can unsweetened pineapple chunks, undrained
1 (8-ounce) carton pineapple low-fat yogurt
10 ice cubes

Combine all ingredients in container of an electric blender; cover and process until smooth. Serve immediately. Yield: 6 cups (serving size: 1 cup).

Calories 151 (3% from fat) **Protein** 1.8g **Fat** 0.5g (sat 0.3g) **Carbohydrate** 34.8g **Fiber** 0.1g **Cholesterol** 2mg **Iron** 0.5mg **Sodium** 22mg **Calcium** 75mg

CINNAMON CANDY PUNCH

To save time, make the cinnamon mixture the day before. Then all you have to do is combine it with the pineapple juice and the ginger ale before serving.

1 cup water
½ cup sugar
¼ cup plus 2 tablespoons cinnamon decorator candies
2 (46-ounce) cans unsweetened pineapple juice, chilled
8 cups raspberry-flavored ginger ale, chilled

Combine first 3 ingredients in a small saucepan; bring to a boil. Reduce heat, and simmer, uncovered, 5 minutes or until candies melt, stirring occasionally. Cool completely.

Combine cinnamon mixture and juice in a large punch bowl; stir well. Add ginger ale, stirring gently. Pour punch into glasses, and serve immediately. Yield: 5½ quarts (serving size: 1 cup).

Calories 125 (0% from fat) **Protein** 0.4g **Fat** 0.1g (sat 0.0g) **Carbohydrate** 32.0g **Fiber** 0.1g **Cholesterol** 0mg **Iron** 0.3mg **Sodium** 6mg **Calcium** 20mg

PINEAPPLE-APRICOT COOLER

1½   cups ice cubes
1   cup apricot nectar, chilled
⅓   cup plain low-fat yogurt
¼   cup frozen pineapple juice
      concentrate, thawed and
      undiluted
1   tablespoon sugar
¼   teaspoon almond extract
1   (8-ounce) can unsweetened
      crushed pineapple,
      undrained and chilled

Combine all ingredients in container of an electric blender; cover and process until smooth, stopping once to scrape down sides. Pour into 4 glasses. Serve immediately. Yield: 4 cups (serving size: 1 cup).

Calories 126 (3% from fat) Protein 1.7g Fat 0.4g (sat 0.2g) Carbohydrate 30.3g Fiber 0.9g Cholesterol 1mg Iron 0.6mg Sodium 16mg Calcium 54mg

CREAMY RASPBERRY SIPPER

1¼   cups fresh raspberries
1¼   cups unsweetened white
      grape juice
1½   cups raspberry sherbet
¼   cup water
1   tablespoon lemon juice
10   ice cubes
Fresh mint sprigs (optional)

Combine raspberries and grape juice in container of an electric blender; cover and process until smooth, stopping once to scrape down sides. Strain mixture through several layers of dampened cheesecloth, reserving liquid and discarding solids.

Combine reserved liquid, sherbet, water, and lemon juice in blender container; cover and process until smooth. Add ice cubes; cover and process until frothy. Serve immediately. Garnish with fresh mint sprigs, if desired. Yield: 4 cups (serving size: 1 cup).

Calories 151 (5% from fat) Protein 1.4g Fat 0.9g (sat 0.0g) Carbohydrate 35.9g Fiber 2.9g Cholesterol 0mg Iron 0.4mg Sodium 53mg Calcium 46mg

COFFEE-KAHLÚA PUNCH

8¼   cups hot strongly brewed
      coffee
⅓   cup sugar
4   cups skim milk
1   tablespoon vanilla extract
1¼   cups Kahlúa or other
      coffee-flavored liqueur
5   cups vanilla nonfat ice
      cream, softened
1   (1-ounce) square semisweet
      chocolate, coarsely grated

Combine coffee and sugar, stirring until sugar dissolves. Stir in milk and vanilla; cover and chill. Combine chilled coffee mixture and Kahlúa in a punch bowl; stir well. Add ice cream, a few tablespoons at a time, stirring until ice cream melts. Sprinkle with chocolate. Yield: 4½ quarts (serving size: 1 cup).

Calories 150 (13% from fat) Protein 3.4g Fat 2.2g (sat 1.4g) Carbohydrate 21.1g Fiber 0.0g Cholesterol 6mg Iron 0.6mg Sodium 62mg Calcium 121mg

ICED VANILLA COFFEE

We prefer hazelnut-flavored coffee, but any flavor would be delicious in this sweet drink.

8   cups hot brewed hazelnut-
      flavored coffee
½   cup sugar
1   tablespoon vanilla extract
2   cups skim milk
⅔   cup vanilla low-fat frozen
      yogurt, softened

Combine first 3 ingredients, stirring until sugar dissolves. Stir in milk; cover and chill. To serve, pour 1 cup coffee mixture into each glass, and top with 1 tablespoon low-fat frozen yogurt. Yield: 10 cups (serving size: 1 cup).

Calories 70 (3% from fat) Protein 2.0g Fat 0.2g (sat 0.2g) Carbohydrate 14.7g Fiber 0.0g Cholesterol 2mg Iron 0.8mg Sodium 32mg Calcium 70mg

COFFEE ROYALE

1¼ cups 1% low-fat milk
1 tablespoon sugar
¼ teaspoon ground cinnamon
2¾ cups hot strongly brewed coffee
½ cup amaretto (almond-flavored liqueur)
6 (3-inch) cinnamon sticks (optional)

Combine first 3 ingredients in a medium saucepan; stir well. Place over medium heat, and cook 2 minutes or until sugar dissolves. Remove from heat; stir in coffee and amaretto. Pour into mugs; garnish with cinnamon sticks, if desired. Yield: 4½ cups (serving size: ¾ cup).

Nonalcoholic version: Omit amaretto; increase coffee to 3¼ cups.

Calories 96 (6% from fat) **Protein** 1.8g **Fat** 0.6g (sat 0.4g) **Carbohydrate** 10.9g **Fiber** 0.0g **Cholesterol** 2mg **Iron** 0.5mg **Sodium** 28mg **Calcium** 66mg

MULLED PEAR PUNCH

2 quarts unsweetened pear juice
1½ quarts pear nectar
¼ teaspoon freshly ground pepper
12 whole cloves
12 whole allspice
6 (3-inch) sticks cinnamon

Combine all ingredients in a Dutch oven; bring to a simmer.

Remove from heat, and let stand, covered, 1 hour. Strain mixture; discard spices. Pour into mugs. Yield: 3½ quarts (serving size: 1 cup).

Calories 120 (2% from fat) **Protein** 0.3g **Fat** 0.2g (sat 0.0g) **Carbohydrate** 29.4g **Fiber** 0.3g **Cholesterol** 0mg **Iron** 0.1mg **Sodium** 8mg **Calcium** 3mg

SPICED TEA MIX

QUICK & EASY

½ cup sugar
½ cup instant orange-flavored breakfast drink mix
¼ cup plus 2 tablespoons instant tea
¾ teaspoon ground cinnamon
½ teaspoon ground cloves
½ teaspoon ground allspice

Combine all ingredients, stirring well. Store mixture in an airtight container. To serve, spoon 1 tablespoon tea mix into a cup. Add ¾ cup boiling water; stir well. Yield: 1¼ cups mix (analysis per 1 tablespoon mix).

Calories 57 (0% from fat) **Protein** 0.1g **Fat** 0.0g (sat 0.0g) **Carbohydrate** 14.4g **Fiber** 0.1g **Cholesterol** 0mg **Iron** 0.1mg **Sodium** 2mg **Calcium** 18mg

RED ZINGER AND APPLE TEA

QUICK & EASY

1 quart unsweetened apple juice
4 red zinger tea bags
4 slices dried apple
4 whole cloves
1 tablespoon golden raisins
1 tablespoon lemon juice

Place apple juice in a medium saucepan; bring to a boil. Add tea bags and next 3 ingredients. Cover, reduce heat, and simmer 10 minutes. Pour mixture through a wire-mesh strainer into a pitcher; press with back of spoon against sides of strainer to squeeze out juice. Discard solids remaining in strainer. Stir in lemon juice, and serve immediately. Yield: 4 cups (serving size: 1 cup).

Calories 117 (2% from fat) **Protein** 0.1g **Fat** 0.2g (sat 0.1g) **Carbohydrate** 29.3g **Fiber** 0.5g **Cholesterol** 0mg **Iron** 0.9mg **Sodium** 7mg **Calcium** 18mg

Cheese Breadsticks,
page 36

We made a believer out of Willard Scott in just one bite. When he tasted our Ham and Cheese Biscuits, he had to agree that low-fat biscuits really can taste great. And so can low-fat coffee cakes, muffins, pancakes, and even ooey, gooey pull-apart breads like Hawaiian Bubble Bread. The

BREADS

secret to making them low-fat is really no secret at all. We just use low-fat and nonfat buttermilk and yogurt, margarine instead of butter, and less vegetable oil. We also use vegetable cooking spray to coat our bread pans.

Want another tip? All of the recipes are great, but if you bake only one, make it Blueberry-Yogurt Muffins. It's an all-time reader favorite.

"Willard Scott once told me that he refused to eat light biscuits because they just didn't taste as good. We both love ham, so I convinced him to try these biscuits when I gave him a basketful as he was headed for the airport. He liked them almost as much as I do. They aren't pretty—no drop biscuit is—but you really can taste the ham and cheese in every bite."

——Deborah Garrison Lowery,
former Executive Editor

HAM AND CHEESE BISCUITS

QUICK & EASY

Vegetable cooking spray
1½ cups chopped low-sodium 96% fat-free ham (about ½ pound)
2 cups all-purpose flour
2 teaspoons baking powder
1 cup (4 ounces) shredded extra-sharp Cheddar cheese
Dash of ground red pepper
1 cup 1% low-fat milk

Coat a medium nonstick skillet with cooking spray; place over medium heat until hot. Add ham; sauté 3 minutes. Combine ham, flour, and next 3 ingredients in a bowl. Add milk, stirring just until dry ingredients are moistened.

Drop biscuit batter by heaping tablespoonfuls onto a baking sheet coated with cooking spray. Bake at 400° for 22 minutes. Yield: 1 dozen (serving size: 1 biscuit).

Calories 141 (29% from fat) **Protein** 8.4g **Fat** 4.6g (sat 2.5g) **Carbohydrate** 16.2g **Fiber** 0.5g **Cholesterol** 20mg **Iron** 1.0mg **Sodium** 265mg **Calcium** 128mg

BUTTERMILK BISCUITS

QUICK & EASY

2 cups all-purpose flour
2 teaspoons baking powder
¼ teaspoon baking soda
¼ teaspoon salt
3 tablespoons plus 1 teaspoon chilled stick margarine, cut into small pieces
¾ cup 1% low-fat buttermilk

Combine first 4 ingredients in a bowl; cut in chilled margarine with a pastry blender until mixture resembles coarse meal. Add buttermilk, stirring just until dry ingredients are moistened.

Turn dough out onto a floured surface; knead 4 or 5 times. Roll dough to ½-inch thickness; cut with a 2½-inch biscuit cutter. Place on a baking sheet. Bake at 450° for 12 minutes or until golden. Yield: 1 dozen (serving size: 1 biscuit).

Calories 112 (29% from fat) **Protein** 2.7g **Fat** 3.6g (sat 0.7g) **Carbohydrate** 16.8g **Fiber** 0.6g **Cholesterol** 0mg **Iron** 1.0mg **Sodium** 161mg **Calcium** 59mg

BUTTERMILK PANCAKES

QUICK & EASY

When we pictured a stack of these pancakes on the March/April 1992 cover, we suggested drizzling them with Fresh Orange Pancake Syrup (on page 150). To freeze any leftovers, place wax paper between pancakes, and wrap tightly in foil.

1 cup all-purpose flour
1 teaspoon baking powder
½ teaspoon baking soda
¼ teaspoon salt
2 tablespoons sugar
1 egg, lightly beaten
1 cup nonfat buttermilk
1 tablespoon vegetable oil
Vegetable cooking spray

Combine first 5 ingredients in a large bowl; make a well in center of mixture. Combine egg, buttermilk, and oil, and add to dry ingredients; stir just until dry ingredients are moistened.

Coat a nonstick griddle with cooking spray, and preheat to 350°. For each pancake, pour ¼ cup batter onto hot griddle. Cook pancakes until tops are covered with bubbles and edges look cooked; turn pancakes, and cook other side. Yield: 9 (4-inch) pancakes (serving size: 1 pancake).

Calories 94 (23% from fat) **Protein** 3.1g **Fat** 2.4g (sat 0.6g) **Carbohydrate** 14.9g **Fiber** 0.4g **Cholesterol** 25mg **Iron** 0.8mg **Sodium** 169mg **Calcium** 67mg

Buttermilk Pancakes with
Fresh Orange Pancake Syrup

TECHNIQUE

For Shaping Scones

1. Coat a baking sheet with cooking spray; then pat the dough into a 9-inch circle. If you don't have a ruler handy, use a 9-inch cake pan as a measurement guide.

2. Before you bake the scones, score deep wedges into the circle of dough, without cutting all the way through to the baking sheet.

3. Brush the unbaked dough with egg white; then sprinkle sugar over the top so the baked scones will develop a sugar-coated crust.

BUTTERMILK-APRICOT SCONES

QUICK & EASY

Delicate scones are best served one way—hot. The wedges that taste heavenly just minutes out of the oven often seem dry and less flavorful after they cool.

2   cups all-purpose flour
1½   teaspoons baking powder
½   teaspoon baking soda
¼   teaspoon salt
¼   cup sugar
¼   cup chilled stick margarine, cut into small pieces
⅓   cup chopped dried apricots
1   egg, lightly beaten
¼   cup nonfat buttermilk
¼   cup apricot nectar
Vegetable cooking spray
1   egg white, lightly beaten
1   tablespoon sugar

Combine first 5 ingredients; cut in margarine with a pastry blender until mixture resembles coarse meal. Add apricots; toss well. Combine egg, buttermilk, and nectar; add to dry ingredients, stirring just until moistened. (Dough will be sticky.)

Turn dough out onto a lightly floured surface; with floured hands, knead 4 or 5 times. Pat dough into a 9-inch circle on a baking sheet coated with cooking spray. Cut dough into 12 wedges, cutting to but not through bottom of dough. Brush with egg white, and sprinkle with 1 tablespoon sugar. Bake at 400° for 15 minutes or until golden. Serve hot. Yield: 1 dozen (serving size: 1 scone).

Calories 149 (27% from fat) **Protein** 3.2g **Fat** 4.5g (sat 0.9g) **Carbohydrate** 24.0g **Fiber** 0.7g **Cholesterol** 18mg **Iron** 1.2mg **Sodium** 184mg **Calcium** 46mg

PINT-SIZE PB & J MUFFINS

1   cup all-purpose flour
1   teaspoon baking powder
½   teaspoon baking soda
⅛   teaspoon salt
½   cup firmly packed brown sugar
½   cup vanilla low-fat yogurt
1   tablespoon vegetable oil
2   tablespoons creamy peanut butter
2   egg whites
Vegetable cooking spray
2   tablespoons strawberry jelly or grape jelly

Combine first 4 ingredients; make a well in center of mixture. Combine sugar and next 4 ingredients; beat at low speed of an electric mixer until blended. Add to dry ingredients; stir just until moistened.

Spoon batter into 24 miniature muffin cups coated with cooking spray, filling half full. Top each with ¼ teaspoon jelly, and top with remaining batter. Bake at 400° for 12 minutes or until a wooden pick inserted in center comes out clean. Remove from pans immediately; let cool on a wire rack. Yield: 2 dozen muffins (serving size: 2 muffins).

Calories 121 (24% from fat) Protein 2.9g Fat 3.2g (sat 0.5g) Carbohydrate 20.7g Fiber 0.4g Cholesterol 0mg Iron 0.9mg Sodium 115mg Calcium 51mg

RASPBERRY-FILLED CINNAMON MUFFINS

QUICK & EASY

1½   cups all-purpose flour
2½   teaspoons baking powder
¼   teaspoon salt
½   cup sugar
1   teaspoon ground cinnamon
1   egg, lightly beaten
⅔   cup low-fat buttermilk
¼   cup margarine, melted
Vegetable cooking spray
¼   cup seedless raspberry
     preserves
1   tablespoon sugar
¼   teaspoon ground cinnamon

Combine first 5 ingredients in a large bowl; make a well in center of mixture. Combine egg, buttermilk, and margarine; add to dry ingredients. Stir just until moistened.

Spoon about 1 tablespoon batter into each of 12 muffin cups coated with cooking spray. Spoon 1 teaspoon preserves onto center of batter in each cup (do not spread), and top evenly with remaining batter.

Combine 1 tablespoon sugar and ¼ teaspoon cinnamon; sprinkle evenly over batter. Bake at 400° for 20 minutes or until muffins spring back when touched lightly in center. Remove from pans immediately; cool on a wire rack. Yield: 1 dozen (serving size: 1 muffin).

Calories 153 (27% from fat) Protein 2.6g Fat 4.6g (sat 1.0g) Carbohydrate 25.7g Fiber 0.5g Cholesterol 18mg Iron 0.9mg Sodium 116mg Calcium 63mg

APPLE-PECAN MUFFINS

QUICK & EASY

The second layer of batter won't cover the apple-nut mixture; crusty, swirled tops form as the muffins bake.

1½   cups all-purpose flour
1¼   teaspoons baking soda
¼   teaspoon salt
1   cup wheat bran flakes cereal
     with raisins
⅔   cup sugar
⅓   cup graham cracker crumbs
1   egg, lightly beaten
1   cup nonfat buttermilk
2   tablespoons margarine,
     melted
1   cup peeled, finely chopped
     Rome apple
⅓   cup chopped pecans, toasted
2   tablespoons sugar
¾   teaspoon ground cinnamon
1   tablespoon margarine,
     melted
Vegetable cooking spray
1   tablespoon sugar

Combine first 6 ingredients in a large bowl; make a well in center of mixture. Combine egg, buttermilk, and 2 tablespoons margarine; add to dry ingredients. Stir just until dry ingredients are moistened. Set aside.

Combine apple and next 4 ingredients; set aside.

Spoon 2 tablespoons batter into each of 12 muffin cups coated with cooking spray. Top evenly with apple mixture. Spoon remaining batter evenly over apple mixture. (Batter will not completely cover apple mixture.) Sprinkle 1 tablespoon sugar evenly over batter. Bake at 350° for 25 minutes. Remove from pans immediately. Yield: 1 dozen (serving size: 1 muffin).

Calories 198 (28% from fat) Protein 3.6g Fat 6.1g (sat 0.9g) Carbohydrate 33.4g Fiber 1.5g Cholesterol 18mg Iron 1.5mg Sodium 240mg Calcium 33mg

MUFFIN MAGIC

The secret to perfect muffins is in the stirring. After you add the milk, margarine, and egg to the flour mixture, stir only until the dry ingredients are moistened (the batter will be lumpy). If you stir the batter too much, the muffin tops will be peaked instead of rounded.

To keep from overstirring, combine all the moist ingredients before you add them to the flour mixture. Then it takes just a few stirs to blend the two mixtures.

Blueberry-Yogurt
Muffins

BLUEBERRY-YOGURT MUFFINS

QUICK & EASY

When just one of these muffins graced the cover of our September 1992 issue, grocers couldn't keep the magazine racks stocked fast enough. The muffin recipe became a staff and reader all-time favorite.

2   cups all-purpose flour
1   teaspoon baking powder
1   teaspoon baking soda
¼   teaspoon salt
⅓   cup sugar
1   egg, lightly beaten
¼   cup unsweetened orange juice
2   tablespoons vegetable oil
1   teaspoon vanilla extract
1   (8-ounce) carton vanilla low-fat yogurt
1   cup fresh or frozen blueberries, thawed
Vegetable cooking spray
1   tablespoon sugar

Combine first 5 ingredients in a large bowl; make a well in center of mixture. Combine egg and next 4 ingredients; add to dry ingredients. Stir just until dry ingredients are moistened. Gently fold in blueberries.

Spoon batter evenly into 12 muffin cups coated with cooking spray; sprinkle 1 tablespoon sugar evenly over batter. Bake at 400° for 18 minutes or until golden. Remove from pans immediately; cool on a wire rack. Yield: 1 dozen (serving size: 1 muffin).

Calories 153 (19% from fat) Protein 3.7g
Fat 3.3g (sat 0.7g) Carbohydrate 27.2g
Fiber 0.9g Cholesterol 19mg Iron 1.1mg
Sodium 172mg Calcium 62mg

Fresh Apple Coffee Cake

This breakfast bread easily doubles as a dessert. Test Kitchens Director Rebecca Pate says that her husband's been requesting it for breakfast—and dessert—since the recipe first ran in 1989. Rebecca prefers using Rome or Granny Smith apples, but any cooking apple will do.

4 cups finely chopped cooking apple
½ cup unsweetened orange juice, divided
1½ teaspoons ground cinnamon
½ cup stick margarine, softened
1 cup sugar
1 (8-ounce) carton fat-free egg substitute
¼ cup skim milk
3 cups sifted cake flour
2 teaspoons baking powder
¼ teaspoon salt
2½ teaspoons vanilla extract
Vegetable cooking spray
2 tablespoons brown sugar

Combine apple, ¼ cup orange juice, and cinnamon; set aside.

Beat margarine at medium speed of an electric mixer until creamy; gradually add 1 cup sugar, beating until light and fluffy (about 5 minutes). Add egg substitute; beat at medium speed 4 minutes or until well blended.

Combine remaining ¼ cup orange juice and milk. Combine flour, baking powder, and salt, and add to margarine mixture alternately with milk mixture, beginning and ending with flour mixture. Stir in vanilla.

Pour half of batter into a 10-inch tube pan coated with cooking spray; top with half of apple mixture. Pour remaining batter into pan, and top with remaining apple mixture; sprinkle with brown sugar.

Bake at 350° for 1 hour or until a wooden pick inserted in center comes out clean. Cool in pan on a wire rack 10 minutes; remove from pan, and cool completely on wire rack. Yield: 18 servings (serving size: 1 slice).

Calories 190 (25% from fat) **Protein** 3.0g **Fat** 5.3g (sat 1.0g) **Carbohydrate** 32.8g **Fiber** 1.1g **Cholesterol** 0mg **Iron** 1.8mg **Sodium** 113mg **Calcium** 49mg

EDITOR'S CHOICE

"I always make this coffee cake when relatives or friends visit. It's great for breakfast, but it's heavenly for dessert when served warm out of the oven with a dollop of frozen vanilla yogurt."

——Cynthia N. LaGrone, Assistant Food Editor

Huckleberry Coffee Cake

In our all-time favorite recipes "taste-off," the *Cooking Light* staff voted this coffee cake as one of the top five recipes from our first 10 years. It's pictured with the other winning recipes on page 8.

¼ cup stick margarine, softened
½ (8-ounce) package nonfat cream cheese
1 cup sugar
1 egg
1 cup all-purpose flour
1 teaspoon baking powder
¼ teaspoon salt
1 teaspoon vanilla extract
2 cups fresh or frozen huckleberries or blueberries, unthawed
Vegetable cooking spray
2 tablespoons sugar
1 teaspoon ground cinnamon

Beat margarine and cream cheese at medium speed of an electric mixer until creamy; gradually add 1 cup sugar, beating well. Add egg; beat well.

Combine flour, baking powder, and salt; stir into margarine mixture. Stir in vanilla; fold in berries. Pour batter into a 9-inch round cake pan coated with cooking spray. Combine 2 tablespoons sugar and cinnamon; sprinkle over batter.

Bake at 350° for 1 hour; cool on a wire rack. Yield: 10 servings (serving size: 1 wedge).

Calories 209 (23% from fat) **Protein** 3.7g **Fat** 5.3g (sat 1.0g) **Carbohydrate** 36.9g **Fiber** 1.7g **Cholesterol** 24mg **Iron** 0.8mg **Sodium** 188mg **Calcium** 70mg

Banana-Nut Bread

BANANA-NUT BREAD

You get extra-rich flavor when you bite into a crunchy toasted pecan. Use your microwave to toast in a hurry. Just spread the nuts in a shallow dish, and microwave at HIGH for 1 to 2 minutes. Open the door every 30 seconds to stir and to sample the nuts for doneness.

1	cup mashed very ripe banana (about 3 small)
½	cup sugar
½	cup plain nonfat yogurt
¼	cup margarine, melted
1	teaspoon vanilla extract
1	egg
1	egg white
2	cups all-purpose flour
1	teaspoon baking powder
½	teaspoon baking soda
¼	teaspoon salt
¼	cup chopped pecans, toasted

Baking spray with flour

Combine first 7 ingredients in a large mixing bowl; beat at medium speed of an electric mixer until blended.

Combine flour and next 3 ingredients; stir in pecans. Add flour mixture to banana mixture, stirring just until dry ingredients are moistened. Spoon batter into an 8½- x 4½- x 3-inch loafpan coated with baking spray with flour. Bake at 350° for 1 hour and 5 minutes or until a wooden pick inserted in center comes out clean. Cool 10 minutes in pan on a wire rack; remove from pan, and cool completely on wire

TRICK FOR NO-STICK BREADS

In the *Cooking Light* test kitchens, we almost always spray our bread pans with vegetable cooking spray. And most of the time it works just fine. But when the bread sticks to a pan coated with vegetable cooking spray, we make the recipe again to see if using baking spray with flour works better. When it does, we let you know by listing baking spray with flour as an ingredient like we did in this recipe.

If you don't have any baking spray with flour on hand, simply coat the pan with vegetable cooking spray; then dust it evenly with a teaspoon of all-purpose flour. In the supermarket, you can find cans of baking spray with flour where you find vegetable cooking sprays.

rack. Yield: 16 servings (serving size: one ½-inch slice).

Calories 143 (30% from fat) **Protein** 3.0g **Fat** 4.7g (sat 0.8g) **Carbohydrate** 22.6g **Fiber** 1.0g **Cholesterol** 14mg **Iron** 0.9mg **Sodium** 123mg **Calcium** 38 mg

CHILE CORN STICKS

Look for a suggested menu with a photograph of Chile Corn Sticks on page 219.

1½	teaspoons vegetable oil
½	cup diced sweet red pepper
⅓	cup seeded, diced Anaheim chile
¼	cup diced onion
1	clove garlic, minced
¾	cup all-purpose flour
2	teaspoons baking powder
¼	teaspoon baking soda
¼	teaspoon salt
¾	cup yellow cornmeal
1½	tablespoons sugar
¾	cup corn cut from cob (about 1½ ears)
1	egg, lightly beaten
1	cup nonfat buttermilk

Vegetable cooking spray

Heat oil in a medium skillet over medium heat. Add red pepper and next 3 ingredients; sauté 5 minutes.

Combine flour and next 5 ingredients in a medium bowl; stir well. Add red pepper mixture and corn, and stir well; make a well in center of mixture. Combine egg and buttermilk; add to flour mixture, stirring just until moistened.

Heavily coat cast-iron corn stick pans with cooking spray, and place in a 400° oven for 10 minutes. Spoon batter evenly into pans. Bake at 400° for 20 minutes or until lightly browned. Remove corn sticks from pans immediately, and serve warm. Yield: 14 corn sticks (serving size: 1 corn stick).

Calories 87 (16% from fat) **Protein** 2.8g **Fat** 1.5g (sat 0.3g) **Carbohydrate** 16.0g **Fiber** 1.1g **Cholesterol** 16mg **Iron** 0.9mg **Sodium** 82mg **Calcium** 51mg

COWBOY CORNBREAD

1	tablespoon plus 1 teaspoon vegetable oil, divided
¾	cup all-purpose flour
1½	teaspoons baking powder
¼	teaspoon baking soda
¼	teaspoon salt
1	cup yellow cornmeal
1	egg, lightly beaten
¾	cup low-fat buttermilk
1	(4.5-ounce) can chopped green chiles, undrained
1	cup frozen whole-kernel corn, thawed
10	sweet red pepper strips

Coat an 8-inch cast-iron skillet with 1 teaspoon oil. Place in a 400° oven for 10 minutes.

Combine flour and next 4 ingredients in a large bowl. Combine remaining 1 tablespoon oil, egg, buttermilk, and chiles; add to cornmeal mixture, stirring just until dry ingredients are moistened. Stir in thawed corn.

Spoon batter into preheated skillet. Arrange pepper strips on top of batter. Bake at 400° for 45 minutes or until a wooden pick inserted in center comes out clean. Yield: 10 servings (serving size: 1 wedge).

Calories 138 (20% from fat) **Protein** 4.3g **Fat** 3.0g (sat 0.5g) **Carbohydrate** 23.9g **Fiber** 1.7g **Cholesterol** 22mg **Iron** 1.4mg **Sodium** 152mg **Calcium** 71mg

SOME LIKE IT HOT

And when they do, cooks pick peppers to add a little heat to the bread, especially to cornbread. Fortunately, Anaheim or other varieties of long, green chiles and canned green chiles are interchangeable, so it's easy to keep spicy hot flavor on hand.

Although fresh Anaheim chiles can range in heat from mild to hot, the canned chiles often are hotter than the fresh ones.

If jalapeños or serranos are your choice of heat, then use pickled jalapeños if you need a substitute for fresh ones. The jarred peppers really don't taste "pickled" and can substitute for fresh yellow hot peppers, too.

TECHNIQUE

To Shape Cheese Breadsticks

1. Roll each half of dough into a 14- x 10-inch rectangle on a floured surface.

2. Brush water and egg white mixture over surface of dough; sprinkle with fresh Romano cheese. Gently press the cheese into the dough with your fingertips. Cut 22 (10-inch) strips from the dough with a very sharp knife.

3. Carefully pick up both ends of each strip, twist the dough, and lay the strips on a baking sheet.

CHEESE BREADSTICKS

Freshly grated cheese makes all the difference in this recipe (pictured on page 26). If you can't find Romano, use freshly grated Parmesan.

3¼ cups bread flour
¾ cup grated fresh Romano cheese, divided
¼ cup instant nonfat dry milk powder
1 teaspoon salt
1 teaspoon sugar
¼ teaspoon ground red pepper
1 package rapid-rise yeast
1 cup plus 2 tablespoons very warm water (120° to 130°)
2 teaspoons olive oil
Vegetable cooking spray
2 teaspoons water
1 egg white, lightly beaten
2 tablespoons cornmeal, divided

Position knife blade in food processor bowl. Add flour, ½ cup cheese, and next 5 ingredients, and pulse 6 times or until blended. With processor running, slowly pour very warm water and oil through food chute; process until dough leaves sides of bowl and forms a ball.

Turn dough out onto a floured surface; knead lightly 5 times. Place dough in a large bowl coated with cooking spray, turning to coat top. Cover and let rise in a warm place (85°), free from drafts, 40 minutes or until doubled in bulk.

Combine 2 teaspoons water and egg white; set aside.

Coat 2 baking sheets with cooking spray, and sprinkle each with 1 tablespoon cornmeal; set aside.

Punch dough down; turn out onto a floured surface. Divide dough in half; roll 1 portion of dough into a 14- x 10-inch rectangle. Brush half of egg white mixture evenly over rectangle, and sprinkle with 2 tablespoons cheese. Using fingertips, press cheese into dough.

Cut rectangle of dough into 22 (10-inch-long) strips. Gently pick up both ends of each strip, and twist dough. Place twisted strips of dough 1 inch apart on a prepared baking sheet. (Dough strips may stretch as they are transferred, creating a unique free-form look as pictured on page 26.) Repeat procedure with remaining dough, egg white mixture, and cheese.

Cover and let rise in a warm place, free from drafts, 20 minutes or until puffy. Bake at 375° for 12 minutes or until golden. Remove from baking sheets, and cool on wire racks. Yield: 44 breadsticks (serving size: 1 breadstick).

Calories 51 (16% from fat) **Protein** 2.2g **Fat** 0.9g (sat 0.4g) **Carbohydrate** 8.2g **Fiber** 0.1g **Cholesterol** 2mg **Iron** 0.5mg **Sodium** 82mg **Calcium** 31mg

CINNAMON ROLLS

1   cup skim milk
3   tablespoons sugar
1   tablespoon margarine
1   package active dry yeast
¼   cup warm water (105° to 115°)
1   large egg, lightly beaten
½   teaspoon salt
3¾   cups plus 2 tablespoons bread flour, divided
Vegetable cooking spray
2   tablespoons margarine, melted
¼   cup plus 2 tablespoons firmly packed brown sugar
2   teaspoons ground cinnamon
1   cup sifted powdered sugar
2   tablespoons skim milk
1   teaspoon vanilla extract

Heat 1 cup milk over medium-high heat in a heavy saucepan to 180° or until tiny bubbles form around edge. (Do not boil.) Remove from heat; add 3 tablespoons sugar and 1 tablespoon margarine, stirring until margarine melts. Cool to 105° to 115°.

Combine yeast and warm water in a 1-cup liquid measuring cup; let stand 5 minutes. Combine milk mixture, yeast mixture, egg, and salt in a large bowl; stir well. Gradually stir in 3½ cups flour to make a soft dough.

Sprinkle 1 tablespoon of remaining flour evenly over work surface. Turn dough out onto floured surface, and knead until smooth and elastic (about 8 minutes). Add enough of remaining flour, 1 tablespoon at a time, to keep dough from sticking to surface. Place dough in a bowl coated with cooking spray, turning to coat top. Cover and let rise in a warm place (85°), free from drafts, 1 hour or until doubled in bulk.

Punch dough down. Turn out onto a lightly floured surface; roll to a 20- x 8-inch rectangle. Brush with 2 tablespoons melted margarine. Combine brown sugar and cinnamon, and sprinkle over dough. Roll up, starting at long side. Pinch seam to seal (do not seal ends). Cut into 20 (1-inch) slices.

Place slices, cut sides down, in a 13- x 9- x 2-inch pan coated with cooking spray. Cover; let rise in a warm place, free from drafts, 30 minutes or until doubled in bulk. Bake at 350° for 22 minutes or until done.

Combine powdered sugar, 2 tablespoons milk, and vanilla; stir well. Drizzle over rolls. Yield: 20 rolls (serving size: 1 roll).

Calories 168 (13% from fat) **Protein** 4.1g **Fat** 2.5g (sat 0.5g) **Carbohydrate** 32.2g **Fiber** 0.2g **Cholesterol** 11mg **Iron** 1.4mg **Sodium** 91mg **Calcium** 30mg

TECHNIQUE

To Measure Flour

Fat tenderizes bread, and flour toughens it—so when we reduce fat in a recipe, it's important to measure the flour correctly for moist, tender breads. Here's how to make sure you don't add more flour than you need:

First stir the flour in the container to make sure it's not compact. Then lightly pile spoonfuls of flour into the correct size measuring cup. Don't pack it into the cup. Level the flour with a flat metal spatula.

MONKEY BREAD

For easy oven cleanup, put a baking sheet or aluminum foil under the Bundt pan while the Monkey Bread bakes. The dough rises high and may force the sugary syrup to drip over the side of the pan.

2   (1-pound) loaves frozen white bread dough
1   cup sugar
¼   cup firmly packed brown sugar
¼   cup 1% low-fat milk
1   tablespoon reduced-calorie stick margarine
1¼ teaspoons ground cinnamon
¼   cup sugar
½   teaspoon ground cinnamon
Vegetable cooking spray

Thaw bread dough in refrigerator for 12 hours.

Combine 1 cup sugar, brown sugar, milk, margarine, and 1¼ teaspoons cinnamon in a small saucepan; bring to a boil. Cook, stirring constantly, 1 minute. Remove sugar syrup from heat; cool 10 minutes.

Cut each loaf of dough into 24 equal portions. Combine ¼ cup sugar and ½ teaspoon cinnamon in a shallow dish; stir well. Roll each portion of dough in sugar mixture, and layer dough in a 12-cup Bundt pan coated with cooking spray. Pour sugar syrup over dough; cover and let rise in a warm place (85°), free from drafts, 35 minutes or until doubled in bulk.

Bake at 350° for 25 minutes or until lightly browned. Immediately loosen edges of bread with a knife. Place a serving plate, upside down, on top of pan, and invert bread onto plate. Remove pan, and drizzle any remaining syrup over bread. Yield: 24 servings (serving size: 2 pull-apart rolls).

Calories 201 (10% from fat) **Protein** 5.2g **Fat** 2.2g (sat 0.5g) **Carbohydrate** 40.1g **Fiber** 0.0g **Cholesterol** 0mg **Iron** 1.4mg **Sodium** 302mg **Calcium** 41mg

TECHNIQUE

To Shape Pull-Apart Breads

For sweet morning treats like Monkey Bread and Hawaiian Bubble Bread, roll pieces of dough into balls, and layer them in a Bundt or tube pan. If the dough is sticky, spray kitchen shears with vegetable cooking spray, and cut uniform dough pieces from the large batch of dough. Then spray your hands with the cooking spray, or rub them with flour to keep the dough from sticking to them as you shape the dough into balls.

HAWAIIAN BUBBLE BREAD

2   packages active dry yeast
1   teaspoon sugar
1   cup warm water (105° to 115°)
1   cup sliced ripe banana
½   cup pineapple-orange-banana juice concentrate, undiluted
¼   cup honey
2   tablespoons margarine, melted
2   drops yellow food coloring (optional)
5¼   cups bread flour, divided
1   teaspoon salt
Vegetable cooking spray
¼   cup cream of coconut
2   tablespoons pineapple-orange-banana juice concentrate, undiluted
½   cup sifted powdered sugar

Combine first 3 ingredients in a 2-cup liquid measuring cup; let stand 5 minutes.

Combine banana and next 3 ingredients in container of an electric blender; add food coloring, if desired. Cover and process until smooth, stopping once to scrape down sides.

Combine 2 cups flour and salt in a large bowl; stir well. Add yeast mixture and banana mixture, stirring until well blended. Add 2¾ cups flour, stirring to form a soft dough.

Turn dough out onto a lightly floured surface, and knead until smooth and elastic (about 8 minutes). Add enough of remaining ½ cup flour, 1 tablespoon at a time, to keep dough from sticking to hands.

Place dough in a large bowl coated with cooking spray, turning to coat top. Cover and let rise in a warm place (85°), free from drafts, 1 hour or until doubled in bulk. Punch dough down; turn out onto a lightly floured surface. Cover and let rest 5 minutes. Shape dough into 1½-inch balls (about 30 balls) on a lightly floured surface. Layer balls in a 10-inch tube pan coated with cooking spray; set aside.

Combine cream of coconut and 2 tablespoons juice concentrate in a bowl; stir well. Pour 3 tablespoons juice mixture over dough, and set aside remaining juice mixture. Cover dough, and let rise in a warm place, free from drafts, 45 minutes or until doubled in bulk.

Bake at 350° for 30 minutes or until loaf sounds hollow when tapped. Cool in pan 20 minutes. Remove from pan; place on a wire rack. Stir powdered sugar into reserved juice mixture; drizzle over top of warm bread. Yield: 30 servings (serving size: 1 pull-apart roll).

Calories 126 (14% from fat) **Protein** 3.2g **Fat** 1.9g (sat 0.8g) **Carbohydrate** 24.0g **Fiber** 0.3g **Cholesterol** 0mg **Iron** 1.2mg **Sodium** 88mg **Calcium** 5mg

Hawaiian Bubble Bread

TENDER YEAST BREAD

Bake this honey-flavored bread, or try its two variations which follow.

2   packages active dry yeast
1   tablespoon sugar
1½ cups warm water (105° to 115°)
6   cups bread flour, divided
½   cup instant nonfat dry milk powder
¼   cup vegetable oil
¼   cup honey
1½ teaspoons salt
1   egg
Vegetable cooking spray

Combine first 3 ingredients in a 2-cup liquid measuring cup; let stand 5 minutes. Combine yeast mixture, 2 cups flour, and next 5 ingredients in a large mixing bowl; beat at medium speed of an electric mixer until well blended. Gradually stir in 3 cups flour to make a soft dough.

Sprinkle ½ cup of remaining flour evenly over a work surface. Turn dough out onto floured surface, and knead until smooth and elastic (about 10 minutes). Add enough of remaining ½ cup flour, 1 table-spoon at a time, to keep dough from sticking to hands.

Place dough in a large bowl coated with cooking spray, turning to coat top. Cover and let rise in a warm place (85°), free from drafts, 1 hour or until doubled in bulk.

Punch dough down; turn out onto a floured surface. Cover and let rest 10 minutes. Divide dough in half;

roll 1 portion into a 14- x 8-inch rectangle. Roll up dough, starting at short side, pressing to eliminate air pockets; pinch ends to seal. Place dough, seam side down, in a 9- x 5- x 3-inch loafpan coated with cooking spray. Repeat procedure with remaining dough.

Cover and let rise in a warm place, free from drafts, 40 minutes or until doubled in bulk. Bake at 350° for 30 minutes or until loaves sound hollow when tapped. Remove from pans immediately; cool on wire racks. Yield: 2 loaves, 18 servings each (serving size: one ½-inch slice).

Calories 114 (17% from fat) **Protein** 3.7g **Fat** 2.1g (sat 0.4g) **Carbohydrate** 19.9g **Fiber** 0.1g **Cholesterol** 6mg **Iron** 1.1mg **Sodium** 110mg **Calcium** 26mg

TECHNIQUE

To Braid Bread

To braid dough for Peppercorn-Cheese Braids, pinch the ends of 3 ropes of dough together, and braid. At the end of the braid, pinch the ends together, and tuck them under a bit for a smooth, round end.

PEPPERCORN-CHEESE BRAIDS

This savory variation of Tender Yeast Bread received the highest rating our food editors give. It's perfect for serving with any holiday dinner.

Recipe for Tender Yeast Bread (at left)
1   tablespoon plus 2 teaspoons coarsely ground pepper, divided
¾   cup grated Romano cheese
⅔   cup no-salt-added whole kernel corn, drained
2   tablespoons bread flour
Vegetable cooking spray
2   teaspoons water
1   egg white, lightly beaten

Prepare dough for Tender Yeast Bread, adding 1 tablespoon plus 1½ teaspoons pepper, cheese, and corn to dough mixture with dry milk powder. Sprinkle 2 tablespoons flour over work surface. After first rising, punch dough down, and turn out onto floured surface; cover and let rest 10 minutes.

Divide dough into 6 equal portions; shape each portion into a 20-inch rope. Place 3 ropes side by side on a baking sheet coated with cooking spray (do not stretch); pinch ropes together at one end to seal. Braid ropes; pinch loose ends to seal. Repeat procedure with remaining 3 portions of dough. Let rise, uncovered, in a warm place (85°), free from drafts, 40 minutes or until doubled in bulk.

Combine water and egg white; brush over tops of braids. Sprinkle remaining ½ teaspoon pepper over braids. Bake at 350° for 23 minutes or until braids sound hollow when tapped. Cool on a wire rack. Yield: 2 loaves, 17 servings each (serving size: one 1-inch slice).

Calories 146 (22% from fat) **Protein** 5.8g **Fat** 3.6g (sat 1.3g) **Carbohydrate** 22.4g **Fiber** 0.2g **Cholesterol** 12mg **Iron** 1.3mg **Sodium** 178mg **Calcium** 82mg

CINNAMON SWIRL BREAD

Like Peppercorn-Cheese Braids, this bread got a perfect score from our test kitchens. Unlike the braids, though, it is sweet—and ideal for breakfast or brunch.

Recipe for Tender Yeast Bread (facing page)
2   tablespoons bread flour
1   egg white, lightly beaten
2   teaspoons water
¼   cup sugar
1   tablespoon plus 1 teaspoon ground cinnamon
⅛   teaspoon ground cloves
Vegetable cooking spray
¾   cup sifted powdered sugar
1   tablespoon skim milk
½   teaspoon vanilla extract

Prepare dough for Tender Yeast Bread. Sprinkle 2 tablespoons flour over a work surface. After first rising, punch dough down, and turn out onto floured surface; cover and let rest 10 minutes.

Combine egg white and water; set mixture aside.

Combine ¼ cup sugar, cinnamon, and cloves in a small bowl; set mixture aside.

Divide dough in half; roll 1 portion of dough into a 14- x 8-inch rectangle. Brush half of egg white mixture over rectangle, and sprinkle with half of cinnamon mixture. Roll up dough, starting at short side, pressing firmly to eliminate air pockets; pinch ends to seal.

Place dough, seam side down, in a 9- x 5- x 3-inch loafpan coated with cooking spray. Repeat procedure with remaining dough, egg white mixture, and cinnamon mixture.

Cover and let rise in a warm place (85°), free from drafts, 40 minutes or until doubled in bulk. Bake at 350° for 30 minutes or until loaves sound hollow when tapped. Remove bread from pans immediately; cool on wire racks.

Combine powdered sugar, milk, and vanilla in a small bowl; stir well. Drizzle over loaves. Yield: 2 loaves, 18 servings each (serving size: one ½-inch slice).

Calories 130 (15% from fat) **Protein** 3.8g **Fat** 2.1g (sat 0.4g) **Carbohydrate** 23.9g **Fiber** 0.2g **Cholesterol** 7mg **Iron** 1.2mg **Sodium** 111mg **Calcium** 29mg

To Shape Cinnamon Swirl Bread

1. Brush egg white and water mixture over rolled dough so the dry sugar-cinnamon filling will stick to it evenly. Sprinkle the cinnamon mixture over the dough.

2. Start at the short side of the rectangle, and roll up the dough. Press the dough firmly as you roll to push out air pockets; then pinch the dough at both ends to seal in the filling.

"This was my first favorite recipe. It smelled so good the first time we made it, we didn't even let it cool before slicing it. And we weren't disappointed; the squash gives the bread a wonderful buttery flavor. I still serve it all the time to family and friends."

——Rebecca J. Pate, Test Kitchens Director

BUTTERNUT-OATMEAL BREAD

2	packages active dry yeast
1¼	cups warm water (105° to 115°)
5½	to 5¾ cups bread flour, divided
1¼	cups mashed cooked fresh butternut squash (about 1 medium squash)
¼	cup molasses
2	tablespoons vegetable oil
1½	teaspoons salt
1	cup plus 2 tablespoons quick-cooking oats, divided
Vegetable cooking spray	
1	tablespoon water

Combine yeast and warm water in a 2-cup liquid measuring cup; let stand 5 minutes. Combine yeast mixture, 3 cups flour, and next 4 ingredients in a large mixing bowl; beat at medium speed of an electric mixer 2 minutes or until smooth. Gradually stir in 1 cup oats and 2 cups flour to make a moderately stiff dough.

Butternut-Oatmeal Bread

Turn dough out onto a lightly floured surface. Knead until smooth and elastic (about 10 minutes), adding enough of remaining flour, ¼ cup at a time, to keep dough from sticking to hands. Place dough in a large bowl coated with cooking spray, turning to coat top. Cover and let rise in a warm place (85°), free from drafts, 35 minutes or until doubled in bulk.

Punch dough down; divide in half. Turn 1 portion out onto work surface; knead 4 or 5 times. Roll into a 14- x 7-inch rectangle. Roll up, starting at short side, pressing firmly to eliminate air pockets; pinch ends to seal. Place dough, seam side down, in an 8½- x 4½- x 3-inch loafpan coated with cooking spray and sprinkled with 1½ teaspoons

oats. Repeat procedure with remaining dough and 1½ teaspoons oats.

Brush loaves evenly with 1 tablespoon water, and sprinkle evenly with remaining 1 tablespoon oats. Cover and let rise in a warm place, free from drafts, 25 minutes or until doubled in bulk. Bake at 350° for 35 minutes or until loaves sound hollow when tapped. Remove from pans immediately; cool on a wire rack. Yield: 2 loaves, 16 servings each (serving size: one ½-inch slice).

Calories 116 (12% from fat) **Protein** 3.5g **Fat** 1.5g (sat 0.3g) **Carbohydrate** 21.8g **Fiber** 0.5g **Cholesterol** 0mg **Iron** 1.4mg **Sodium** 112mg **Calcium** 14mg

Dinner Roll Variation: Prepare dough as directed. After first rising, divide dough in half, and shape half of dough into 15 balls. Place in a 9-inch round cake pan coated with cooking spray. Cover and let rise in a warm place (85°), free from drafts, 25 minutes or until doubled in bulk. Bake at 350° for 20 to 22 minutes or until browned. Repeat procedure with remaining dough. Yield: 30 rolls (serving size: 1 roll).

Calories 117 (12% from fat) **Protein** 3.3g **Fat** 1.4g (sat 0.2g) **Carbohydrate** 21.3g **Fiber** 0.3g **Cholesterol** 0mg **Iron** 1.4mg **Sodium** 120mg **Calcium** 14mg

MOCHA BABKA

4½ to 4¾ cups bread flour, divided
¾ cup medium rye flour
⅓ cup firmly packed brown sugar
¼ cup instant nonfat dry milk powder
1 teaspoon instant coffee granules
¾ teaspoon salt
2 packages active dry yeast
1¼ cups water
½ cup semisweet chocolate morsels
¼ cup plus 2 tablespoons reduced-calorie stick margarine
4 egg whites
2 tablespoons bread flour
Vegetable cooking spray
Chocolate Streusel

Combine 1 cup bread flour and next 6 ingredients in a large bowl; stir well. Combine water, chocolate, and margarine in a small saucepan; cook over medium heat, stirring constantly, until chocolate and margarine melt. Cool to 120° to 130°.

Gradually add liquid mixture to flour mixture, beating well at low speed of an electric mixer 1 minute. Add egg whites; beat at medium-high 1 minute. Gradually stir in enough of remaining 3¾ cups bread flour to make a soft dough.

Sprinkle 2 tablespoons bread flour evenly over a work surface. Turn out onto surface; knead until smooth and elastic (about 8 minutes). Place dough in a bowl coated with cooking spray, turning to coat top. Cover; let rise in a warm place (85°), free from drafts, 55 minutes or until doubled in bulk. (While dough is rising, prepare Chocolate Streusel.)

Punch dough down; turn out onto floured surface, and knead 4 or 5 times. Divide dough in half. Roll 1 portion into a 12- x 8-inch rectangle. Sprinkle half of Chocolate Streusel over rectangle, leaving a 1-inch margin around edges.

Roll up dough, starting at long side, pressing firmly to eliminate air pockets; pinch long edge to seal. Place dough, seam side down, in a 10-cup tube pan coated with cooking spray; pinch ends together. Repeat procedure with remaining dough and Chocolate Streusel.

Place 1 roll, seam side down, directly on top of other roll. Cover and let rise in a warm place, free from drafts, 45 minutes or until doubled in bulk. Bake at 350° for 40 minutes or until loaf sounds hollow when tapped. (Cover loaf with foil the last 10 minutes of baking to prevent excessive browning, if necessary.) Let bread stand 10 minutes. Remove bread from pan, and cool on a wire rack. Yield: 28 servings (serving size: one 1-inch slice).

CHOCOLATE STREUSEL:

½ cup firmly packed dark brown sugar
¼ cup bread flour
2 tablespoons unsweetened cocoa
½ teaspoon ground cinnamon
3 tablespoons reduced-calorie stick margarine, chilled and cut into small pieces

Position knife blade in food processor bowl; add first 4 ingredients. Process until combined. Add margarine; pulse 5 times or until mixture resembles coarse meal. Yield: 1 cup.

Calories 167 (22% from fat) **Protein** 4.4g **Fat** 4.1g (sat 1.1g) **Carbohydrate** 28.8g **Fiber** 0.6g **Cholesterol** 0mg **Iron** 1.5mg **Sodium** 115mg **Calcium** 26mg

WHAT'S BABKA?

Babka is a sweet Polish yeast bread that usually contains almonds and raisins—but this decadent version is baked in a tube pan and has a chocolate streusel baked inside.

Smoked Rosemary-Scented
Salmon, page 52

FISH

It was 10 a.m. when we first sampled Smoked Rosemary-Scented Salmon, yet we all reached for seconds and thirds of the hickory-smoked fish. The smoke is the secret to making this and other fish and shellfish sensational. The flavor of any type of hardwood-smoked coals or lava

& SHELLFISH

rocks transforms the taste. But if grilling's not your style, don't worry. The delicate flavors of fish also respond to marinades, crunchy coatings, fiery peppers, and about anything in your spice cabinet. Our favorite? Just look to the left. For a less adventurous (but outstanding) recipe, try Crispy Fish Sticks.

SEARED SEA BASS WITH GARLIC SAUCE

QUICK & EASY

1   (1-pound) sea bass fillet
     (about 2 inches thick)
2   teaspoons vegetable oil
¼   cup water
¼   cup dry vermouth
¼   teaspoon salt
¼   teaspoon pepper
4   cloves garlic, minced
2   tablespoons chopped fresh
     parsley
4   lemon wedges

Cut fish fillet crosswise into 4 equal pieces. Heat vegetable oil in a large nonstick skillet over high heat. Add fish pieces; cook 1 minute. Turn each piece of fish over; gradually add water, vermouth, salt, pepper, and minced garlic to skillet. Cover, reduce heat to medium, and cook 3 minutes or until fish flakes easily when tested with a fork.

Remove fish from skillet; set aside, and keep warm.

Continue cooking vermouth mixture in skillet over high heat 1 minute or until slightly thickened. Place fish on a serving platter; pour vermouth mixture over fish. Sprinkle with parsley. Serve with lemon wedges. Yield: 4 servings (serving size: 3 ounces fish and 1 lemon wedge).

Calories 156 (38% from fat) Protein 21.7g Fat 6.5g (sat 1.3g) Carbohydrate 1.4g Fiber 0.2g Cholesterol 77mg Iron 2.0mg Sodium 229mg Calcium 101mg

CREOLE CATFISH FILLETS

QUICK & EASY

Use either Creole or Dijon mustard to add spicy hotness to this recipe. Creole mustard, with its touch of horseradish, adds more pungency. Find it in supermarkets or gourmet shops. The flavor of the more commonly available Dijon mustard also works well in the sauce—just look for one of the hotter varieties.

2   tablespoons minced onion
3   tablespoons plain low-fat
     yogurt
1½   tablespoons nonfat
     mayonnaise
1½   tablespoons Creole or Dijon
     mustard
1   tablespoon reduced-calorie
     ketchup
½   teaspoon dried thyme
¼   teaspoon grated lemon rind
⅛   teaspoon ground red pepper
1   teaspoon paprika
½   teaspoon onion powder
⅛   teaspoon salt
⅛   teaspoon ground red pepper
4   (4-ounce) farm-raised catfish
     fillets
Vegetable cooking spray
4   lemon wedges

Combine first 8 ingredients; stir well. Cover sauce, and chill.

Combine paprika and next 3 ingredients; stir well. Rub mixture over both sides of fish. Arrange fish in a wire grilling basket coated with cooking spray; place on grill rack over hot coals (400° to 500°). Cook 6 minutes on each side or until fish flakes easily when tested with a fork. Serve with sauce and lemon wedges. Yield: 4 servings (serving size: 3 ounces fish, 2 tablespoons sauce, and 1 lemon wedge).

Calories 178 (30% from fat) Protein 22.7g Fat 6.0g (sat 1.3g) Carbohydrate 14.8g Fiber 0.7g Cholesterol 66mg Iron 2.1mg Sodium 372mg Calcium 138mg

GRILLED HALIBUT WITH PINEAPPLE-LIME SALSA

QUICK & EASY

To make this an even quicker recipe, make the salsa ahead, and chill it until you're ready to serve the fish.

Pineapple-Lime Salsa
1   teaspoon vegetable oil
1   large clove garlic, minced
4   (4-ounce) halibut steaks
     (about ¾ inch thick)
¼   teaspoon salt
Vegetable cooking spray
Lime wedges (optional)

Prepare Pineapple-Lime Salsa, and set aside.

Combine vegetable oil and minced garlic; brush mixture over fish. Sprinkle fish with ¼ teaspoon salt. Coat grill rack with cooking spray. Place fish on rack, and grill, covered, over medium-hot coals (350° to 400°) 5 to 6 minutes or until fish flakes easily when tested with a fork.

Spoon Pineapple-Lime Salsa over fish. Serve with lime wedges, if desired. Yield: 4 servings (serving size: 3 ounces fish and ¼ cup salsa).

Note: To broil fish instead of grilling, coat rack of a broiler pan with cooking spray. Place fish on rack, and broil 5½ inches from heat (with electric oven door partially opened) 3 minutes on each side or until fish flakes easily when tested with a fork. Serve as directed.

Calories 222 (17% from fat) **Protein** 24.2g **Fat** 4.1g (sat 0.6g) **Carbohydrate** 22.5g **Fiber** 0.8g **Cholesterol** 53mg **Iron** 1.4mg **Sodium** 293mg **Calcium** 73mg

PINEAPPLE-LIME SALSA:

⅓ cup pineapple preserves
¼ cup finely chopped sweet red pepper
2 tablespoons finely chopped purple onion
2 tablespoons fresh lime juice
1 tablespoon seeded, finely chopped jalapeño pepper
1 teaspoon dried mint flakes
⅛ teaspoon salt
1 (8-ounce) can unsweetened pineapple tidbits, drained

Combine all ingredients; stir well. Serve chilled or at room temperature. Yield: 1 cup (serving size: ¼ cup).

Calories 96 (1% from fat) **Protein** 0.3g **Fat** 0.1g (sat 0.0g) **Carbohydrate** 25.0g **Fiber** 0.9g **Cholesterol** 0mg **Iron** 0.3mg **Sodium** 114mg **Calcium** 5mg

GINGERED FLOUNDER

QUICK & EASY

See page 21 for easy step-by-step instructions for peeling and grating gingerroot.

¾ cup peeled, coarsely grated gingerroot
2 tablespoons low-sodium soy sauce
2 tablespoons dry sherry
2 tablespoons lemon juice
2 teaspoons sugar
4 (4-ounce) flounder fillets
Vegetable cooking spray
1 teaspoon dark sesame oil

Place gingerroot on several layers of damp cheesecloth. Gather edges of cheesecloth together, and squeeze cheesecloth bag over a small bowl. Reserve 3 tablespoons gingerroot juice.

Combine 2 tablespoons of reserved gingerroot juice, soy sauce, and next 3 ingredients in a shallow dish; add fish, turning to coat. Cover and marinate in refrigerator 20 minutes, turning occasionally. Remove fish from marinade; discard marinade.

Place fish on rack of a broiler pan coated with cooking spray, and broil 5½ inches from heat (with electric oven door partially opened) 3 minutes or until lightly browned (do not turn). Brush oil over fish, and broil 1 additional minute or until fish flakes easily when tested with a fork. Place fish on individual serving plates, and drizzle remaining 1 tablespoon gingerroot juice over fish. Yield: 4 servings (serving size: 3 ounces fish).

Calories 191 (19% from fat) **Protein** 31.0g **Fat** 4.0g (sat 0.7g) **Carbohydrate** 5.0g **Fiber** 0.0g **Cholesterol** 87mg **Iron** 0.5mg **Sodium** 427mg **Calcium** 25mg

GREAT GINGER FLAVOR

The best ginger flavor comes from the flesh just under the skin of the knobby root. So peel the skin carefully to cut away only the tough outer skin, not the flesh just beneath it. To store the unused portion, wrap it tightly. The gingerroot will keep for a week in the refrigerator or up to two months in the freezer.

To pick the freshest gingerroot, look for one with smooth skin. If the skin is wrinkled, it means the gingerroot is old and that the flesh is dry.

PECAN-CRUSTED FLOUNDER WITH CRAB-PECAN RELISH

New Orleans chef Emeril (EM-er-ul) Lagasse combines traditional Creole and Cajun cooking with French, Asian, and Italian flavors.

2	tablespoons plus 2 teaspoons Emeril's Creole Seasoning, divided
4	(4-ounce) flounder fillets
½	pound fresh lump crabmeat, drained
¼	cup chopped pecans, toasted
¼	cup chopped green onions
1	tablespoon minced sweet red pepper
1	tablespoon fresh lemon juice
¼	teaspoon salt
⅛	teaspoon pepper
½	cup all-purpose flour, divided
1	egg, lightly beaten
¼	cup 1% low-fat milk
3	tablespoons ground pecans
1	tablespoon olive oil
8	lemon wedges

Rub 2 teaspoons Emeril's Creole Seasoning over fish; set fish aside.

Combine crabmeat and next 6 ingredients; stir well, and set aside. Combine ¼ cup flour and 1 tablespoon Emeril's Creole Seasoning in a shallow dish; set aside. Combine egg and milk in a shallow dish; set aside. Combine remaining ¼ cup flour, remaining 1 tablespoon Emeril's Creole Seasoning, and ground pecans in a shallow dish.

Dredge each piece of fish in flour-seasoning mixture, dip into milk mixture, and then dredge in flour-seasoning-pecan mixture.

Heat oil in a large nonstick skillet over high heat until hot. Add fish; cook 1½ minutes on each side or until fish flakes easily when tested with a fork. Serve immediately with crabmeat mixture and lemon wedges. Yield: 4 servings (serving size: 3 ounces fish, ⅓ cup crabmeat mixture, and 2 lemon wedges).

Calories 376 (39% from fat) Protein 38.4g Fat 16.4g (sat 2.2g) Carbohydrate 20.7g Fiber 2.2g Cholesterol 165mg Iron 3.3mg Sodium 891mg Calcium 161mg

EMERIL'S CREOLE SEASONING:

2½	tablespoons paprika
2	tablespoons garlic powder
1	tablespoon salt
1	tablespoon onion powder
1	tablespoon dried whole oregano
1	tablespoon dried whole thyme
1	tablespoon ground red pepper
1	tablespoon black pepper

Combine all ingredients; stir well. Store in an airtight container. Use to season fish, chicken, salad dressings, dips, or vegetables. Yield: about ⅔ cup (serving size: 1 tablespoon).

Calories 19 (19% from fat) Protein 0.8g Fat 0.4g (sat 0.1g) Carbohydrate 4.0g Fiber 0.9g Cholesterol 0mg Iron 1.4mg Sodium 705mg Calcium 30mg

GOLDEN FISH NUGGETS WITH DILLED TARTAR SAUCE

QUICK & EASY

2	tablespoons reduced-fat mayonnaise
2	tablespoons plain nonfat yogurt
1	tablespoon plus 1 teaspoon sweet pickle relish
1	teaspoon lemon juice
¼	teaspoon onion powder
¼	teaspoon dried dillweed
¼	cup plus 2 tablespoons crushed corn flakes cereal
2	tablespoons grated Parmesan cheese
1	teaspoon paprika
¼	teaspoon salt
1	pound grouper or other firm white fish fillets, cut into 1-inch pieces
2	egg whites, lightly beaten
	Vegetable cooking spray

Combine first 6 ingredients; stir well. Cover sauce, and chill.

Combine cereal and next 3 ingredients in a shallow bowl.

Dip fish in egg whites; dredge in cereal mixture. Place on a baking sheet coated with cooking spray. Bake at 500° for 8 minutes or until crispy. Serve with sauce. Yield: 4 servings (serving size: 3 ounces fish and 1½ tablespoons sauce).

Calories 166 (22% from fat) Protein 25.5g Fat 4.1g (sat 1.1g) Carbohydrate 5.5g Fiber 0.2g Cholesterol 47mg Iron 1.4mg Sodium 408mg Calcium 83mg

Golden Fish Nuggets
With Dilled Tartar Sauce

CRISPY FISH STICKS

QUICK & EASY

3   (1-ounce) slices French
    bread, cubed
3   tablespoons reduced-fat
    mayonnaise
2   teaspoons water
½   teaspoon grated lemon rind
1   teaspoon lemon juice
1½ pounds grouper or other
    firm white fish fillets, cut
    into 1-inch-wide strips
Vegetable cooking spray

Position knife blade in food
processor bowl; add bread cubes.
Process 30 seconds or until crumbs
are fine. Sprinkle crumbs on an
ungreased baking sheet; bake at
350° for 12 minutes or until
browned. Set aside.

Combine mayonnaise and next 3
ingredients in a shallow bowl; stir
well. Dip fish in mayonnaise mixture, and dredge in breadcrumbs.
Place fish on a baking sheet coated
with cooking spray. Bake at 425°
for 22 to 25 minutes or until crispy
and browned. Yield: 6 servings
(serving size: 3 ounces fish).

Calories 167 (19% from fat) **Protein** 23.3g
Fat 3.6g (sat 0.5g) **Carbohydrate** 8.4g
Fiber 0.3g **Cholesterol** 45mg **Iron** 1.3mg
Sodium 198mg **Calcium** 37mg

GLAZED MAHIMAHI

QUICK & EASY

Find a photo of and a menu to serve
with this recipe on page 220.

3   tablespoons honey
3   tablespoons sherry vinegar
1   teaspoon peeled, minced
    gingerroot
4   cloves garlic, crushed
4   (4-ounce) mahimahi fillets
1½ teaspoons olive oil
¼   teaspoon salt
⅛   teaspoon freshly ground
    pepper

Combine first 4 ingredients in a
shallow dish; stir well. Place fish in a
single layer over mixture in dish,
turning to coat. Cover and marinate
in refrigerator 20 minutes, turning
fish once. Remove fish from marinade, reserving marinade.

Heat oil in a nonstick skillet over
medium-high heat until hot. Add
fish, and cook 6 minutes. Turn fish;
sprinkle with salt and pepper. Cook
3 minutes or until fish flakes easily
when tested with a fork. Remove
from skillet; keep warm.

Add reserved marinade to skillet;
cook over medium-high heat 1
minute, deglazing skillet by scraping
particles that cling to bottom.
Spoon glaze over fish. Yield: 4 servings (serving size: 3 ounces fish).

Calories 173 (13% from fat) **Protein** 20.5g
Fat 2.5g (sat 0.4g) **Carbohydrate** 14.7g
Fiber 0.1g **Cholesterol** 49mg **Iron** 0.6mg
Sodium 275mg **Calcium** 25mg

LEMON-DILL FISH FILLETS

QUICK & EASY

4   (4-ounce) orange roughy or
other firm white fish fillets
Vegetable cooking spray
¼   teaspoon salt
½   cup Lemon-Dill Coating
Lemon wedges (optional)

Coat both sides of fish with cooking spray; sprinkle with salt. Place Lemon-Dill Coating in a shallow dish; dredge fish in coating. Place fish in an 11- x 7- x 2-inch baking dish coated with cooking spray. Bake at 400° for 15 minutes or until fish flakes easily when tested with a fork. Serve with lemon wedges, if desired. Yield: 4 servings (serving size: 3 ounces fish).

Calories 125 (16% from fat) **Protein** 18.3g **Fat** 2.2g (sat 0.2g) **Carbohydrate** 7.6g **Fiber** 0.2g **Cholesterol** 23mg **Iron** 0.9mg **Sodium** 307mg **Calcium** 8mg

Lemon-Dill Fish Fillets

LEMON-DILL COATING:

2   cups finely crushed plain
Melba toast rounds
(about 54)
2   tablespoons paprika
2   tablespoons grated lemon
rind
1   tablespoon plus 1 teaspoon
dried dillweed
1½   teaspoons dry mustard

Combine all ingredients in a large heavy-duty, zip-top plastic bag; seal bag, and shake well. Store, tightly sealed, in refrigerator; shake well before each use. Use to coat fish or chicken. Yield: 2 cups (serving size: 2 tablespoons).

Calories 43 (19% from fat) **Protein** 1.6g **Fat** 0.9g (sat 0.2g) **Carbohydrate** 7.5g **Fiber** 0.2g **Cholesterol** 0mg **Iron** 0.7mg **Sodium** 89mg **Calcium** 6mg

SHAKE ON FLAVOR

Commercial coating mixes often contain high amounts of sodium, fat, and preservatives. It's healthier—and cheaper—to make your own. Just combine flavorful seasonings with crushed Melba toast, cornmeal, corn flake crumbs, or seasoned breadcrumbs.

LEMON-BROILED ORANGE ROUGHY

QUICK & EASY

3   tablespoons lemon juice
1   tablespoon Dijon mustard
1   tablespoon margarine,
    melted
¼   teaspoon coarsely ground
    pepper
4   (4-ounce) orange roughy
    fillets
Vegetable cooking spray
Coarsely ground pepper
    (optional)
Lemon wedges (optional)

Combine first 4 ingredients in a small bowl; stir well. Divide mixture in half.

Place fish on rack of a broiler pan coated with cooking spray; brush with half of lemon juice mixture. Broil 5½ inches from heat (with electric oven door partially opened) 5 minutes or until fish flakes easily when tested with a fork. Drizzle with remaining half of lemon juice mixture. If desired, sprinkle with additional pepper, and serve with lemon wedges. Yield: 4 servings (serving size: 3 ounces fish).

Calories 92 (36% from fat) Protein 12.6g Fat 3.7g (sat 0.6g) Carbohydrate 1.4g Fiber 0.0g Cholesterol 17mg Iron 0.2mg Sodium 198mg Calcium 2mg

SMOKED TROUT

Pecan shell chips or hickory chips
1¼ cups water
⅓   cup firmly packed dark
    brown sugar
¼   cup lemon juice
¼   teaspoon ground red pepper
3   (8-ounce) trout fillets, each
    halved lengthwise
Vegetable cooking spray
¼   teaspoon salt

Soak chips in water to cover 1 hour. Drain well.

Combine 1¼ cups water and next 3 ingredients in a large heavy-duty, zip-top plastic bag; add fish. Seal bag; marinate in refrigerator 2 hours, turning bag occasionally. Remove fish from bag, reserving marinade. Set aside.

Prepare charcoal fire in meat smoker; let burn 15 to 20 minutes. Place soaked chips on top of hot coals. Place water pan in smoker; add reserved marinade. Add hot tap water to fill pan.

Coat grill rack with cooking spray; place rack in smoker. Arrange fish on rack, skin side down, allowing enough room between fish pieces for air to circulate. Cover with smoker lid, and cook 1 hour or until fish flakes easily when tested with a fork. Sprinkle with salt. Yield: 6 servings (serving size: 3 ounces fish).

Calories 185 (19% from fat) Protein 23.7g Fat 4.0g (sat 0.8g) Carbohydrate 12.8g Fiber 0.0g Cholesterol 66mg Iron 2.4mg Sodium 133mg Calcium 88mg

TECHNIQUE

For Using Wood Chips

When you're using a smoker or grill-smoking meats for long periods of time, soak wood chips or chunks in water for 1 to 24 hours. In a smoker or a charcoal grill, place the wet chips directly on the hot coals. This allows the wood to smoke instead of burn so the flavor penetrates the fish or meat.

Hickory and mesquite wood impart the strongest smoked flavor. Apple, pecan, cherry, and maple chips add a milder smoked flavor. Find wood chips at your local supermarket, or order them from the following sources:

Apple, Cherry, Hickory, Maple Sugar Chips:
Sugartown Products Company
2330 East Heil Road
P.O. Box 641
Gladwin, MI 48624
517-426-4189
Mesquite:
Pecos Valley Spice Company
2429 Monroe Street NE
Albuquerque, NM 87110
800-473-8226

SMOKE IT ON THE GRILL

To smoke salmon in a charcoal or gas grill, use the following instructions:

For a charcoal grill:

Soak hickory or alder wood chips in water to cover 1 to 24 hours; drain. Pile charcoal on each side of grill, leaving center empty. Place a drip pan between coals. Prepare fire, and let burn 10 to 15 minutes. Place soaked hickory or alder wood chips on hot coals. Coat grill rack with cooking spray; place over coals. Arrange fish on rack over drip pan; cover and cook 50 minutes or until fish flakes easily when tested with a fork.

For a gas grill:

Soak hickory or alder wood chips in water 1 to 24 hours; drain. Wrap chips in heavy-duty aluminum foil, and make several holes in foil. Light gas grill on one side; place foil-wrapped chips directly on hot coals. Coat grill rack on opposite side with cooking spray, and place on grill. Let grill preheat 10 to 15 minutes; turn to lowest setting. Arrange fish on rack opposite hot coals; cover fish, and cook 50 minutes or until fish flakes easily when tested with a fork.

SMOKED ROSEMARY-SCENTED SALMON

Smoking is a slow-cooking process that makes fish, poultry, and meat especially tender and flavorful—the wood chips add unforgettable taste. We tested this recipe (pictured on page 44) with a meat smoker. However, you can use your charcoal or gas grill with equally satisfying results.

Hickory or alder wood chips
1   (3-pound) salmon fillet, halved crosswise
¾   cup fresh lime juice
3   tablespoons minced fresh rosemary
2   tablespoons olive oil
1½ teaspoons prepared horseradish
1½ teaspoons cracked pepper
¾   teaspoon salt
Vegetable cooking spray
Fresh rosemary sprig (optional)
Lime wedges (optional)

Soak wood chips in water to cover 1 to 24 hours. Drain well.

Place fish in a large heavy-duty, zip-top plastic bag. Combine lime juice and next 3 ingredients. Pour over fish; seal bag, and shake gently until fish is well coated. Marinate in refrigerator 3 hours, turning bag occasionally. Remove fish from bag, reserving marinade. Sprinkle fish with pepper and salt; set aside.

Prepare charcoal fire in meat smoker; let burn 15 to 20 minutes. Place soaked wood chips on top of coals. Place water pan in smoker; add reserved marinade. Add hot tap water to fill pan.

Coat grill rack with cooking spray; place rack in smoker. Arrange fish on rack, skin side down, allowing enough room between fish pieces for air to circulate. Cover with smoker lid, and cook 50 minutes or until fish flakes easily when tested with a fork. If desired, garnish with fresh rosemary sprig, and serve with lime wedges. Yield: 12 servings (serving size: 3 ounces fish).

Calories 130 (43% from fat) Protein 16.1g Fat 6.2g (sat 1.1g) Carbohydrate 2.0g Fiber 0.2g Cholesterol 20mg Iron 1.0mg Sodium 833mg Calcium 20mg

FRESH TUNA WITH TANGY ONIONS

QUICK & EASY

1   tablespoon olive oil
2   cups chopped onion
½   cup red wine vinegar
¼   teaspoon salt, divided
¼   teaspoon pepper, divided
½   cup all-purpose flour
8   (4-ounce) tuna steaks (about ¾ inch thick)
2   teaspoons olive oil

Heat 1 tablespoon olive oil in a large nonstick skillet over medium-high heat. Add chopped onion, and sauté 5 minutes or until lightly browned. Add vinegar, ⅛ teaspoon salt, and ⅛ teaspoon pepper; cook mixture 2 minutes or until most of

Maryland Crab Cakes

liquid evaporates. Remove onion mixture from skillet; set aside, and keep warm. Wipe skillet clean with a paper towel.

Combine remaining ⅛ teaspoon salt, remaining ⅛ teaspoon pepper, and flour in a shallow dish; stir well. Dredge fish in flour mixture.

Heat 2 teaspoons olive oil in a large skillet over medium heat. Add half of fish, and cook 2 minutes on each side until fish is medium-rare or to desired degree of doneness. Repeat procedure with remaining fish. Serve fish with onion mixture. Yield: 8 servings (serving size: 3 ounces fish and 2 tablespoons onion mixture).

Calories 228 (33% from fat) **Protein** 26.7g **Fat** 8.3g (sat 1.8g) **Carbohydrate** 10.2g **Fiber** 1.0g **Cholesterol** 42mg **Iron** 1.6mg **Sodium** 117mg **Calcium** 10mg

MARYLAND CRAB CAKES

Tear fresh or slightly stale bread into small pieces to make soft breadcrumbs.

1	pound fresh lump crabmeat, shell pieces removed
1⅓	cups soft breadcrumbs
⅓	cup minced green onions
⅓	cup chopped fresh parsley
2	tablespoons lemon juice
1	tablespoon 2% low-fat milk
1	teaspoon hot sauce
½	teaspoon salt
¼	teaspoon pepper
4	egg whites, lightly beaten
1⅓	cups soft breadcrumbs
2	tablespoons vegetable oil, divided

Lemon wedges (optional)

Combine first 10 ingredients in a bowl, and stir well. Shape mixture into 8 (½-inch-thick) patties. Place 1⅓ cups soft breadcrumbs in a shallow dish, and coat patties with breadcrumbs.

Heat 1 tablespoon vegetable oil in a large nonstick skillet over medium-high heat. Add 4 coated patties, and cook 3 minutes. Carefully turn patties, and cook 3 minutes or until patties are golden. Repeat procedure with remaining 1 tablespoon vegetable oil and remaining 4 coated patties. Serve crab cakes with lemon wedges, if desired. Yield: 4 servings (serving size: 2 crab cakes).

Calories 282 (32% from fat) **Protein** 29.4g **Fat** 10.0g (sat 1.8g) **Carbohydrate** 17.2g **Fiber** 1.0g **Cholesterol** 114mg **Iron** 2.2mg **Sodium** 830mg **Calcium** 162mg

*For Wrapping Crab
Spring Rolls*

1. Fold the lower right, lower left, and then top right corners of the egg roll over the crab mixture.

2. Brush egg white onto the top left corner so it will cling to the dry egg roll wrapper and seal in the filling.

3. Roll up the crab-filled portion of the egg roll toward the corner brushed with egg white.

CRAB SPRING ROLLS

Find pickled ginger, preserved in sweet vinegar, on the ethnic aisle of supermarkets or at Asian markets. Or order pickled ginger from Cinnabar Specialty Foods, Inc., at 1134 W. Haining Street, Prescott, AZ 86301 (800-824-4563).

2	tablespoons sugar
1	cup pink grapefruit juice
2	tablespoons fresh lime juice
⅛	teaspoon freshly ground pepper
Vegetable cooking spray	
2	cups thinly sliced bok choy
⅔	cup finely chopped green onions
6	ounces fresh lump crabmeat, shell pieces removed
2	tablespoons fresh lime juice
2	teaspoons minced fresh cilantro
½	teaspoon minced pickled ginger
⅛	teaspoon salt
⅛	teaspoon freshly ground pepper
8	egg roll wrappers
1	egg white, lightly beaten
2	tablespoons olive oil
2	cups mixed baby salad greens
12	pink grapefruit sections
2	tablespoons slivered almonds, toasted

Place sugar in a small saucepan over medium-high heat; caramelize by stirring often until sugar melts and is golden (about 2 minutes). Remove from heat; carefully stir in grapefruit juice and 2 tablespoons lime juice (caramelized sugar will harden and stick to spoon). Place pan over medium-high heat until caramelized sugar melts. Bring to a boil, and cook 8 minutes or until reduced to ½ cup, stirring often. Remove from heat; stir in ⅛ teaspoon pepper. Set aside.

Coat a nonstick skillet with cooking spray; place over medium heat until hot. Add bok choy and green onions. Sauté until bok choy wilts. Combine bok choy mixture, crabmeat, 2 tablespoons lime juice, cilantro, pickled ginger, salt, and ⅛ teaspoon pepper; stir mixture well.

Working with 1 egg roll wrapper at a time (keeping remaining wrappers covered), spoon ¼ cup crabmeat mixture onto center of wrapper. Fold lower right corner over crabmeat mixture; fold lower left and top right corners over mixture. Moisten top left corner with egg white; roll up, jellyroll fashion, and seal roll with moistened corner. Repeat procedure with remaining wrappers, crabmeat mixture, and egg white.

Heat oil in skillet over medium-high heat. Add egg rolls; cook 5 minutes or until golden, turning rolls often.

Arrange ½ cup salad greens and 3 grapefruit sections on each of 4 serving plates; top each with 2 egg rolls. Drizzle 2 tablespoons caramelized sugar mixture over each serving; sprinkle each serving with

1½ teaspoons slivered almonds. Yield: 4 servings (serving size: ½ cup salad greens, 3 grapefruit sections, and 2 egg rolls).

Calories 414 (23% from fat) **Protein** 18.2g **Fat** 10.4g (sat 1.4g) **Carbohydrate** 62.2g **Fiber** 1.5g **Cholesterol** 48mg **Iron** 4.8mg **Sodium** 602mg **Calcium** 154mg

ITALIAN-STYLE SCALLOP KABOBS

QUICK & EASY

36 sea scallops (about 1 pound)
1   (6-ounce) package lean, smoked sliced ham, cut into 36 strips
Vegetable cooking spray
2   cloves garlic, minced
¼   cup lemon juice
2   tablespoons minced fresh parsley
¾   teaspoon minced fresh oregano

Wrap each scallop with a strip of ham; thread 6 scallops onto each of 6 (12-inch) skewers. Set aside.

Coat a medium nonstick skillet with cooking spray; place over medium-high heat until hot. Add garlic, and sauté until browned. Remove from heat, and stir in lemon juice, parsley, and oregano.

Coat grill rack with cooking spray, and place on grill over medium-hot coals (350° to 400°). Place kabobs on rack; grill, uncovered, 9 minutes or until scallops are done, turning and basting often with lemon

mixture. Serve warm. Yield: 6 servings (serving size: 1 kabob).

Calories 102 (15% from fat) **Protein** 17.8g **Fat** 1.7g (sat 0.1g) **Carbohydrate** 3.1g **Fiber** 0.1g **Cholesterol** 35mg **Iron** 0.4mg **Sodium** 482mg **Calcium** 24mg

COQUILLES ST. JACQUES À LA PROVENÇALE

Coquilles St. Jacques (koh-KEEL sahn-ZHAHK) is a French specialty made with scallops and a creamy white sauce. *Coquille* is French for "scallop" and "shell," and the dish is usually served in scallop shells or individual gratin dishes. *Provençale* refers to foods characteristic of the Provence region in France.

1½ tablespoons margarine, divided
⅓   cup minced onion
2   tablespoons minced shallots
1   clove garlic, minced
½   cup all-purpose flour
1¼ pounds sea scallops
⅔   cup dry white wine
½   teaspoon chopped fresh thyme
⅛   teaspoon salt
½   bay leaf
Dash of ground white pepper
¼   cup plus 2 tablespoons (1½ ounces) shredded Swiss cheese

Melt 1½ teaspoons margarine in a nonstick skillet over medium heat; add onion. Sauté 3 minutes or until

lightly browned. Add shallots and garlic, and sauté 1 minute. Remove from skillet, and set aside.

Place flour in a heavy-duty, zip-top plastic bag; add scallops. Seal bag; shake until scallops are coated.

Melt remaining 1 tablespoon margarine in skillet over medium heat. Add scallops; sauté 4 minutes or until scallops are opaque. Return onion mixture to skillet; add wine and next 4 ingredients. Cover, reduce heat, and simmer 4 minutes. Uncover mixture, and bring to a boil; cook 1 minute. Remove and discard bay leaf.

Spoon scallop mixture evenly into 6 individual gratin dishes. Top each with 1 tablespoon cheese. Broil 5½ inches from heat (with electric oven door partially opened) 30 seconds or until cheese melts. Serve immediately. Yield: 6 servings.

Calories 197 (26% from fat) **Protein** 19.2g **Fat** 5.6g (sat 1.9g) **Carbohydrate** 12.2g **Fiber** 0.5g **Cholesterol** 38mg **Iron** 1.0mg **Sodium** 253mg **Calcium** 100mg

Skewered Mustard-
Beer Shrimp

SKEWERED MUSTARD-
BEER SHRIMP

To make this recipe quickly and
easily, buy already-peeled shrimp.

2	**pounds (about 48) unpeeled large fresh shrimp**
½	**teaspoon garlic powder**
½	**teaspoon ground red pepper**
¼	**cup spicy brown mustard**
¼	**cup light beer**
	Vegetable cooking spray

Peel and devein shrimp, leaving
tails intact. Thread 6 shrimp onto
each of 8 (12-inch) skewers. Sprinkle
shrimp evenly with garlic powder
and pepper.

Combine mustard and beer; stir
mixture well.

Coat grill rack with cooking spray;
place on grill over medium-hot
coals (350° to 400°). Place skewers
on rack; grill, uncovered, 5 minutes
on each side, basting shrimp often
with mustard mixture. Yield: 4 servings (serving size: 2 kabobs).

Calories 136 (16% from fat) **Protein** 24.8g
Fat 2.4g (sat 0.3g) **Carbohydrate** 1.6g
Fiber 0.1g **Cholesterol** 221mg **Iron** 3.5mg
Sodium 400mg **Calcium** 46mg

A HANDY WAY TO
CHECK THE COALS

A quick way to judge the temperature of the coals is to hold
your hand, palm down, over
coals at grill rack level. Count
the seconds you can hold your
hand at that level before it
becomes too hot.

5 seconds = low heat

4 seconds = medium heat

3 seconds = medium-hot heat

2 seconds = high heat

CHILLED LOBSTER SALAD WITH BASIL-LIME SALSA

½ cup seeded, chopped tomato
2 tablespoons fresh lime juice
1 tablespoon balsamic vinegar
1 tablespoon olive oil
1 small clove garlic
1½ cups seeded, chopped tomato
⅓ cup peeled, seeded, and diced cucumber
⅓ cup finely chopped green onions
2 tablespoons finely chopped fresh basil
¼ teaspoon salt
⅛ teaspoon pepper
2½ ears fresh corn, cooked
4 cups tightly packed sliced romaine lettuce
1 cup tightly packed torn fresh watercress
¾ pound cooked lobster meat, cut into bite-sized pieces

Position knife blade in food processor bowl; add ½ cup tomato, lime juice, balsamic vinegar, olive oil, and garlic. Process until smooth. Pour mixture into a medium bowl; stir in 1½ cups tomato and next 5 ingredients. Set mixture aside.

Cut whole kernels from ears of corn to measure 2 cups. Combine cut corn, lettuce, and watercress in a large bowl; toss well. Add tomato mixture, and toss gently to coat. Place salad evenly on 4 serving plates, and top evenly with lobster.

Yield: 4 servings (serving size: about 2 cups salad and 3 ounces lobster).

Calories 183 (25% from fat) Protein 19.3g Fat 5.1g (sat 0.8g) Carbohydrate 17.4g Fiber 4.0g Cholesterol 81mg Iron 1.5mg Sodium 171mg Calcium 47mg

PAELLA

Arborio is a rice valued for the creamy texture it lends to any recipe.

1 pound unpeeled medium-size fresh shrimp
16 fresh mussels
8 small clams in shells
2 tablespoons yellow cornmeal
2 (10½-ounce) cans low-sodium chicken broth, undiluted
¼ teaspoon salt
⅛ teaspoon black pepper
½ teaspoon threads of saffron
Vegetable cooking spray
1 tablespoon olive oil
1 pound skinned, boned chicken breasts, cut into 1-inch pieces
1 cup chopped onion
2 cloves garlic, minced
2 cups julienne-sliced sweet red pepper
2 cups chopped tomato
1½ cups Arborio rice, uncooked
½ cup water
1 cup frozen English peas, thawed

Peel and devein shrimp; set aside. Remove beards on mussels, and scrub shells with a brush. Discard opened, cracked, or heavy mussels (they're filled with sand). Wash clams thoroughly, discarding any opened shells. Place mussels and clams in a large bowl; cover with cold water. Sprinkle with cornmeal; let stand 30 minutes. Drain; rinse mussels and clams under running water, and set aside.

Combine broth, salt, and black pepper in a medium saucepan; place over medium heat. Add saffron, and simmer 10 minutes. Reduce heat to low; keep warm (do not boil).

Coat a nonstick skillet with cooking spray, and add oil. Place over medium heat until hot, and add chicken, onion, and garlic. Sauté 5 minutes or until chicken is lightly browned. Add red pepper and tomato; sauté 3 minutes. Add rice; cook, stirring constantly, 2 minutes.

Add ½ cup broth mixture to rice mixture, stirring constantly until most of liquid is absorbed. Add remaining broth mixture, ½ cup at a time, cooking and stirring constantly until each addition is absorbed (about 30 minutes). (Rice will be tender.)

Stir in ½ cup water. Add shrimp, mussels, clams, and peas. Cover and cook 10 minutes or until mussels and clams open and shrimp are done. (Discard any unopened mussels and clams.) Yield: 8 servings (serving size: 1 cup rice and shrimp mixture, 2 mussels, and 1 clam).

Calories 339 (12% from fat) Protein 30.4g Fat 4.6g (sat 1.0g) Carbohydrate 41.8g Fiber 2.2g Cholesterol 113mg Iron 7.2mg Sodium 325mg Calcium 48mg

Seven-Layer Tortilla Pie,
page 68

You study the menu while the waiter waits, pen in hand. Will it be the burger or the taco salad? Of course, the chicken pot pie looks tempting...but then you spy the veggie-topped pizza. Decision made. It's a meatless meal. But that's not how you think about it.

MEATLESS MAIN

You picked it for the pure enjoyment of flavor, not because your moral conscience bids you to forego meat. The recipes in this chapter, like soul-satisfying Polenta With Italian Vegetable Sauce and hearty Seven-Layer Tortilla Pie, make it easy to enjoy the same flavor at home. In fact, if tomatoes are ripe, don't wait. Make Fresh Tomato, Basil, and Cheese Pizza—one of our favorites—tonight.

EGGS SARDOU

A lighter cheese sauce replaces traditional egg-based hollandaise sauce in this New Orleans brunch classic.

Vegetable cooking spray
¼   cup chopped green onions
1   (9-ounce) package frozen artichoke hearts, thawed
4   cups tightly packed torn spinach leaves
2   hard-cooked eggs, peeled and sliced
1½ tablespoons all-purpose flour
1   cup skim milk
2   tablespoons grated Parmesan cheese, divided
1   tablespoon plus 1 teaspoon lemon juice
⅛   teaspoon dried whole thyme
⅛   teaspoon freshly ground pepper
⅛   teaspoon paprika
¼   cup nonfat sour cream

Coat a nonstick skillet with cooking spray; place over medium heat until hot. Add green onions and artichokes; sauté 5 minutes. Remove from heat; stir in spinach. Spoon mixture into 2 individual gratin dishes coated with cooking spray. Arrange egg over mixture; set aside.
Place flour in a small saucepan; gradually add milk, stirring with a wire whisk until blended. Place over medium heat; cook, stirring constantly, 5 minutes or until thickened. Remove from heat; stir in 1 tablespoon cheese and next 3 ingredients.

Pour ½ cup sauce over egg in each casserole. Combine remaining 1 tablespoon cheese and paprika; sprinkle over sauce. Place dishes on a baking sheet. Cover with foil, and bake at 350° for 20 minutes. To serve, top each with 2 tablespoons sour cream. Yield: 2 servings.

Calories 272 (30% from fat) Protein 22.0g Fat 9.0g (sat 3.0g) Carbohydrate 28.6g Fiber 6.0g Cholesterol 219mg Iron 5.0mg Sodium 390mg Calcium 393mg

MUSHROOM AND CHEESE SOUFFLÉ

Use a food processor with a steel shredding blade to grate nutty-tasting Asiago (ah-SYAH-goh) cheese.

Vegetable cooking spray
2   teaspoons fine, dry breadcrumbs
3   tablespoons all-purpose flour
⅛   teaspoon black pepper
Dash of ground red pepper
1   cup skim milk
2   egg yolks
1   cup finely chopped fresh shiitake mushroom caps
½   cup finely chopped fresh mushrooms
¾   cup (2¼ ounces) finely grated Asiago cheese
¼   cup sliced green onions
⅔   cup mashed cooked potato
5   egg whites
¼   teaspoon cream of tartar

Coat a 1½-quart soufflé dish with cooking spray; sprinkle bottom and sides of dish with breadcrumbs. Set dish aside.
Combine flour, black pepper, and red pepper in a small bowl. Gradually add milk, stirring with a wire whisk until blended. Set aside.
Place egg yolks in a small bowl; stir well, and set aside. Coat a small saucepan with cooking spray, and place over medium-high heat until hot. Add mushrooms; sauté 3 minutes. Add milk mixture; cook over medium heat 2 minutes or until thickened and bubbly.
Gradually stir about one-fourth of hot milk mixture into egg yolks; add to remaining milk mixture in saucepan, stirring constantly. Stir in cheese and green onions, and cook over medium heat, stirring constantly, 1½ minutes or until thickened. Spoon into a large bowl; stir in potato. Set aside.
Beat egg whites and cream of tartar at high speed of an electric mixer until stiff peaks form. Gently stir one-fourth of egg white mixture into potato mixture. Gently fold in remaining egg white mixture. Pour mixture into prepared soufflé dish. Bake at 375° for 45 minutes or until puffed and golden. Serve immediately. Yield: 4 servings.

Calories 192 (34% from fat) Protein 15.4g Fat 7.3g (sat 3.5g) Carbohydrate 15.9g Fiber 1.1g Cholesterol 121mg Iron 1.3mg Sodium 382mg Calcium 288mg

FRESH TOMATO AND BASIL QUICHE

Find a photograph of this recipe, along with a menu that includes it, on page 221.

1	(7-ounce) package refrigerated breadstick dough
	Vegetable cooking spray
1	teaspoon olive oil
1	cup slivered onion
1	clove garlic, minced
¾	cup (3 ounces) shredded part-skim mozzarella cheese
1	cup (¼-inch-thick) sliced plum tomato
¼	cup shredded fresh basil
1	cup evaporated skimmed milk
1½	teaspoons cornstarch
¼	teaspoon freshly ground pepper
2	eggs
1	egg white

Unroll dough; separate into strips. Working on a flat surface, coil 1 strip of dough around itself in a spiral pattern. Add a second strip to end of first strip, and pinch ends together to seal; continue coiling dough. Repeat procedure with remaining dough to make an 8-inch flat circle. Roll dough into a 13-inch circle; fit into a 9-inch quiche dish or pieplate coated with cooking spray. Fold edges under, and flute.

Coat a nonstick skillet with cooking spray; add oil, and place over medium heat until hot. Add onion and garlic; sauté 8 minutes or until lightly browned. Spread onion mixture in bottom of prepared crust; sprinkle with cheese. Arrange tomato slices over cheese; top with basil.

Combine milk and remaining 4 ingredients in container of an electric blender; cover and process until smooth. Pour over tomatoes. Bake, uncovered, at 350° for 45 minutes or until a knife inserted 1 inch from center comes out clean; let stand 10 minutes. Yield: 6 servings (serving size: 1 wedge).

Calories 207 (30% from fat) **Protein** 12.4g **Fat** 6.9g (sat 2.8g) **Carbohydrate** 18.0g **Fiber** 0.8g **Cholesterol** 84mg **Iron** 0.6mg **Sodium** 341mg **Calcium** 234mg

TECHNIQUE

For Low-Fat Quiche Crust

Refrigerated breadstick dough (yes, the kind in a can) turns into a low-fat crust for Fresh Tomato and Basil Quiche.

1. Coil one strip of breadstick dough around itself in a spiral pattern.

2. Add a second strip to the end of the first strip, pinching ends together to seal. Continue coiling to make a flat 8-inch circle.

3. Roll 8-inch dough circle into a 13-inch circle.

4. Fit rolled dough into a 9-inch quiche dish coated with cooking spray; fold edges under, and flute edges with your fingertips.

Squash and Potato Frittata

If you like omelets, you'll like frittatas. To make a frittata, mix the ingredients together, and cook slowly over low heat in a skillet for a sort of egg "pie."

¾ pound small round red potatoes
Vegetable cooking spray
1 cup thinly sliced zucchini
1 cup thinly sliced yellow squash
¼ cup loosely packed parsley
½ teaspoon grated lemon rind
¼ teaspoon salt
¼ teaspoon ground pepper
1 clove garlic, crushed
2 teaspoons olive oil
½ cup (2 ounces) crumbled feta cheese
1½ cups fat-free egg substitute

Place potatoes in a medium saucepan; cover with water, and bring to a boil over medium-high heat. Cook, uncovered, 20 minutes or just until tender. Drain; let cool. Peel potatoes, and cut into ¼-inch slices.

Coat a large nonstick skillet with cooking spray; place over low heat until hot. Add zucchini and yellow squash. Cover and cook 10 minutes or until tender. Combine squash mixture, parsley, and next 4 ingredients in a bowl; toss gently.

Wipe skillet with paper towels. Heat oil in skillet over medium heat. Arrange potato slices in skillet, overlapping slices. Cook over medium heat, without turning, 10 minutes or until potato slices begin to brown. Spoon half of squash mixture evenly over potato layer. Top with feta cheese, and layer remaining squash mixture over cheese.

Pour egg substitute over squash mixture; cover and cook over medium-low heat 20 minutes or until set. Serve warm. Yield: 4 servings (serving size: 1 wedge).

Calories 168 (30% from fat) Protein 13.3g Fat 5.6g (sat 2.5g) Carbohydrate 16.5g Fiber 1.9g Cholesterol 13mg Iron 2.8mg Sodium 447mg Calcium 124mg

Chicago Deep-Dish Pizza With Mushrooms, Peppers, and Onions

Deep-Dish Pizza Dough
1 tablespoon olive oil
1½ cups chopped green pepper
1½ cups chopped onion
1 clove garlic, crushed
2½ cups sliced mushrooms
2 teaspoons dried oregano
¼ teaspoon salt
1½ cups canned crushed tomatoes
1¼ cups (5 ounces) shredded reduced-fat Monterey Jack cheese
¾ cup (3 ounces) shredded provolone cheese

Prepare Deep-Dish Pizza Dough, and set aside.

Heat oil in a large nonstick skillet over medium heat. Add pepper, onion, and garlic, and sauté 5 minutes. Add mushrooms, oregano, and salt; sauté 3 minutes or until tender. Remove from heat; cool.

Spread half of tomatoes over each prepared crust, and top each with half of vegetable mixture. Sprinkle Monterey Jack cheese and provolone cheese evenly over pizzas.

Bake at 475° for 15 minutes. Reduce oven temperature to 375°, and bake 15 additional minutes. Cut each pizza into 8 wedges. Yield: 8 servings (serving size: 2 wedges).

Calories 342 (28% from fat) Protein 14.8g Fat 10.6g (sat 4.4g) Carbohydrate 47.2g Fiber 3.4g Cholesterol 19mg Iron 3.6mg Sodium 417mg Calcium 261mg

DEEP-DISH PIZZA DOUGH:

1 teaspoon sugar
1 package active dry yeast
1 cup warm water (105° to 115°)
2½ cups all-purpose flour
½ cup yellow cornmeal
¼ teaspoon salt
1 tablespoon olive oil
Vegetable cooking spray
2 tablespoons yellow cornmeal

Combine first 3 ingredients in a small bowl, and let stand 5 minutes. Position knife blade in food processor bowl; add flour, ½ cup cornmeal, and salt, and pulse 2 times or until blended. With processor running, slowly add yeast mixture and oil through food chute, and process until dough forms a ball. Process 1 additional minute.

Turn dough out onto a lightly floured surface; knead lightly 4 or 5 times. Place dough in a large bowl coated with cooking spray, turning to coat top. Cover dough, and let rise in a warm place (85°), free from drafts, 45 minutes or until doubled in bulk.

Punch dough down; cover and let rest 5 minutes. Divide dough in half; roll each half into an 11-inch circle on a lightly floured surface. Coat 2 (9-inch) round cake pans with cooking spray, and sprinkle each with 1 tablespoon cornmeal. Place dough in prepared pans; press dough up sides of pans. Cover and let rise 20 minutes or until puffy. Top and bake according to recipe directions. Yield: dough for 2 (9-inch) deep-dish pizza crusts.

Chicago Deep-Dish Pizza With Mushrooms, Peppers, and Onions

"I make this a lot during the summer when I can use fresh tomatoes and when the basil tastes best. My husband is crazy about pizza and especially likes this recipe. You could probably use a commercial crust to make it more quickly, but I always make my own crust—the flavor is worth it."

——Telia Johnson, former Test Kitchens Staff

FRESH TOMATO, BASIL, AND CHEESE PIZZA

Homemade Pizza Dough
2   teaspoons olive oil
½   cup freshly grated Parmesan cheese, divided
3   large ripe tomatoes, cut into ¼-inch-thick slices (about 1½ pounds)
6   cloves garlic, thinly sliced
¼   teaspoon salt
⅛   teaspoon pepper
¼   teaspoon chopped fresh basil

Prepare Homemade Pizza Dough. Brush prepared dough for 1 pizza with oil. Sprinkle with ¼ cup Parmesan cheese, leaving a ½-inch border. Arrange tomato slices over cheese, overlapping slices. Top with garlic, remaining ¼ cup Parmesan cheese, salt, and pepper. Bake at 500° for 10 to 12 minutes on bottom rack of oven. Remove pizza to a cutting board; top with basil. Cool 5 minutes. Yield: 6 servings (serving size: 1 wedge).

Calories 194 (23% from fat) **Protein** 7.7g **Fat** 4.9g (sat 1.9g) **Carbohydrate** 30.0g **Fiber** 1.9g **Cholesterol** 6mg **Iron** 2.0mg **Sodium** 303mg **Calcium** 129mg

HOMEMADE PIZZA DOUGH:

1   package active dry yeast
1   tablespoon sugar
1   cup warm water (105° to 115°)
3   cups all-purpose flour, divided
¼   teaspoon salt
1   teaspoon olive oil
Vegetable cooking spray
1   tablespoon yellow cornmeal

Combine first 3 ingredients in a 2-cup liquid measuring cup; let stand 5 minutes. Combine yeast mixture, 2¾ cups flour, salt, and oil in a large bowl, stirring to form a soft dough.

Turn dough out onto a lightly floured surface. Knead until smooth and elastic (about 5 minutes); add enough of remaining ¼ cup flour, 1 tablespoon at a time, to keep dough from sticking to hands.

Place dough in a bowl coated with cooking spray, turning to coat top. Cover and let rise in a warm place (85°), free from drafts, 1 hour or until doubled in bulk.

Punch dough down, and divide in half. Roll each half of dough into a 12-inch circle on a lightly floured surface. Coat 2 (12-inch) pizza pans or baking sheets with cooking spray; sprinkle each with ½ tablespoon cornmeal. Place dough on prepared pans. Crimp edges of dough with fingers to form a rim. Cover; let rise in a warm place, free from drafts, 30 minutes. Top and bake according to recipe directions. Yield: dough for 2 (12-inch) pizza crusts.

Note: Freeze dough up to 1 month, if desired. To freeze, wrap tightly in plastic wrap; place in a heavy-duty, zip-top plastic bag. To use, thaw the frozen dough in the refrigerator overnight.

INDIAN CORN CASSEROLE

Because Native Americans always planted and ate corn, beans, and squash together, they called the three vegetables "The Inseparable Sisters."

4   ears fresh corn with husks
1   quart water
3   cups grated zucchini
1   cup minced onion
1   (4.5-ounce) can chopped green chiles, drained
½   cup all-purpose flour
1   teaspoon ground cumin
1   teaspoon chili powder
½   teaspoon freshly ground black pepper
¼   teaspoon salt
¼   teaspoon ground red pepper
2   (15-ounce) cans black beans, drained

Husk corn, reserving 12 husks; rinse husks thoroughly. Bring water to a boil in a saucepan; add husks.

1. Line a 2-quart casserole with softened corn husks, and allow the excess length of husks to extend over the sides.

2. Fold the extended ends of the husks toward the center, and overlap the tops over the casserole.

Remove from heat. Cover and let stand 15 minutes. Drain; pat dry with paper towels. Line a 2-quart casserole with softened husks, allowing excess to extend over sides.

Cut whole kernels from 2 ears of corn. Grate corn from remaining 2 ears, pressing firmly to remove pulp. Add grated corn to cut corn.

Combine zucchini, onion, and chiles in a large nonstick skillet. Cover; cook over medium-low heat 10 minutes, stirring occasionally. Add flour and next 5 ingredients; stir well. Stir in corn and beans. Cook, uncovered, over medium heat 4 minutes, stirring often.

Spoon mixture into prepared dish. Fold extended ends of husks toward center, overlapping ends of husks. Bake at 325° for 25 minutes. Yield: 4 servings (serving size: 1½ cups).

Calories 461 (6% from fat) **Protein** 25.0g **Fat** 2.7g (sat 0.6g) **Carbohydrate** 90.4g **Fiber** 14.1g **Cholesterol** 0mg **Iron** 6.8mg **Sodium** 656mg **Calcium** 94mg

CURRIED VEGETABLE FRIED RICE

QUICK & EASY

1	cup coarsely chopped fresh cauliflower flowerets
½	cup diced carrot
2	teaspoons curry powder
1	teaspoon chili powder
½	teaspoon salt
⅛	teaspoon ground red pepper
1	tablespoon water
2	teaspoons vegetable oil
¼	cup finely chopped onion
1	clove garlic, minced
4	cups cooked long-grain rice (cooked without salt or fat)
½	cup frozen English peas, thawed
¼	cup raisins
1	(8-ounce) carton fat-free egg substitute
½	cup chopped almonds, toasted

Cook cauliflower and carrot in boiling water to cover 3 minutes. Drain and rinse under cold water; set aside.

Combine curry powder and next 4 ingredients; stir well. Heat oil in a large nonstick skillet over medium heat. Add curry powder mixture, onion, and garlic; stir-fry 3 minutes. Add cauliflower mixture, rice, peas, and raisins; stir-fry 2 minutes or until heated. Add egg substitute; cook, stirring constantly, 1 minute or until egg is done. Add almonds; toss well. Yield: 4 servings (serving size: 1½ cups).

Calories 425 (24% from fat) **Protein** 15.1g **Fat** 11.4g (sat 1.3g) **Carbohydrate** 66.9g **Fiber** 5.9g **Cholesterol** 0mg **Iron** 4.5mg **Sodium** 417mg **Calcium** 110mg

Rice and Beans
With Pesto

BLACK BEAN AND RICE BURRITOS

1   tablespoon salt-free
    garlic-and-herb spice blend
¼   teaspoon ground cumin
1   (15-ounce) can black beans,
    undrained
1¾ cups cooked long-grain rice
    (cooked without salt or fat)
6   (8-inch) flour tortillas
¾   cup (3 ounces) shredded
    reduced-fat sharp Cheddar
    cheese
¼   cup plus 2 tablespoons
    sliced green onions
¼   cup plus 2 tablespoons
    salsa
¼   cup plus 2 tablespoons
    nonfat sour cream

RICE AND BEANS WITH PESTO

Q U I C K   &   E A S Y

Vegetable cooking spray
1½ cups chopped onion
1½ cups instant brown rice,
    uncooked
2¾ cups canned vegetable broth,
    undiluted
1½ cups seeded, chopped
    tomato
⅓   cup pesto basil sauce
2   (16-ounce) cans red beans,
    drained
Fresh basil (optional)

Coat a large nonstick skillet with
cooking spray, and place over

medium-high heat until hot. Add
onion, and sauté 2 minutes; stir in
rice and broth. Bring to a boil;
reduce heat, and simmer, uncovered,
15 minutes or until rice is tender
and liquid is absorbed.

Stir in tomato, pesto sauce, and
beans. Cook over medium-high heat
2 minutes or until mixture is thoroughly heated. Spoon into a serving
dish; garnish with fresh basil, if
desired. Yield: 4 servings (serving
size: 2 cups).

Calories 414 (27% from fat) Protein 18.2g
Fat 12.6g (sat 2.0g) Carbohydrate 62.3g
Fiber 8.8g Cholesterol 2mg Iron 6.7mg
Sodium 997mg Calcium 203mg

Combine first 3 ingredients in a
medium saucepan, and bring to a
boil. Reduce heat, and simmer,
uncovered, 5 minutes, stirring mixture occasionally. Remove from
heat, and stir in rice.

Spoon about ⅓ cup bean mixture
down center of each tortilla. Top
each tortilla with 2 tablespoons
cheese, 1 tablespoon green onions, 1
tablespoon salsa, and 1 tablespoon
sour cream; roll up. Yield: 6 servings
(serving size: 1 burrito).

Calories 332 (15% from fat) Protein 16.1g
Fat 5.7g (sat 2.1g) Carbohydrate 53.9g
Fiber 5.1g Cholesterol 9mg Iron 3.8mg
Sodium 573mg Calcium 212mg

Rice Enchiladas With Black Bean Sauce

Black Bean Sauce
½   cup 1% low-fat cottage cheese
¼   cup low-fat sour cream
1½ ounces goat cheese, crumbled
1   cup cooked long-grain rice (cooked without salt or fat)
¼   cup finely chopped onion
1   tablespoon seeded, minced jalapeño pepper
1   cup water
8   (6-inch) corn tortillas
Vegetable cooking spray
¾   cup (3 ounces) shredded reduced-fat Monterey Jack cheese
1   cup seeded, chopped tomato
1   tablespoon minced fresh cilantro
½   cup low-fat sour cream

Prepare Black Bean Sauce, and set aside.

Position knife blade in food processor bowl, and add cottage cheese, ¼ cup sour cream, and goat cheese. Process until smooth. Spoon into a bowl. Stir in rice, onion, and jalapeño pepper; set rice mixture aside.

Bring water to a boil in a large skillet. Working quickly, dip 1 tortilla in water. Spread about 3 tablespoons rice mixture down center of tortilla; fold sides over, and place, seam side down, in a 13- x 9- x 2-inch baking dish coated with cooking spray. Repeat procedure with remaining tortillas and rice mixture.

Pour 2¼ cups Black Bean Sauce over tortillas; cover tortillas, and bake at 350° for 25 minutes. Uncover and sprinkle with Monterey Jack cheese. Bake, uncovered, 5 additional minutes or until cheese melts.

Combine tomato and cilantro in a bowl, and stir well. Spoon 2 tablespoons Black Bean Sauce onto each of 8 serving plates; top each with a filled tortilla and 2 tablespoons tomato mixture. Dollop each serving with 1 tablespoon low-fat sour cream. Yield: 8 servings (serving size: 1 enchilada).

Calories 294 (27% from fat) **Protein** 13.9g **Fat** 8.9g (sat 4.1g) **Carbohydrate** 39.0g **Fiber** 4.8g **Cholesterol** 21mg **Iron** 2.9mg **Sodium** 488mg **Calcium** 196mg

BLACK BEAN SAUCE:

1   ancho chile
1   (15-ounce) can no-salt-added black beans, undrained
1   (14½-ounce) can vegetable broth
½   cup chopped onion
2   cloves garlic
1   bay leaf
½   teaspoon hot sauce

Cut chile in half lengthwise, and discard seeds and stem. Combine chile, beans, and next 4 ingredients in a large saucepan. Bring bean mixture to a boil, and simmer, uncovered, 5 minutes. Remove and discard bay leaf.

Position knife blade in food processor bowl, and add bean mixture. Process until beans are chopped; pour into a bowl. Stir in hot sauce. Yield: 3¼ cups (serving size: 1 tablespoon).

Calories 9 (0% from fat) **Protein** 0.1g **Fat** 0.0g (sat 0.0g) **Carbohydrate** 0.4g **Fiber** 0.5g **Cholesterol** 0mg **Iron** 0.2mg **Sodium** 19mg **Calcium** 1mg

Team Up Proteins

Pasta, grains, legumes, vegetables, and seeds contain incomplete proteins. But when you team up just two of them, the incomplete protein in each pairs with the other to provide a complete protein equivalent to that of meat. That's why meatless main recipes often mix protein-powered rice or pasta with legumes such as dried or canned beans.

If a meatless dish includes cheese or milk, there's no need to worry about the amount of protein. Like meat, dairy foods contain complete proteins.

SEVEN-LAYER TORTILLA PIE

1	tablespoon olive oil
1	cup chopped sweet red pepper
¾	cup chopped green pepper
½	cup chopped purple onion
½	cup seeded, chopped Anaheim chile or
1	(4.5-ounce) can chopped green chiles, drained
2	tablespoons minced fresh cilantro
1	teaspoon dried oregano
1	teaspoon chili powder
½	teaspoon ground cumin
2	cups no-salt-added tomato juice
2	(15-ounce) cans black beans, drained
2	(15-ounce) cans cannellini beans or other white beans, drained
1	cup (4 ounces) shredded reduced-fat Monterey Jack cheese
1	cup (4 ounces) shredded reduced-fat sharp Cheddar cheese
	Vegetable cooking spray
7	(8-inch) flour tortillas
	Cilantro sprigs (optional)

Heat oil in a large nonstick skillet over medium heat. Add red pepper and next 7 ingredients; sauté 5 minutes or until tender. Add tomato juice; cook 8 minutes or until reduced to 2½ cups.

Combine black beans and half of tomato juice mixture in a bowl; stir well, and set aside. Stir cannellini beans into remaining tomato juice mixture; set aside.

Combine cheeses in a bowl; toss well. Line a 9-inch pieplate with aluminum foil, allowing 6 inches of foil to extend over opposite edges of pieplate. Repeat procedure, extending foil over remaining edges of pieplate. Coat foil with cooking spray, and place 1 tortilla in bottom of dish. Spread 1 cup cannellini bean mixture over tortilla; sprinkle with ¼ cup cheeses. Place 1 tortilla over cheeses, pressing gently. Spread 1 cup black bean mixture over tortilla; sprinkle with ¼ cup cheeses. Place 1 tortilla over cheeses, pressing gently. Repeat layers, ending with remaining cannellini bean mixture and cheeses.

Bring edges of foil to center; fold to seal. Bake at 325° for 40 minutes. Remove from oven, and let stand, covered, 10 minutes. Remove foil packet from dish; unwrap pie, and slide onto a serving plate using a spatula. Cut into wedges; garnish with cilantro sprigs, if desired. Yield: 8 servings (serving size: 1 wedge).

Calories 423 (23% from fat) **Protein** 24.5g **Fat** 11.0g (sat 4.1g) **Carbohydrate** 59.3g **Fiber** 7.4g **Cholesterol** 18mg **Iron** 5.0mg **Sodium** 758mg **Calcium** 353mg

POLENTA WITH ITALIAN VEGETABLE SAUCE

Polenta is a fancy name for cooked cornmeal. It can be soft (like hot grits) or firm enough to cut. The conventional way to cook polenta is in a pot on the stove, but we like the firmer texture polenta gets when microwaved.

3	cups water
1	cup yellow cornmeal
½	teaspoon salt
⅛	teaspoon pepper
	Vegetable cooking spray
1¼	cups peeled, finely chopped eggplant
1¼	cups frozen whole kernel corn, thawed
¾	cup finely chopped onion
1	teaspoon dried Italian seasoning
2	teaspoons olive oil
⅛	teaspoon salt
1	(8-ounce) can no-salt-added tomato sauce
1	clove garlic, crushed
1	cup (4 ounces) shredded part-skim mozzarella cheese

Combine first 4 ingredients in a 2-quart casserole; cover with heavy-duty plastic wrap, and vent. Microwave at HIGH 10 minutes, stirring after 5 minutes. Stir mixture well; cover and microwave at HIGH 2 additional minutes, stirring after 1 minute.

Spoon cornmeal mixture into an 8½- x 4½- x 3-inch loafpan coated

Polenta With Italian
Vegetable Sauce

with cooking spray. Cover and chill at least 45 minutes.

Turn polenta out onto a cutting board; cut crosswise into 16 slices, dipping knife into cold water after each slice. Set aside.

Combine chopped eggplant and next 7 ingredients in a 2-quart casserole. Microwave, uncovered, at HIGH 9 to 12 minutes, stirring every 3 minutes.

Arrange 4 polenta slices on each of 4 microwave-safe serving plates. Top evenly with eggplant mixture and mozzarella cheese, and microwave at HIGH 30 seconds or until mozzarella cheese melts. Yield: 4 servings (serving size: 4 polenta slices, ½ cup eggplant mixture, and ¼ cup cheese).

Calories 272 (28% from fat) **Protein** 11.6g **Fat** 8.4g (sat 3.4g) **Carbohydrate** 40.1g **Fiber** 6.0g **Cholesterol** 16mg **Iron** 1.9mg **Sodium** 522mg **Calcium** 212mg

Pork Tenderloins With
Blackberry Mustard Sauce, page 84

You probably don't beef about light entrées you can cook in a matter of minutes and serve to the tune of rave reviews. If that's your style, you'll want Filet Mignon With Mushroom-Wine Sauce and Three-Pepper Pork Cutlets on your must-try list.

MEATS

Of course, certain occasions call for fanfare. In those cases, you can ham it up by starring Pork Tenderloins With Blackberry Mustard Sauce. Before dessert is served, you'll be the star.

Then, when you relish a return to your roots, turn to Corn Meat Loaf and Vegetable-Beef Pot Pie for comfort food without all the fat or the guilt. All you'll need is your mom. So invite her over for Onion-Topped Pot Roast. And don't forget the mashed potatoes.

CORN MEAT LOAF

2   teaspoons vegetable oil
2   cups chopped onion
1   cup diced celery
1¼ teaspoons dried basil
¾   teaspoon dried oregano
½   teaspoon salt
½   teaspoon celery salt
⅛   teaspoon pepper
1   large clove garlic, crushed
2   tablespoons cider vinegar
1½ pounds ground round
½   cup dry breadcrumbs
1½ cups fresh corn kernels,
    divided
¼   cup chopped fresh parsley
1   egg
Vegetable cooking spray
¼   cup tomato sauce

Heat oil in a large skillet over medium-high heat. Add onion and celery, and sauté 5 minutes or until tender and lightly browned. Add basil and next 5 ingredients; cook 2 minutes. Remove from heat; stir in vinegar. Combine onion mixture, meat, breadcrumbs, ½ cup corn, and parsley in a large bowl; set mixture aside.

Position knife blade in food processor bowl. Add remaining 1 cup corn and egg; process until almost smooth. Add to meat mixture; stir well (mixture will be wet).

Shape meat mixture into a 9- x 4- x 3-inch loaf; place on rack of a broiler pan coated with cooking spray. Bake at 350° for 30 minutes. Brush tomato sauce over loaf; bake 35 additional minutes. Let stand 5 minutes before slicing. Yield: 6 servings (serving size: 1 slice).

Calories 293 (32% from fat) **Protein** 28.8g **Fat** 10.4g (sat 3.2g) **Carbohydrate** 21.3g **Fiber** 3.3g **Cholesterol** 107mg **Iron** 3.8mg **Sodium** 601mg **Calcium** 66mg

DEEP-DISH PIZZA

QUICK & EASY

To crush fennel seeds, press them against a cutting board with a knife handle.

¾   cup water
½   cup no-salt-added tomato
    paste
1   teaspoon dried whole basil
½   teaspoon dried whole
    oregano
½   teaspoon fennel seeds,
    crushed
⅛   teaspoon ground red pepper
⅛   teaspoon black pepper
Vegetable cooking spray
6   ounces ground chuck
1   cup chopped onion
1   cup chopped green pepper
6   large cloves garlic, crushed
1   tablespoon yellow cornmeal
2   (11-ounce) packages
    refrigerated French bread
    dough
¾   cup (3 ounces) shredded
    part-skim mozzarella cheese
¼   cup grated Romano cheese
Crushed red pepper (optional)

Combine first 7 ingredients in a small saucepan; stir well. Cook over low heat until mixture is thoroughly heated. Set aside.

Coat a large skillet with cooking spray, and place over medium-high heat until hot. Add meat and next 3 ingredients; cook until meat is browned, stirring until it crumbles. Drain and set aside.

Coat 2 (9-inch) round cakepans with cooking spray, and sprinkle each with 1½ teaspoons cornmeal. Unroll 1 package bread dough; fold each corner in toward center to form a diamond. Pat dough, folded corners up, into a prepared pan. Repeat procedure with remaining bread dough.

Spread ½ cup tomato mixture over each prepared crust; top each with 1 cup meat mixture. Sprinkle each with ¼ cup plus 2 tablespoons mozzarella cheese and 2 tablespoons Romano cheese. Bake at 475° for 12 minutes. Let pizzas stand 5 minutes. Cut each pizza into 4 wedges. Sprinkle with crushed red pepper, if desired. Yield: 8 servings (serving size: 1 wedge).

Calories 315 (24% from fat) **Protein** 15.3g **Fat** 8.3g (sat 3.3g) **Carbohydrate** 43.8g **Fiber** 0.9g **Cholesterol** 22mg **Iron** 1.1mg **Sodium** 499mg **Calcium** 130mg

ZUCCHINI-BEEF PARMIGIANA

The most tender, succulent zucchini are firm, shiny, and about 8 to 10 inches long. To pick the right size, choose squash that's a little longer than the span from the end of your thumb to the tip of your little finger.

½   pound ground round
1½ cups chopped onion
3   tablespoons chopped fresh basil
2   tablespoons chopped fresh oregano
2   large cloves garlic, minced
2   tablespoons tomato paste
1   teaspoon sugar
⅛   teaspoon salt
2   (14½-ounce) cans no-salt-added whole tomatoes, undrained and chopped
1   teaspoon all-purpose flour
6   medium zucchini, cut crosswise into ¼-inch slices (about 2 pounds)
¼   cup all-purpose flour
¼   teaspoon salt
⅛   teaspoon ground nutmeg
2   cups 1% low-fat milk
1   clove garlic, minced
½   cup plus 3 tablespoons freshly grated Parmesan cheese, divided
Vegetable cooking spray

Combine first 5 ingredients in a large nonstick skillet, and cook mixture over medium-high heat until meat is browned, stirring until it crumbles. Add tomato paste and next 3 ingredients. Bring to a boil; reduce heat, and simmer, uncovered, 30 minutes, stirring occasionally. Stir in 1 teaspoon flour, and cook 2 additional minutes; set aside.

Cook zucchini in boiling water 3 minutes; drain zucchini, and gently press between paper towels to remove excess moisture. Set aside.

Combine ¼ cup flour, ¼ teaspoon salt, and nutmeg in a medium saucepan; stir well. Gradually add milk, stirring constantly with a wire whisk until smooth. Stir in 1 clove minced garlic. Cook over medium heat, stirring constantly, 10 to 12 minutes or until thickened and bubbly. Remove from heat. Add ½ cup plus 1 tablespoon Parmesan cheese, stirring until cheese melts. Set aside.

Arrange zucchini slices in 6 (15-ounce) individual casseroles coated with cooking spray. Spoon ⅔ cup meat mixture over zucchini in each dish. Spread ⅓ cup white sauce over meat mixture in each dish. Sprinkle each with 1 teaspoon cheese. Place dishes on a baking sheet. Bake at 450° for 15 to 20 minutes or until golden. Serve immediately. Yield: 6 servings.

Calories 246 (40% from fat) **Protein** 15.2g **Fat** 10.8g (sat 4.7g) **Carbohydrate** 23.5g **Fiber** 2.7g **Cholesterol** 36mg **Iron** 2.5mg **Sodium** 331mg **Calcium** 257mg

CLIP AND SAVE YOUR HERBS

Herbs will stay fresh long after you've clipped them if you store them right. Wrap fresh stems in a damp paper towel, place them in a zip-top plastic bag, and store them in the refrigerator. They'll keep about five days.

For longer storage—up to a week or more—arrange the herbs, stems down, in a glass of cool water, and secure a plastic bag over the tops. (A rubber band holds the bag in place nicely.) Change the water every couple of days.

The same cold water trick usually works for herbs that have wilted a bit. They'll perk up pretty enough for a garnish in just an hour or so. Place the herbs, stem ends down, in a glass of cold water; then set the glass in the refrigerator.

BEEF BURGUNDY

Cut up the steak ahead of time, and buy mushrooms already sliced to turn this into a quick recipe.

2½ pounds lean, boneless round steak
Vegetable cooking spray
4 cloves garlic, minced
2 cups Burgundy or other dry red wine
1 (10¾-ounce) can reduced-fat, reduced-sodium cream of mushroom soup, undiluted
1 (10½-ounce) can beef consommé, undiluted
1 (1-ounce) envelope onion recipe soup mix
6 cups sliced fresh mushrooms
1 (16-ounce) package frozen pearl onions
3 tablespoons all-purpose flour
½ cup water
2 (12-ounce) packages medium egg noodles, uncooked
¼ cup grated Parmesan cheese
¾ cup nonfat sour cream

Beef Burgundy

Trim fat from steak. Cut steak into 1-inch cubes. Coat an ovenproof Dutch oven with cooking spray; place over medium heat until hot. Add steak; cook 9 minutes or until steak is no longer pink. Drain well; set aside. Wipe drippings from Dutch oven with a paper towel.

Coat Dutch oven with cooking spray; place over medium heat. Add garlic; sauté 1 minute. Add wine and next 3 ingredients; stir well, and bring to a boil. Return steak to Dutch oven; stir in mushrooms and onions. Remove from heat.

Place flour in a small bowl. Gradually add water, blending with a wire whisk; add to steak mixture, stirring well. Cover and bake at 350° for 1½ hours.

Cook egg noodles according to package directions, omitting salt and fat. Drain noodles well, and place in a large serving bowl. Add Parmesan cheese and sour cream; toss mixture gently to coat. Serve steak mixture over noodle mixture. Yield: 12 servings (serving size: ¾ cup steak mixture and 1 cup noodle mixture).

Calories 416 (17% from fat) Protein 32.8g Fat 7.7g (sat 2.3g) Carbohydrate 52.5g Fiber 2.3g Cholesterol 115mg Iron 5.3mg Sodium 583mg Calcium 64mg

QUICK BEEF WITH BROCCOLI

¾ ounce sun-dried tomatoes, packed without oil (about 10 tomatoes)
½ cup boiling water
½ pound lean, boneless top round steak
Vegetable cooking spray
½ teaspoon vegetable oil
2 cups fresh broccoli flowerets
¼ cup sliced green onions
1 clove garlic, minced
¼ cup plus 2 tablespoons dry white wine
¼ cup low-sodium soy sauce
2 teaspoons cornstarch
2 cups hot cooked long-grain rice (cooked without salt or fat)

Combine tomatoes and water; let stand 5 minutes. Drain; thinly slice, and set aside.

Trim fat from steak. Slice steak diagonally across grain into thin strips. Coat a wok or large nonstick skillet with cooking spray; place over medium-high heat until hot. Add steak, and stir-fry 2 minutes. Remove steak from wok; set aside, and keep warm.

Add oil to wok, and place over medium-high heat until hot. Add broccoli; stir-fry 3 minutes. Add sliced tomato, green onions, and garlic; stir-fry 1 minute.

Combine wine, soy sauce, and cornstarch; stir well. Add cornstarch mixture and steak to wok; stir-fry 1 minute or until sauce is thickened and bubbly. Serve over rice. Yield: 2 servings (serving size: 1 cup steak mixture and 1 cup rice).

Calories 509 (17% from fat) Protein 33.5g Fat 9.4g (sat 2.9g) Carbohydrate 62.7g Fiber 4.1g Cholesterol 72mg Iron 5.3mg Sodium 1086mg Calcium 94mg

VEGETABLE-BEEF POT PIE

Convenience products help you put this one-dish meal on the table in less than an hour from start to finish.

Vegetable cooking spray
1 cup chopped onion
½ pound lean boneless sirloin steak, cut into ½-inch cubes
1 cup peeled, cubed baking potato
1 (10-ounce) package frozen mixed vegetables
2 tablespoons cornstarch
2 cups canned no-salt-added beef broth, undiluted
½ teaspoon dried thyme
½ teaspoon dried basil
¼ teaspoon salt
¼ teaspoon pepper
1 tablespoon all-purpose flour
1 (4-ounce) package refrigerated crescent dinner rolls

Coat a nonstick skillet with cooking spray; place over medium-high heat until hot. Add onion and steak, and sauté 3 to 4 minutes or until onion is tender. Add potato and mixed vegetables; sauté 2 minutes.

Place cornstarch in a bowl. Gradually add broth, blending with a wire whisk; add to skillet. Stir in thyme and next 3 ingredients; bring to a boil over medium heat, stirring occasionally. Reduce heat, and simmer, uncovered, 15 minutes or until thickened. Spoon steak mixture into a 2-quart baking dish coated with cooking spray; set aside.

Sprinkle flour over a work surface. Unroll dinner roll dough, and separate into 2 rectangles; roll each portion into an 8- x 4-inch rectangle on floured surface. Cut each rectangle lengthwise into 4 (1-inch) strips. Arrange dough strips in a lattice design over steak mixture. Bake at 375° for 20 minutes or until filling is bubbly and crust is golden. Yield: 4 servings.

Calories 312 (26% from fat) Protein 18.2g Fat 9.0g (sat 2.4g) Carbohydrate 37.9g Fiber 4.3g Cholesterol 35mg Iron 3.0mg Sodium 436mg Calcium 40mg

"I could never be a vegetarian because of my weakness for this recipe. It's perfect for special occasions; it's very easy, and I can cook the steaks to each person's preference (rare for me, please!). French bread is a must so you'll be able to sop up every bit of the delicious juices."

——Elizabeth J. Taliaferro, former Assistant Foods Editor and current freelance recipe developer

FILET MIGNON WITH MUSHROOM-WINE SAUCE

QUICK & EASY

Filet Mignon With Mushroom-Wine Sauce

1	tablespoon margarine, divided
	Vegetable cooking spray
⅓	cup finely chopped shallots
½	pound fresh shiitake mushrooms, stems removed
1½	cups dry red wine, divided
1	(10½-ounce) can beef consommé, undiluted and divided
	Cracked pepper
4	(4-ounce) filet mignon steaks (about 1 inch thick)
1	tablespoon low-sodium soy sauce
2	teaspoons cornstarch
1	tablespoon fresh chopped thyme or 1 teaspoon dried thyme
	Fresh thyme sprigs (optional)

Melt 1½ teaspoons margarine in a nonstick skillet coated with cooking spray over medium heat. Add shallots and mushrooms; sauté 4 minutes. Add 1 cup wine and ¾ cup consommé; cook 5 minutes, stirring often. Remove mushrooms, and place in a bowl. Increase heat to high; cook wine mixture 5 minutes or until reduced to ½ cup. Add to mushrooms in bowl; set aside. Wipe skillet with a paper towel.

Sprinkle desired amount of cracked pepper over steaks. Melt remaining 1½ teaspoons margarine in skillet coated with cooking spray over medium heat. Add steaks; cook 3 minutes on each side or until browned. Reduce heat to medium-low, and cook 1½ minutes on each side or to desired degree of doneness. Place on a serving platter, and keep warm.

Combine soy sauce and cornstarch; stir well. Add remaining ½ cup wine and consommé to skillet; scrape skillet with a wooden spoon to loosen browned bits. Bring to a boil; cook 1 minute. Add mushroom mixture, cornstarch mixture, and chopped thyme; bring to a boil, and cook, stirring constantly, 1 minute. Serve with steaks. Garnish with thyme sprigs, if desired. Yield: 4 servings (serving size: 3 ounces steak and ½ cup sauce).

Calories 250 (39% from fat) **Protein** 28.5g **Fat** 10.7g (sat 3.6g) **Carbohydrate** 9.4g **Fiber** 0.9g **Cholesterol** 84mg **Iron** 5.1mg **Sodium** 712mg **Calcium** 30mg

ONION-TOPPED POT ROAST

Lean cuts of meat like round roast need to be marinated or cooked in wine or citrus juices, or else simmered for long periods to make them tender. This roast is so good that we listed the recipe with a handful of other favorites in a special *Cooking Light* publication in the early '90s.

1   (2-pound) lean, boneless bottom round roast
Vegetable cooking spray
¼   teaspoon pepper
2   cloves garlic
1   cup coarsely chopped onion
½   cup dry red wine
½   cup canned no-salt-added beef broth, undiluted
¼   cup no-salt-added tomato juice
½   teaspoon salt
1   cup water
18 small round red potatoes (about 1½ pounds)
18 baby carrots (about ½ pound)

Trim fat from roast. Coat an oven-proof Dutch oven with cooking spray; place over medium-high heat until hot. Add roast, and brown on all sides. Remove roast from Dutch oven, and sprinkle with pepper; set roast aside. Wipe drippings from Dutch oven with a paper towel.

Position knife blade in food processor bowl. Drop garlic through food chute with processor running; process 5 seconds. Add onion; process 1 minute or until smooth. Spread onion puree over roast. Return roast to Dutch oven. Bake, uncovered, at 350° for 1 hour.

Add wine and next 3 ingredients to Dutch oven. Cover and bake 2½ hours. Add water, potatoes, and carrots; cover and bake 1 additional hour or until roast is tender.

Place roast and vegetables on a platter; serve with gravy. Yield: 6 servings (serving size: 3 ounces roast, 3 carrots, 3 potatoes, and 2 tablespoons gravy).

Calories 293 (17% from fat) Protein 33.1g Fat 5.6g (sat 2.0g) Carbohydrate 26.4g Fiber 3.8g Cholesterol 74mg Iron 4.6mg Sodium 288mg Calcium 39mg

PEPPERCORN BEEF TENDERLOIN

1   (4-pound) beef tenderloin
½   cup low-sodium soy sauce, divided
2   teaspoons freshly ground pink peppercorns
2   teaspoons freshly ground green peppercorns
2   teaspoons freshly ground black peppercorns
2   teaspoons ground ginger
1½   teaspoons ground cardamom
8   cloves garlic, minced
Vegetable cooking spray

Trim fat from tenderloin. Combine 2 tablespoons soy sauce and next 6 ingredients; stir well. Rub tenderloin with soy sauce mixture. Place tenderloin in a large heavy-duty, zip-top plastic bag. Pour remaining ¼ cup plus 2 tablespoons soy sauce over tenderloin. Seal bag, and shake until meat is well coated. Marinate tenderloin in refrigerator 8 hours, turning bag occasionally.

Remove tenderloin from bag, reserving marinade. Place marinade in a small saucepan; bring to a boil. Remove from heat, and set aside.

Place tenderloin on a rack coated with cooking spray, and place rack in a shallow roasting pan. Insert meat thermometer into thickest part of tenderloin, if desired. Bake at 425° for 45 minutes or until meat thermometer registers 140° (rare) or 160° (medium), basting often with reserved marinade. Remove from oven, and let stand 10 minutes before slicing. Yield: 14 servings (serving size: 3 ounces).

Calories 209 (39% from fat) Protein 27.7g Fat 9.1g (sat 3.6g) Carbohydrate 1.5g Fiber 0.3g Cholesterol 82mg Iron 3.8mg Sodium 285mg Calcium 16mg

Phyllo Facts

Working with delicate sheets of phyllo (FEE-lo) pastry, the thinnest of pastries, is like handling butterfly wings. Even though the dough dries out quickly and tears easily, using it as a pastry wrapper for meats or appetizers is easier than making other types of pastry from scratch. That's because you can buy the dough already layered in handy sheets ready to pull apart and use.

Find boxes of phyllo pastry in the freezer section of the supermarket. Before you use it, place the entire package in the refrigerator to thaw overnight. Don't try to thaw it quickly at room temperature, or else the dough will develop soggy spots that will stick and tear when you separate the sheets.

An unopened box of phyllo will stay fresh in the refrigerator about one month. The pastry in an opened package will keep two or three days in the refrigerator.

Individual Beef Wellingtons

¾   pound fresh mushrooms, quartered
Butter-flavored vegetable cooking spray
¼   cup chopped shallots
2   cloves garlic, minced
2   teaspoons all-purpose flour
½   teaspoon dried marjoram
⅛   teaspoon pepper
1   (10½-ounce) can beef consommé, undiluted and divided
2   tablespoons minced fresh parsley
6   (4-ounce) beef tenderloin steaks (1 inch thick)
1½ teaspoons 72%-less-sodium Worcestershire sauce
6   sheets frozen phyllo pastry, thawed in refrigerator
½   cup Marsala
1½ tablespoons cornstarch

Position knife blade in food processor bowl; add mushrooms, and process until finely chopped.

Coat a large skillet with cooking spray; place over medium-high heat until hot. Add mushrooms, shallots, and garlic; sauté 2 minutes or until tender. Stir in flour, marjoram, and pepper. Gradually add ¼ cup consommé; stir well. Cook, stirring constantly, 5 minutes or until liquid evaporates. (Mixture will be very thick.) Remove from heat, and stir in parsley; set aside.

Trim fat from steaks. Coat skillet with cooking spray, and place over medium-high heat until hot. Add steaks, and cook 1½ minutes on each side or until browned. Drain on paper towels. Place steaks on a rack coated with cooking spray, and place rack in a shallow roasting pan. Drizzle ¼ teaspoon Worcestershire sauce over each steak; top each with 3 tablespoons mushroom mixture.

Place 1 phyllo sheet on a work surface (keeping remaining phyllo covered); lightly coat phyllo sheet with cooking spray. Fold phyllo sheet in thirds crosswise to form a 13- x 5½-inch rectangle; lightly coat with cooking spray. Fold rectangle in half crosswise to form a 6½- x 5½-inch rectangle; lightly coat with cooking spray. Cut a ¼-inch strip from short side of rectangle; set aside. Drape phyllo rectangle over a steak, tucking edges under steak. Lightly coat with cooking spray. Crumple ¼-inch phyllo strip into a ball, and place on top of phyllo-wrapped steak. Return steak to rack in roasting pan. Repeat procedure with remaining phyllo sheets and cooked steaks. Bake at 425° for 15 minutes or to desired degree of doneness.

Combine remaining consommé, wine, and cornstarch in a small saucepan; stir well. Bring to a boil; cook, stirring constantly, 1 minute. Serve with steaks. Yield: 6 servings (serving size: 3 ounces steak and ¼ cup sauce).

Calories 297 (28% from fat) Protein 28.6g Fat 9.4g (sat 3.3g) Carbohydrate 18.4g Fiber 0.9g Cholesterol 71mg Iron 4.7mg Sodium 497mg Calcium 20mg

STEP BY STEP

Wrapping Individual Beef Wellingtons

Instead of buttery puff pastry, low-fat phyllo pastry encases the meat in this recipe. The thin sheets dry out quickly; work with one at a time, and keep the other phyllo sheets loosely covered with a damp towel. Prepare the steaks as directed, and follow the steps below to wrap each in a crispy phyllo crust.

1. Lightly spray a sheet of phyllo with cooking spray.

2. Fold phyllo in thirds, starting from a short side, to form a 13- x 5½-inch rectangle. Lightly spray the phyllo rectangle with cooking spray.

3. Fold the rectangle in half, matching short sides together to make a 6½- x 5½-inch rectangle. Coat the rectangle with cooking spray.

4. Use a sharp knife to cut a ¼-inch strip from the short side of the rectangle, and then set the strip aside.

5. Drape the phyllo rectangle over the steak, tucking phyllo edges under the steak. Lightly spray the wrapped steak with cooking spray.

6. Crumple the reserved strip of phyllo into a ball; place it on top of the wrapped steak. Place on the rack of a roasting pan. Bake as directed, and serve the steaks with wine sauce.

A Flavor of Their Own

The recipe for Veal Medaillons With Mushroom-Wine Sauce takes advantage of the flavor of two types of mushrooms. You can use sliced button mushrooms instead, but the flavor of the sauce won't be quite the same.

Oyster mushrooms have a peppery, robust flavor.

Shiitake *(she-TAHK-ee)* mushrooms taste rich and almost like steak. Although the tough stems have to be removed from shiitakes, they can be saved to flavor stocks.

Veal Medaillons With Mushroom-Wine Sauce

QUICK & EASY

You can substitute slices of pork tenderloin for the veal tenderloin.

2	tablespoons all-purpose flour
¼	teaspoon salt, divided
¼	teaspoon pepper, divided
8	(2-ounce) pieces veal tenderloin (½ inch thick)
2	teaspoons olive oil, divided
¼	cup finely chopped shallots
1	small clove garlic, minced
1¼	cups diced fresh shiitake mushroom caps (3 ounces)
1	cup diced fresh oyster mushroom caps (3 ounces)
2	tablespoons finely chopped fresh parsley
¼	teaspoon dried thyme
¼	cup dry white wine
⅔	cup plus 1 tablespoon canned no-salt-added beef broth, undiluted and divided
1	teaspoon cornstarch

Combine flour, ⅛ teaspoon salt, and ⅛ teaspoon pepper; sprinkle over both sides of veal pieces. Heat 1 teaspoon oil in a large nonstick skillet over medium-high heat. Add veal, and cook 3 minutes on each side or until browned. Remove veal from skillet, and place on a serving platter; set aside, and keep warm.

Heat remaining 1 teaspoon oil in skillet over medium heat. Add shallots and garlic; sauté 2 minutes. Add remaining ⅛ teaspoon salt, remaining ⅛ teaspoon pepper, mushrooms, parsley, and thyme; sauté 2 minutes. Add wine, and cook, stirring constantly, 2 minutes. Add ⅔ cup broth, and cook 3 additional minutes. Combine remaining 1 tablespoon broth and cornstarch in a bowl; stir well. Add cornstarch mixture to skillet; cook, stirring constantly, 1 minute or until thickened. Spoon sauce over veal. Yield: 4 servings (serving size: 3 ounces veal and 3 tablespoons sauce).

Calories 186 (28% from fat) **Protein** 24.6g **Fat** 5.7g (sat 1.3g) **Carbohydrate** 7.9g **Fiber** 0.8g **Cholesterol** 94mg **Iron** 2.1mg **Sodium** 250mg **Calcium** 31mg

Marinated Lamb Chops With Herbs

4	(3-ounce) lean lamb rib chops
¼	cup dry red wine
2	tablespoons low-sodium soy sauce
2	tablespoons chopped fresh mint or ½ teaspoon dried mint flakes
1½	teaspoons chopped fresh rosemary or ¼ teaspoon dried rosemary
½	teaspoon coarsely ground pepper
1	clove garlic, crushed
	Vegetable cooking spray

Trim fat from chops; set chops aside. Combine wine and next 5 ingredients in a large heavy-duty, zip-top plastic bag. Add chops; seal bag, and marinate in refrigerator 8 hours, turning bag occasionally.

Remove chops from bag, reserving marinade. Place marinade in a small saucepan; bring to a boil. Remove from heat, and set aside.

Coat grill rack with cooking spray; place on grill over medium-hot coals (350° to 400°). Place chops on rack, and grill, covered, 4 minutes on each side or to desired degree of doneness. Baste often with reserved marinade. Yield: 2 servings (serving size: 2 chops).

Note: To broil chops instead of grilling, place chops on rack of a broiler pan coated with cooking spray. Broil 5½ inches from heat (with electric oven door partially opened) 4 minutes on each side or to desire degree of doneness.

Calories 301 (45% from fat) **Protein** 32.5g **Fat** 14.9g (sat 5.3g) **Carbohydrate** 2.7g **Fiber** 0.3g **Cholesterol** 103mg **Iron** 3.5mg **Sodium** 584mg **Calcium** 39mg

LAMB CHOPS MARSALA

QUICK & EASY

If you want the same great flavor that made this recipe one of our favorites, use only Marsala wine. No other wine provides the same distinctively sweet taste.

4	(4-ounce) lean lamb loin chops
	Vegetable cooking spray
½	cup water
½	cup Marsala
2	tablespoons tomato paste
1	cup sliced fresh mushrooms
¼	cup chopped onion

Trim fat from chops. Coat a large skillet with cooking spray; place over medium heat until hot. Add chops, and cook 7 minutes on each side or to desired degree of doneness. Remove chops from skillet. Drain; set aside, and keep warm. Wipe drippings from skillet with a paper towel.

Combine water, wine, and tomato paste; stir well with a wire whisk. Add wine mixture, mushrooms, and onion to skillet; cook over high heat, stirring constantly, 2 minutes or until thickened. Spoon sauce over chops. Yield: 2 servings (serving size: 2 chops and ¼ cup plus 1 tablespoon sauce).

Calories 283 (37% from fat) **Protein** 35.9g **Fat** 11.7g (sat 4.0g) **Carbohydrate** 7.5g **Fiber** 1.6g **Cholesterol** 108mg **Iron** 3.6mg **Sodium** 113mg **Calcium** 38mg

MAKE-AHEAD BREAKFAST CASSEROLE

	Vegetable cooking spray
¾	pound lean ground pork
¾	teaspoon Italian seasoning
¼	teaspoon fennel seeds, crushed
2	cloves garlic, minced
1	cup skim milk
¼	cup (1 ounce) shredded Cheddar cheese
¾	teaspoon dry mustard
¼	teaspoon salt
¼	teaspoon ground red pepper
3	green onions, chopped
2	(8-ounce) cartons fat-free egg substitute
6	(1-ounce) slices white bread, cut into ½-inch cubes

Coat a skillet with cooking spray; place over medium heat until hot. Add pork and next 3 ingredients; cook until meat is browned, stirring until it crumbles. Drain; set aside.

Combine milk and next 6 ingredients in a large bowl; stir well. Add pork mixture and bread, stirring until well blended. Pour into an 11- x 7- x 2-inch baking dish coated with cooking spray. Cover and chill 8 to 12 hours.

Bake, uncovered, at 350° for 50 minutes or until set and lightly browned. Yield: 6 servings (serving size: one 3¾- x 3½-inch piece).

Calories 258 (31% from fat) **Protein** 24.2g **Fat** 8.8g (sat 3.3g) **Carbohydrate** 18.8g **Fiber** 0.8g **Cholesterol** 45mg **Iron** 2.9mg **Sodium** 436mg **Calcium** 148mg

COOKING WITH CASCABELS

Hot little **cascabel chiles** add a rich smoky, woodsy flavor to salsas and stews. They get their name, the Spanish word for "jingle bell," from the seeds that rattle inside when the dried chiles are shaken.

If cascabels aren't available in your area, order them from **Don Alfonso Foods, P.O. Box 201988, Austin, TX 78720 (800-456-6100).**

You can also substitute cayenne peppers or dried New Mexican chiles for cascabels.

PORK FAJITAS WITH APPLE-AVOCADO SALSA

4	dried cascabel chiles (about ½ ounce)
1	cup water
2	tablespoons fresh lime juice
¼	teaspoon salt
3	large cloves garlic
1	(1-pound) pork tenderloin

Apple-Avocado Salsa
Vegetable cooking spray

8	(7-inch) flour tortillas

Fresh cilantro sprigs (optional)

Remove stems and seeds from chiles. Combine chiles and water in a small saucepan, and bring to a boil; remove from heat. Cover and let stand 1 hour. Drain well, reserving 2 tablespoons soaking liquid. Combine chiles, reserved soaking liquid, lime juice, salt, and garlic in container of an electric blender; cover and process until smooth.

Trim fat from pork; place pork in a shallow dish. Pour chile mixture over pork; cover and chill 1½ hours.

Prepare Apple-Avocado Salsa, and set aside.

Drain pork, reserving marinade. Place pork on a rack coated with cooking spray; place rack in a shallow roasting pan. Brush reserved marinade over pork. Insert meat thermometer into thickest part of pork, if desired. Bake at 375° for 30 minutes or until meat thermometer registers 160°. Set aside; keep warm.

Wrap tortillas tightly in foil, and bake at 350° for 10 minutes.

Cut pork diagonally across grain into thin slices. Arrange one-eighth of pork slices and 2 tablespoons Apple-Avocado Salsa in center of each tortilla. Fold bottom half of tortilla over filling, and fold sides over filling. Top each fajita with 2 tablespoons salsa, and garnish with cilantro sprigs, if desired. Yield: 4 servings (serving size: 2 fajitas).

Calories 375 (27% from fat) **Protein** 30.1g **Fat** 11.1g (sat 2.4g) **Carbohydrate** 38.7g **Fiber** 4.1g **Cholesterol** 79mg **Iron** 3.7mg **Sodium** 531mg **Calcium** 90mg

APPLE-AVOCADO SALSA:

1	cup diced Granny Smith apple
½	cup peeled, diced ripe avocado
¼	cup diced sweet red pepper
¼	cup diced purple onion
1	tablespoon chopped fresh cilantro
1½	teaspoons seeded, minced jalapeño pepper
½	teaspoon grated lime rind
1½	tablespoons fresh lime juice
⅛	teaspoon salt

Dash of pepper

1	small clove garlic, minced

Combine all ingredients in a bowl, and toss well. Serve salsa as an alternative to tomato salsa with pork, chicken, or beef. Yield: 2 cups (serving size: ¼ cup).

Calories 27 (50% from fat) **Protein** 0.4g **Fat** 1.5g (sat 0.2g) **Carbohydrate** 3.8g **Fiber** 0.8g **Cholesterol** 0mg **Iron** 0.2mg **Sodium** 38mg **Calcium** 5mg

Pork Fajitas With
Apple-Avocado Salsa

PORK TENDERLOINS WITH BLACKBERRY MUSTARD SAUCE

Find this recipe pictured on page 70.

¼ cup Blackberry Mustard
1½ teaspoons minced fresh thyme, divided
½ teaspoon ground pepper
¼ teaspoon salt
¼ teaspoon ground allspice
¼ teaspoon ground cinnamon
2 cloves garlic, minced
2 (¾-pound) pork tenderloins
Vegetable cooking spray
1 tablespoon olive oil
1¼ cups canned no-salt-added chicken broth, undiluted and divided
2 tablespoons balsamic vinegar
1 tablespoon brown sugar
½ teaspoon cornstarch
2 tablespoons water
¾ cup fresh blackberries
Fresh thyme sprigs (optional)

Prepare Blackberry Mustard, and set aside.

Combine ½ teaspoon minced thyme and next 5 ingredients; stir well. Trim fat from pork; rub pork with thyme mixture. Place in a shallow dish; cover and chill 2 hours.

Coat a large nonstick skillet with cooking spray; add oil. Place over medium-high heat until hot. Add pork; cook 4 minutes or until browned on all sides. Add ¼ cup broth and vinegar to skillet; bring to a boil. Insert a meat thermometer into thickest part of pork, if desired. Cover, reduce heat, and simmer 25 minutes or until meat thermometer registers 160°. Remove pork from skillet; set aside, and keep warm.

Add remaining 1 cup broth and sugar to skillet. Bring to a boil; cook 5 minutes or until reduced to ½ cup. Strain mixture; discard solids.

Place cornstarch in a small saucepan; gradually add water, blending with a wire whisk. Stir in strained mixture and ¼ cup Blackberry Mustard. Bring to a boil over medium heat; cook, stirring constantly, 1 minute. Remove from heat; stir in remaining 1 teaspoon minced thyme.

Cut pork into ½-inch-thick slices. Spoon sauce evenly onto 6 serving plates, and arrange pork evenly on top of sauce. Top servings evenly with blackberries. Garnish with thyme sprigs, if desired. Yield: 6 servings (serving size: 3 ounces pork, 2 tablespoons sauce, and 2 tablespoons blackberries).

Calories 188 (27% from fat) Protein 24.2g Fat 5.6g (sat 1.3g) Carbohydrate 8.4g Fiber 1.9g Cholesterol 74mg Iron 1.8mg Sodium 285mg Calcium 22mg

BLACKBERRY MUSTARD:

1 cup fresh blackberries
¼ cup plus 3 tablespoons hot Dijon mustard
3 tablespoons honey
1 tablespoon balsamic vinegar
1 teaspoon dry mustard

Position knife blade in food processor bowl; add blackberries. Process 1 minute or until smooth; strain and discard seeds.

Combine blackberry puree, Dijon mustard, and remaining ingredients in a bowl; stir well. Serve sauce with grilled or roasted pork, beef, or chicken. Store in an airtight container in the refrigerator up to two weeks. Yield: 1 cup (serving size: 1 tablespoon).

Calories 25 (18% from fat) Protein 0.1g Fat 0.5g (sat 0.0g) Carbohydrate 4.9g Fiber 0.7g Cholesterol 0mg Iron 0.1mg Sodium 195mg Calcium 3mg

LIME-BASTED PORK CHOPS WITH PLUM RELISH

½ cup fresh lime juice, divided
⅓ cup pitted, finely chopped plums
2 tablespoons finely chopped tomato
1 tablespoon finely chopped green onions
1 tablespoon brown sugar
2 drops hot sauce
2 (4-ounce) boneless center-cut pork loin chops (¾ inch thick)
1 teaspoon chopped fresh thyme
⅛ teaspoon salt
⅛ teaspoon pepper
Vegetable cooking spray

Combine ½ teaspoon lime juice and next 5 ingredients in a bowl; stir well. Cover relish, and chill.

Place pork between 2 sheets of heavy-duty plastic wrap; flatten to ½-inch thickness, using a meat mallet or rolling pin. Sprinkle both sides of pork evenly with thyme, pressing thyme into pork chops. Sprinkle with salt and pepper.

Place pork chops in a heavy-duty, zip-top plastic bag. Pour remaining lime juice over pork. Seal bag; shake well. Marinate in refrigerator 1 hour, turning bag occasionally.

Remove pork from marinade, reserving marinade. Place marinade in a small saucepan; bring to a boil. Remove from heat, and set aside.

Coat grill rack with cooking spray; place on grill over medium-hot coals (350° to 400°). Place pork on rack; grill, covered, 8 minutes on each side or until done, basting occasionally with marinade. Serve with relish. Yield: 2 servings (serving size: 1 pork chop and ¼ cup relish).

Calories 274 (39% from fat) **Protein** 25.1g **Fat** 11.8g (sat 3.9g) **Carbohydrate** 17.8g **Fiber** 1.2g **Cholesterol** 77mg **Iron** 2.2mg **Sodium** 207mg **Calcium** 38mg

THREE-PEPPER PORK CUTLETS

QUICK & EASY

Find a simple supper suggestion featuring this recipe on page 219.

1   (1-pound) pork tenderloin
2   teaspoons sweet Hungarian paprika
1   teaspoon dried thyme
1   teaspoon olive oil
½   teaspoon dried oregano
½   teaspoon dried rosemary, crushed
¼   teaspoon salt
¼   teaspoon ground white pepper
¼   teaspoon freshly ground black pepper
⅛   teaspoon ground red pepper
2   cloves garlic, minced
Vegetable cooking spray

Trim fat from pork. Cut crosswise into 8 slices. Place pork between 2 sheets of heavy-duty plastic wrap, and flatten each slice to ¼-inch thickness, using a meat mallet or rolling pin.

Combine paprika and next 9 ingredients, and stir mixture well. Rub both sides of pork slices with paprika mixture.

Place pork slices on a rack coated with cooking spray; place rack in a shallow roasting pan. Broil 5½ inches from heat (with electric oven door partially opened) 5 minutes. Turn pork, and broil 3 additional minutes or until done. Yield: 4 servings (serving size: 2 cutlets).

Calories 172 (31% from fat) **Protein** 26.9g **Fat** 5.9g (sat 1.7g) **Carbohydrate** 1.8g **Fiber** 0.4g **Cholesterol** 86mg **Iron** 2.3mg **Sodium** 209mg **Calcium** 26mg

SUNDAY BAKED HAM

1   (6½- to 7-pound) lower-sodium smoked, fully cooked ham half
40   whole cloves
Vegetable cooking spray
¼   cup firmly packed brown sugar
¼   cup honey
3   tablespoons unsweetened pineapple juice
½   teaspoon dry mustard

Trim fat and rind from ham. Score outside of ham in a diamond pattern, and stud with cloves. Place ham on a rack coated with cooking spray; place rack in a roasting pan.

Combine sugar and remaining 3 ingredients in a small saucepan; stir well. Bring to a boil; cook 1 minute. Remove from heat; let cool. Brush over ham. Bake at 425° for 5 minutes. Reduce heat to 325°; bake 1 additional hour, basting ham with sugar mixture every 15 minutes. Transfer ham to a platter; let stand 15 minutes before slicing. Yield: 23 servings (serving size: 3 ounces).

Calories 126 (30% from fat) **Protein** 15.3g **Fat** 4.2g (sat 1.6g) **Carbohydrate** 7.4g **Fiber** 0.0g **Cholesterol** 42mg **Iron** 0.1mg **Sodium** 659mg **Calcium** 3mg

Hearty Lasagna, page 93

It's a sure bet. Put a pasta recipe on the cover of *Cooking Light*, and sales of that issue are sure to go through the roof. Maybe you remember some of the classics: Pasta With Roasted Peppers and Basil... Fettuccine Alfredo... Hearty Lasagna.

PASTA

Inside our covers, the list is even longer. And best of all, you can pick a pasta to fill any spot on the menu—entrée, salad, or side. Of course, pasta's popularity has been around a long time. Just ask any kid. Then feed him our lightened version of Macaroni and Cheese. Our preferred pick? We voted Greek Spaghetti With Tomatoes and Feta as an all-time staff favorite. Enough said.

MACARONI AND CHEESE

1   egg, lightly beaten
2   cups (8 ounces) shredded reduced-fat sharp Cheddar cheese
1   cup 1% low-fat cottage cheese
¾   cup nonfat sour cream
½   cup skim milk
2   tablespoons grated onion
1½   teaspoons reduced-calorie stick margarine, melted
½   teaspoon salt
¼   teaspoon pepper
4   cups cooked elbow macaroni (cooked without salt or fat)
Vegetable cooking spray
¼   cup dry breadcrumbs
1   tablespoon reduced-calorie stick margarine, melted
¼   teaspoon paprika

Combine first 10 ingredients; stir well. Spoon into a 2-quart casserole coated with cooking spray.

Combine breadcrumbs, 1 tablespoon margarine, and paprika; stir well. Sprinkle breadcrumb mixture over casserole. Cover and bake at 350° for 30 minutes. Uncover casserole, and bake 5 additional minutes or until set. Yield: 6 servings (serving size: 1 cup).

Calories 356 (28% from fat) **Protein** 24.9g **Fat** 11.2g (sat 5.2g) **Carbohydrate** 37.5g **Fiber** 1.2g **Cholesterol** 63mg **Iron** 2.0mg **Sodium** 724mg **Calcium** 402mg

EDITOR'S CHOICE

"Pasta With Roasted Peppers and Basil is easy to make if you roast the peppers ahead of time, which I always do. I serve it often to family and friends with French bread and a glass of Chardonnay. For variety, I may toss in grilled vegetables—eggplant, yellow squash, and zucchini—or strips of grilled chicken. Any way, the flavor's great!"

—————Katherine M. Eakin,
Founding Editor

HOW MUCH PASTA TO COOK?

Uncooked pasta of similar sizes and shapes may be interchanged in recipes if it is measured by weight, not volume. Just follow this guide:

Linguine, Spaghetti, or Vermicelli:
4 ounces dry = 2 to 3 cups cooked
8 ounces dry = 4 to 5 cups cooked
16 ounces dry = 8 to 9 cups cooked

Macaroni, Penne, or Rotini:
4 ounces dry = 2½ cups cooked
8 ounces dry = 4½ cups cooked

Fine or Medium Egg Noodles:
4 ounces dry = 2 to 3 cups cooked
8 ounces dry = 4 to 5 cups cooked

PASTA WITH ROASTED PEPPERS AND BASIL

Look for photographed step-by-step instructions for roasting peppers on page 167.

1   tablespoon olive oil
2   cups chopped onion
½   teaspoon fennel seeds, crushed
2   cloves garlic, minced
2   (14½-ounce) cans no-salt-added whole tomatoes, undrained and chopped
1   pound green peppers, roasted and peeled (about 2 large)
1   pound sweet red peppers, roasted and peeled (about 2 large)
1   pound sweet yellow peppers, roasted and peeled (about 2 large)
½   teaspoon salt
¼   teaspoon freshly ground pepper
8   cups cooked penne (short tubular pasta), (cooked without salt or fat)
½   cup thinly sliced fresh basil
½   cup freshly grated Parmesan cheese

Heat olive oil in a large nonstick skillet over medium-low heat. Add chopped onion, fennel seeds, and garlic; cover mixture, and cook 10 minutes or until tender, stirring occasionally. Add chopped tomatoes to onion mixture, and bring to a boil. Reduce heat, and simmer, uncovered, 30 minutes, stirring occasionally.

Cut roasted green, red, and yellow peppers into julienne strips. Add roasted pepper strips, salt, and freshly ground pepper to tomato mixture; cook 3 minutes or until thoroughly heated.

Combine tomato mixture, cooked pasta, and basil in a large bowl, and toss mixture well. Sprinkle with Parmesan cheese. Yield: 8 servings (serving size: 1½ cups).

Calories 279 (15% from fat) **Protein** 10.7g **Fat** 4.8g (sat 1.6g) **Carbohydrate** 48.9g **Fiber** 4.4g **Cholesterol** 5mg **Iron** 3.2mg **Sodium** 278mg **Calcium** 144mg

Pasta With Roasted Peppers and Basil

Fettuccine Alfredo

"Fettuccine Alfredo is one of my favorite menu choices when I'm eating out. I make this lighter version at home when I need to be comforted or indulged. And it's just as delicious as the higher fat ones served at restaurants."

——Karen Mitchell Wilcher, former Test Kitchens Staff

FETTUCCINE ALFREDO

QUICK & EASY

1 tablespoon margarine
2 small cloves garlic, minced
1 tablespoon all-purpose flour
1⅓ cups skim milk
2 tablespoons light process cream cheese
1¼ cups freshly grated Parmesan cheese, divided
4 cups hot cooked fettuccine (cooked without salt or fat)
2 teaspoons chopped fresh parsley
Freshly ground pepper

Melt margarine in a saucepan over medium heat. Add minced garlic, and sauté 1 minute. Stir in flour. Gradually add skim milk, stirring with a wire whisk until mixture is blended. Cook, stirring constantly, 8 minutes or until mixture is thickened and bubbly.

STEP BY STEP

Fettuccine Alfredo

1. Sauté garlic in margarine in a saucepan; then stir in flour. Gradually add milk, stirring with a wire whisk until blended. Cook mixture 8 minutes or until thickened. Stir in cream cheese, and cook 2 minutes.

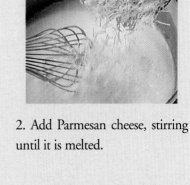

2. Add Parmesan cheese, stirring until it is melted.

3. Pour the cheese sauce over the hot cooked fettuccine, tossing well to coat the fettuccine.

4. Top the fettuccine with additional Parmesan cheese, chopped fresh parsley, and freshly ground pepper.

Stir in cream cheese; cook 2 minutes. Add 1 cup Parmesan cheese, stirring constantly until Parmesan cheese melts.

Pour sauce over hot cooked fettuccine, and toss well to coat. Top fettuccine with remaining ¼ cup Parmesan cheese, chopped parsley, and pepper. Yield: 4 servings (serving size: 1 cup).

Calories 345 (25% from fat) **Protein** 16.8g **Fat** 9.7g (sat 4.4g) **Carbohydrate** 46.7g **Fiber** 2.3g **Cholesterol** 18mg **Iron** 2.3mg **Sodium** 401mg **Calcium** 333mg

"I crave feta cheese, so I have to claim this recipe as my favorite. I serve it with just a salad and bread to make a great meatless meal. Sometimes I vary the recipe by adding cucumbers, black olives, fresh herbs, or shrimp."

———L. Alyson Moreland,
Assistant Food Editor

GREEK SPAGHETTI WITH TOMATOES AND FETA

QUICK & EASY

Garlic, onion, lemon juice, parsley, and feta are the ingredients that give this spaghetti recipe a Greek twist. Look for a photo of the recipe on page 218.

2   teaspoons olive oil
1   teaspoon dried oregano
1   large clove garlic, minced
3   cups diced tomato
½   cup sliced green onions
¼   cup chopped fresh parsley, divided
2   tablespoons lemon juice
4   cups hot cooked thin spaghetti (cooked without salt or fat)
1   cup (4 ounces) crumbled feta cheese, divided
Freshly ground pepper

Heat oil in a large nonstick skillet over medium-high heat. Add oregano and garlic, and sauté 30

seconds. Add tomato, onions, 2 tablespoons parsley, and juice; cook 2 minutes or until heated.

Combine tomato mixture, spaghetti, and ¾ cup cheese; toss gently. Top with remaining ¼ cup cheese and 2 tablespoons parsley, and sprinkle with pepper. Yield: 4 servings (serving size: 1¼ cups).

Calories 334 (26% from fat) **Protein** 12.5g **Fat** 9.8g (sat 4.8g) **Carbohydrate** 50.2g **Fiber** 4.8g **Cholesterol** 25mg **Iron** 3.4mg **Sodium** 336mg **Calcium** 179mg

LINGUINE WITH GARLIC-RED PEPPER OIL

QUICK & EASY

3   tablespoons olive oil
½   teaspoon dried crushed red pepper
4   large cloves garlic, minced
6   cups hot cooked linguine (cooked without salt or fat)
½   cup chopped fresh parsley
1   teaspoon salt
½   teaspoon pepper

Heat oil in a nonstick skillet over medium-high heat. Add red pepper; cook 2 minutes. Add garlic; sauté 30 seconds or until garlic is lightly browned. Remove from heat; stir in pasta and remaining ingredients. Yield: 6 servings (serving size: 1 cup).

Calories 330 (22% from fat) **Protein** 11.4g **Fat** 7.9g (sat 1.1g) **Carbohydrate** 58.2g **Fiber** 9.3g **Cholesterol** 0mg **Iron** 3.2mg **Sodium** 401mg **Calcium** 46mg

FOUR-CHEESE VEGETABLE LASAGNA

1   (10-ounce) package frozen chopped spinach, thawed
Vegetable cooking spray
2   teaspoons vegetable oil
2   cups chopped fresh broccoli
1½   cups thinly sliced carrot
1   cup sliced green onions
½   cup chopped sweet red pepper
3   cloves garlic, crushed
½   cup all-purpose flour
3   cups 1% low-fat milk
½   cup freshly grated Parmesan cheese, divided
¼   teaspoon salt
¼   teaspoon pepper
1½   cups 1% low-fat cottage cheese
1   cup (4 ounces) shredded part-skim mozzarella cheese
½   cup (2 ounces) shredded Swiss cheese
12   cooked lasagna noodles (cooked without salt or fat)

Drain spinach; press between paper towels to remove moisture; set aside.

Coat a Dutch oven with cooking spray. Add oil; place over medium heat until hot. Add broccoli and next 4 ingredients; sauté 7 minutes. Set broccoli mixture aside.

Place flour in a medium saucepan. Gradually add milk, stirring with a wire whisk until blended. Bring to a boil over medium heat, and cook, stirring constantly, 5 minutes or until thickened. Add ¼ cup

Parmesan cheese, salt, and pepper; cook, stirring constantly, 1 minute. Remove from heat; stir in spinach. Set aside ½ cup spinach mixture.

Combine cottage cheese, mozzarella, and Swiss cheese, and stir well. Spread ½ cup spinach mixture in a 13- x 9- x 2-inch baking dish coated with cooking spray. Arrange 4 lasagna noodles over spinach mixture; top with half of cottage cheese mixture, half of broccoli mixture, and half of remaining spinach mixture. Repeat layers, ending with noodles. Spread reserved ½ cup spinach mixture over noodles, and sprinkle with remaining ¼ cup Parmesan cheese. Cover and bake at 375° for 35 minutes. Let stand 5 minutes before serving. Yield: 9 servings.

Calories 340 (22% from fat) **Protein** 21.6g **Fat** 8.4g (sat 4.3g) **Carbohydrate** 44.6g **Fiber** 3.7g **Cholesterol** 21mg **Iron** 3.1mg **Sodium** 457mg **Calcium** 395mg

FOR GREAT LASAGNA

• To prevent "watery" lasagna, cook the noodles first. Let them drain while you prepare the rest of the recipe. They will be slightly sticky, but will pull apart easily when you are ready to use them.
• Let the baked lasagna stand 5 minutes after removing it from the oven. This will let it "set," making it easier to cut and serve.

HEARTY LASAGNA

Grate the Parmesan cheese as finely as possible to distribute the fresh cheese flavor evenly throughout the filling.

¾	pound ground round
	Vegetable cooking spray
1	cup chopped onion
3	cloves garlic, minced
¼	cup chopped fresh parsley, divided
2	teaspoons dried oregano
1	teaspoon dried basil
¼	teaspoon pepper
1	(28-ounce) can whole tomatoes, undrained and chopped
1	(14½-ounce) can Italian-style stewed tomatoes, undrained and chopped
1	(8-ounce) can no-salt-added tomato sauce
1	(6-ounce) can tomato paste
2	cups nonfat cottage cheese
½	cup freshly grated Parmesan cheese
1	(15-ounce) container nonfat ricotta cheese
1	egg white, lightly beaten
12	cooked lasagna noodles (cooked without salt or fat)
2	cups (8 ounces) shredded provolone cheese
	Fresh oregano sprigs (optional)

Cook ground round in a large saucepan over medium heat until browned, stirring until it crumbles. Drain meat, and set aside. Wipe pan with a paper towel. Coat pan with cooking spray; add onion and garlic, and sauté 5 minutes. Return meat to pan. Add 2 tablespoons parsley and next 7 ingredients; bring mixture to a boil. Cover, reduce heat, and simmer 15 minutes. Uncover and simmer 20 minutes. Remove from heat.

Combine remaining 2 tablespoons parsley, cottage cheese, and next 3 ingredients; stir well, and set aside.

Spread ¾ cup tomato mixture over bottom of a 13- x 9- x 2-inch baking dish coated with cooking spray. Arrange 4 noodles over tomato mixture; top with half of cottage cheese mixture, 2¼ cups tomato mixture, and ⅔ cup provolone. Repeat layers, ending with noodles. Spread remaining tomato mixture over noodles.

Cover and bake at 350° for 1 hour. Sprinkle with remaining ⅔ cup provolone; bake, uncovered, 10 additional minutes. Let stand 10 minutes before serving. Garnish with oregano sprigs, if desired. Yield: 9 servings.

Calories 380 (25% from fat) **Protein** 33.4g **Fat** 10.5g (sat 5.7g) **Carbohydrate** 40.5g **Fiber** 2.8g **Cholesterol** 50mg **Iron** 3.8mg **Sodium** 703mg **Calcium** 394mg

PICK YOUR PASTA

Orzo

Couscous

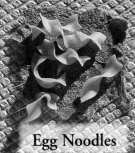

Egg Noodles

Mostaccioli

Wagon Wheel

Fusilli

Farfalle

Shell

Elbow Macaroni

Rotini

Tortellini

Penne

Linguine

Angel Hair

Spaghetti

Ziti

Fettuccine

Manicotti

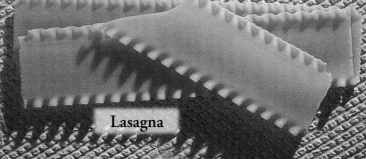

Lasagna

CHILI MAC

QUICK & EASY

For a menu including this recipe and a photo, see page 219.

1   pound ground round
½   cup chopped onion
½   cup chopped green pepper
3   cloves garlic, minced
2   cups cooked elbow
    macaroni (cooked without
    salt or fat)
½   cup water
1   tablespoon chili powder
1   teaspoon ground cumin
½   teaspoon salt
¼   teaspoon pepper
1   (15¼-ounce) can kidney
    beans, drained
1   (14½-ounce) can no-salt-
    added whole tomatoes,
    undrained and chopped
1   (8¾-ounce) can no-salt-
    added whole kernel corn,
    drained
1   (8-ounce) can no-salt-added
    tomato sauce
1   (6-ounce) can no-salt-added
    tomato paste
1   cup (4 ounces) shredded
    reduced-fat sharp Cheddar
    cheese

Cook first 4 ingredients in a Dutch oven over medium-high heat until meat is browned, stirring until meat crumbles. Drain well; wipe drippings from Dutch oven with a paper towel. Return beef mixture to Dutch oven; add macaroni and next 10 ingredients; stir well. Bring to a boil; cover, reduce heat, and simmer 20 minutes, stirring occasionally. Spoon into individual serving bowls; sprinkle 2 tablespoons cheese over each serving. Yield: 8 servings (serving size: 1 cup).

Calories 309 (21% from fat) Protein 25.1g Fat 7.2g (sat 2.9g) Carbohydrate 36.9g Fiber 4.4g Cholesterol 44mg Iron 4.2mg Sodium 420mg Calcium 165mg

ZITI CASSEROLE

½   pound ground chuck
½   pound freshly ground raw
    turkey breast
Vegetable cooking spray
1   cup chopped onion
1   cup sliced fresh mushrooms
¾   cup chopped green pepper
2   cloves garlic, minced
1   cup water
¼   cup chopped fresh parsley
1½ teaspoons dried Italian
    seasoning
½   teaspoon salt
½   teaspoon pepper
2   (14½-ounce) cans no-salt-
    added whole tomatoes,
    undrained and chopped
1   (6-ounce) can Italian-style
    tomato paste
3   cups cooked ziti (short
    tubular pasta), (cooked
    without salt or fat)
½   cup freshly grated Parmesan
    cheese

Cook ground chuck and turkey in a Dutch oven over medium-high heat until browned, stirring until meat crumbles. Drain meat well, and set aside. Wipe drippings from Dutch oven with a paper towel.

Coat Dutch oven with cooking spray; place over medium-high heat until hot. Add onion and next 3 ingredients; sauté until vegetables are tender.

Add beef mixture to vegetable mixture in Dutch oven. Add water and next 6 ingredients. Bring mixture to a boil; reduce heat, and simmer, uncovered, 25 minutes, stirring occasionally. Remove from heat, and stir in pasta.

Spoon beef mixture into a 13- x 9- x 2-inch baking dish coated with cooking spray. Bake, covered, at 375° for 25 minutes or until thoroughly heated. Top with Parmesan cheese. Cover casserole, and let stand 5 minutes or until cheese melts. Yield: 8 servings (serving size: 1⅓ cups).

Calories 251 (32% from fat) Protein 16.8g Fat 8.8g (sat 3.3g) Carbohydrate 26.5g Fiber 3.3g Cholesterol 34mg Iron 3.4mg Sodium 285mg Calcium 122mg

BEEF CARBONNADE

You don't often see regular bacon in our recipes. But in this case, we found that it added a lot of flavor and kept the recipe authentic, without compromising our nutritional standards.

2 slices bacon, finely diced
2 pounds lean, boneless chuck roast, cut into 1-inch cubes
½ teaspoon salt
½ teaspoon pepper
1 clove garlic, minced
5 cups thinly sliced onion
3 tablespoons all-purpose flour
1 cup canned beef broth, undiluted
2 teaspoons white wine vinegar
½ teaspoon sugar
½ teaspoon dried thyme
1 bay leaf
1 (12-ounce) can light beer
7 cups hot cooked egg noodles (cooked without salt or fat)

Cook bacon in an ovenproof Dutch oven over medium heat until crisp; remove bacon with a slotted spoon, reserving drippings in Dutch oven. Set bacon aside.

Cook beef, salt, and pepper in drippings over medium-high heat 3 minutes, browning beef well on all sides. Add garlic; cook 30 seconds. Remove beef with a slotted spoon; set aside.

Add onion to drippings in Dutch oven; cover and cook 10 minutes, stirring occasionally. Stir in flour; cook 2 minutes. Add broth and next 5 ingredients; bring to a boil. Remove from heat; stir in reserved bacon and beef. Cover and bake at 325° for 2 hours and 45 minutes or until beef is tender; remove and discard bay leaf. Serve over noodles. Yield: 7 servings (serving size: 1 cup beef mixture and 1 cup noodles).

Calories 553 (31% from fat) **Protein** 36.4g **Fat** 18.9g (sat 6.9g) **Carbohydrate** 54.8g **Fiber** 5.9g **Cholesterol** 73mg **Iron** 6.3mg **Sodium** 462mg **Calcium** 21mg

BEEF STROGANOFF

1 pound lean boneless top sirloin steak
Vegetable cooking spray
3 cups sliced fresh mushrooms
½ cup chopped onion
1 teaspoon beef-flavored bouillon granules
1 cup hot water
1 tablespoon margarine
2 tablespoons all-purpose flour
¼ cup dry sherry
½ teaspoon salt
⅛ teaspoon pepper
¾ cup low-fat sour cream
3½ cups cooked wide egg noodles (cooked without salt or fat)
3 tablespoons minced fresh parsley
Fresh parsley sprigs (optional)

Partially freeze steak; trim fat from steak. Slice steak diagonally across grain into ¼-inch-wide strips; cut strips into 2-inch pieces.

Coat a large nonstick skillet with cooking spray; place over medium-high heat until hot. Add steak strips, sliced mushrooms, and chopped onion; sauté 6 minutes or until steak is done and mushrooms are tender. Remove steak mixture from skillet. Drain well, and set aside. Wipe drippings from skillet with a paper towel.

Combine bouillon granules and hot water, stirring well. Melt margarine in skillet over medium heat, and add flour. Cook, stirring constantly with a wire whisk, 1 minute. Gradually add bouillon mixture, stirring constantly. Cook, stirring constantly, until thickened and bubbly.

Add steak mixture to flour mixture in skillet; add sherry, salt, and pepper. Bring to a boil; reduce heat, and simmer, uncovered, 6 minutes. Remove from heat, and let stand 30 seconds. Stir sour cream into steak mixture.

Combine cooked noodles and minced parsley; toss mixture well. Serve steak mixture over noodles. Garnish with parsley sprigs, if desired. Yield: 7 servings (serving size: ½ cup steak mixture and ½ cup noodles).

Calories 293 (32% from fat) **Protein** 23.0g **Fat** 10.4g (sat 4.2g) **Carbohydrate** 26.0g **Fiber** 2.7g **Cholesterol** 87mg **Iron** 4.1mg **Sodium** 380mg **Calcium** 56mg

Tuna Noodle Casserole

Vegetable cooking spray
¾ cup sliced fresh mushrooms
¼ cup chopped sweet red pepper
2 tablespoons finely chopped onion
3 tablespoons margarine
3 tablespoons all-purpose flour
2 cups skim milk
4 cups cooked medium egg noodles (cooked without salt or fat)
1 cup frozen English peas, thawed
¼ teaspoon salt
⅛ teaspoon pepper
1 (12-ounce) can solid white tuna in water, drained
¼ cup fine, dry breadcrumbs
½ cup (2 ounces) shredded sharp Cheddar cheese

Coat a medium saucepan with cooking spray; place over medium heat until hot. Add mushrooms, red pepper, and onion; sauté 3 minutes or until crisp-tender. Remove from saucepan; set aside.

Add margarine to saucepan; place over medium-low heat until margarine melts. Add flour; cook, stirring constantly with a wire whisk, 1 minute. Gradually add milk, stirring constantly. Cook over medium heat, stirring constantly, 6 minutes or until thickened and bubbly.

Pour sauce into a bowl. Stir in mushroom mixture, noodles, and next 4 ingredients. Spoon into a shallow 2-quart baking dish coated with cooking spray. Top with breadcrumbs and cheese. Cover and bake at 350° for 30 minutes; uncover and bake 5 additional minutes or until cheese melts. Yield: 8 servings (serving size: 1 cup).

Calories 289 (28% from fat) **Protein** 19.9g **Fat** 9.0g (sat 2.8g) **Carbohydrate** 32.0g **Fiber** 2.9g **Cholesterol** 51mg **Iron** 2.3mg **Sodium** 424mg **Calcium** 188mg

Pasta Pointers

• Use a Dutch oven or a stockpot to allow room for the pasta to move freely in the boiling water, and it will cook evenly.
• Use 4 to 6 quarts of water to cook spaghetti and other "long" pastas or to cook 1 pound of shaped pasta.
• A bundle of long pasta about the diameter of a quarter weighs 4 ounces and will yield 2 cups of cooked pasta.
• It isn't necessary to add salt or oil to the water. We omit them when preparing pasta for *Cooking Light* recipes to avoid adding sodium and fat, but you can add lemon juice to the water to add subtle flavor.
• Bring the water to a rolling boil, and add the pasta gradually so the water will continue to boil. Once all the pasta has been added, stir and begin timing. Stir often—you can't stir too much!

Lemony Shrimp and Couscous Salad

1 cup water
¾ cup couscous, uncooked
1½ quarts water
1¼ pounds unpeeled medium-size fresh shrimp
½ cup chopped sweet red pepper
¼ cup chopped fresh parsley
3 tablespoons chopped fresh basil
2 tablespoons chopped green onions
2 teaspoons grated lemon rind
2 tablespoons lemon juice
1 tablespoon olive oil
½ teaspoon ground allspice
¼ teaspoon salt
¼ teaspoon pepper

Bring 1 cup water to a boil in a saucepan; stir in couscous. Remove from heat. Cover; let stand 5 minutes or until couscous is tender and liquid is absorbed. Fluff with a fork.

Bring 1½ quarts water to a boil; add shrimp, and cook 3 to 5 minutes or until shrimp turn pink. Drain well; rinse with cold water. Peel, devein, and coarsely chop shrimp. Add chopped shrimp and sweet pepper to cooked couscous.

Combine parsley and remaining 8 ingredients. Add to couscous mixture; toss well. Cover; chill. Yield: 4 servings (serving size: 1 cup).

Calories 239 (18% from fat) **Protein** 22.4g **Fat** 4.8g (sat 0.9g) **Carbohydrate** 26.6g **Fiber** 1.8g **Cholesterol** 166mg **Iron** 3.8mg **Sodium** 343mg **Calcium** 48mg

Chilled Broccoli-Pasta Salad

3 cups fresh broccoli flowerets
3 cups cooked rotini (corkscrew pasta), (cooked without salt or fat)
1 cup thinly sliced red cabbage
1 clove garlic
3 tablespoons white wine vinegar
3 tablespoons mango chutney
1 tablespoon Dijon mustard
2 teaspoons sugar
¼ teaspoon pepper
2 tablespoons vegetable oil

Drop broccoli into a large saucepan of boiling water; return to a boil. Cook 1 minute; drain. Pour cold water over broccoli; drain. Combine broccoli, pasta, and cabbage in a large bowl; set aside.

Place garlic in container of an electric blender; cover and process until minced. Add vinegar and next 4 ingredients; cover and process until smooth. With blender running, add oil through opening in lid; process until blended. Pour over pasta mixture; toss gently. Cover and chill 30 minutes. Yield: 5 servings (serving size: 1 cup).

Calories 193 (29% from fat) **Protein** 4.9g **Fat** 6.3g (sat 1.1g) **Carbohydrate** 29.9g **Fiber** 3.0g **Cholesterol** 0mg **Iron** 1.6mg **Sodium** 127mg **Calcium** 41mg

Balsamic Pasta Salad

QUICK & EASY

Asiago cheese adds a sharp, nutty flavor to any salad. If you can't find it, try substituting fresh Parmesan or Romano cheese.

¼ cup balsamic vinegar
3 tablespoons water
1½ teaspoons olive oil
¼ teaspoon salt
¼ teaspoon pepper
1 large clove garlic, minced
½ cup small broccoli flowerets
½ cup small cauliflower flowerets
½ cup julienne-sliced carrot
½ cup julienne-sliced sweet red pepper
4 cups cooked farfalle (bow tie pasta), (cooked without salt or fat)
2 tablespoons thinly sliced fresh basil
¼ cup (1 ounce) grated Asiago cheese

Combine first 6 ingredients in a jar; cover tightly, and shake vigorously. Set aside.

Drop broccoli, cauliflower, and carrot into a large saucepan of boiling water; cook 30 seconds. Drain. Pour cold water over vegetables, and drain.

Combine drained vegetables, red pepper, cooked pasta, basil, and Asiago cheese in a large bowl. Add vinegar mixture; toss gently. Cover

salad, and chill. Yield: 5 servings (serving size: 1 cup).

Calories 199 (15% from fat) **Protein** 7.7g **Fat** 3.4g (sat 1.1g) **Carbohydrate** 34.3g **Fiber** 2.9g **Cholesterol** 3mg **Iron** 2.0mg **Sodium** 203mg **Calcium** 81mg

Tortellini Salad

QUICK & EASY

1 (9-ounce) package fresh cheese tortellini, uncooked
2 cups (2-inch) julienne-sliced zucchini
1 cup cherry tomato halves
½ cup chopped sweet red pepper
⅓ cup sliced green onions
2 tablespoons grated Parmesan cheese
⅓ cup fat-free red wine vinaigrette
1½ teaspoons chopped fresh dillweed
¼ teaspoon pepper

Cook tortellini in boiling water 6 minutes, omitting salt and fat; drain. Rinse under cold running water, and drain well. Combine tortellini, zucchini, and next 4 ingredients in a large bowl. Combine vinaigrette, dillweed, and ¼ teaspoon pepper; stir well. Pour over tortellini mixture; toss gently. Yield: 6 servings (serving size: 1 cup).

Calories 168 (20% from fat) **Protein** 8.2g **Fat** 3.8g (sat 2.2g) **Carbohydrate** 25.1g **Fiber** 1.0g **Cholesterol** 21mg **Iron** 0.7mg **Sodium** 335mg **Calcium** 42mg

Vegetable Salad With Pasta Wheels

2   cups cooked wagon wheel pasta (cooked without salt or fat)
1   cup drained canned pinto beans
2   tablespoons sliced green onions
1   (9-ounce) package frozen Sugar Snap peas, thawed and diagonally sliced in half
⅓   cup plain low-fat yogurt
3   tablespoons reduced-calorie mayonnaise
½   teaspoon dried tarragon
¼   teaspoon salt
¼   teaspoon cracked black pepper
5   large red leaf lettuce leaves
5   large plum tomatoes, each cut into 6 wedges
20 peeled, diagonally sliced cucumber slices

Combine pasta, beans, green onions, and peas in a large bowl. Combine yogurt, mayonnaise, tarragon, salt, and pepper; stir well. Pour yogurt mixture over pasta mixture; toss gently.

Arrange lettuce leaves on individual salad plates. Spoon 1 cup pasta mixture on each. Top each serving with 6 tomato wedges and 4 cucumber slices. Yield: 5 servings (serving size: 1 cup).

Calories 204 (15% from fat) **Protein** 8.9g **Fat** 3.5g (sat 0.3g) **Carbohydrate** 34.9g **Fiber** 5.0g **Cholesterol** 4mg **Iron** 3.2mg **Sodium** 312mg **Calcium** 86mg

Cool Couscous Salad

QUICK & EASY

Couscous is a beadlike pasta from the Middle East that cooks in just 5 minutes. Look for it in boxes on the pasta or rice aisles.

1   cup plus 2 tablespoons canned no-salt-added chicken broth, undiluted
¾   cup couscous, uncooked
2   cups seeded, chopped tomato
1   cup chopped sweet red pepper
½   cup chopped celery
½   cup seeded, chopped cucumber
¼   cup chopped green onions
¼   cup chopped fresh parsley
3   tablespoons balsamic vinegar
1   tablespoon olive oil
1   tablespoon Dijon mustard
½   teaspoon grated lemon rind
¼   teaspoon pepper

Bring broth to a boil in a medium saucepan; stir in couscous. Remove from heat; cover and let stand 5 minutes or until couscous is tender and liquid is absorbed. Fluff with a fork. Cool, uncovered, 10 minutes.

Combine couscous, tomato, and next 5 ingredients in a large bowl, and toss gently.

Combine vinegar and remaining 4 ingredients in a small bowl, and stir with a wire whisk. Add to couscous mixture; toss to coat. Serve chilled or at room temperature. Yield: 6 servings (serving size: 1 cup).

Calories 121 (23% from fat) **Protein** 3.7g **Fat** 3.1g (sat 0.4g) **Carbohydrate** 19.8g **Fiber** 1.7g **Cholesterol** 0mg **Iron** 1.3mg **Sodium** 117mg **Calcium** 24mg

Mostaccioli Pizza Salad

QUICK & EASY

3   tablespoons white vinegar
2   tablespoons water
1   tablespoon olive oil
¾   teaspoon dried Italian seasoning
¼   teaspoon salt
¼   teaspoon pepper
2   cloves garlic, crushed
2¼ cups cooked mostaccioli (tubular pasta), (cooked without salt or fat)
1   cup sliced mushrooms
¾   cup cherry tomatoes, halved
½   cup chopped green pepper
½   cup (2 ounces) shredded part-skim mozzarella cheese

Combine first 7 ingredients in a medium bowl, stirring with a wire whisk until blended. Add cooked pasta and remaining ingredients, and toss gently to coat. Cover salad, and chill. Yield: 5 servings (serving size: 1 cup).

Calories 164 (28% from fat) **Protein** 6.6g **Fat** 5.2g (sat 1.6g) **Carbohydrate** 22.3g **Fiber** 0.8g **Cholesterol** 7mg **Iron** 0.8mg **Sodium** 174mg **Calcium** 86mg

Tortellini With Cherry
Tomatoes and Corn

TORTELLINI WITH CHERRY TOMATOES AND CORN

QUICK & EASY

1   (9-ounce) package fresh
    cheese tortellini, uncooked
1   (10-ounce) package frozen
    whole kernel corn
1   clove garlic, halved
2   cups quartered cherry
    tomatoes
¼   cup sliced green onions
¼   cup chopped fresh
    basil
2   tablespoons grated
    Parmesan cheese
1   teaspoon olive oil
⅛   teaspoon pepper

Cook tortellini in boiling water 3 minutes, omitting salt and fat. Add corn, and cook 3 additional minutes; drain well.

Rub the inside of a large serving bowl with garlic halves, and discard garlic halves. Add tortellini mixture, tomato quarters, and remaining ingredients, tossing gently to coat. Serve warm. Yield: 6 servings (serving size: 1 cup).

Calories 207 (21% from fat) Protein 9.3g
Fat 4.9g (sat 1.5g) Carbohydrate 33.8g
Fiber 2.2g Cholesterol 21mg Iron 0.6mg
Sodium 194mg Calcium 33mg

MEDITERRANEAN PASTA

QUICK & EASY

4   cups chopped tomato
2   tablespoons chopped fresh
    basil
1   tablespoon olive oil
1   tablespoon red wine vinegar
¼   teaspoon salt
⅛   teaspoon crushed red pepper
1   clove garlic, minced
4   cups cooked angel hair pasta
    (cooked without salt or fat)
¼   cup (1 ounce) crumbled feta
    cheese

Combine first 7 ingredients in a large bowl, and stir mixture well.

Let stand 10 minutes. Serve at room temperature over cooked pasta, and sprinkle with feta cheese. Yield: 4 servings (serving size: 1 cup tomato mixture, 1 cup pasta, and 1 tablespoon cheese).

Calories 286 (20% from fat) **Protein** 9.3g **Fat** 6.4g (sat 1.7g) **Carbohydrate** 48.8g **Fiber** 4.6g **Cholesterol** 6mg **Iron** 2.9mg **Sodium** 243mg **Calcium** 58mg

ORZO WITH SPINACH AND PINE NUTS

QUICK & EASY

Pine nuts are expensive and turn rancid quickly. Look for them where they're sold in bulk, and buy just the amount you need.

1	tablespoon pine nuts
1	teaspoon margarine
1	clove garlic, minced
1¾	cups water
¾	cup orzo (rice-shaped pasta), uncooked
⅛	teaspoon salt
1	cup tightly packed chopped fresh spinach
2	tablespoons grated Parmesan cheese

Spread pine nuts in a shallow pan. Bake at 350° for 5 to 10 minutes or until nuts are lightly toasted, stirring occasionally. Set aside.

Melt margarine in a medium saucepan over medium heat. Add garlic; sauté 1 minute. Add water, orzo, and salt, and bring to a boil.

Reduce heat to medium-low, and cook 13 minutes or until liquid is absorbed. Stir in spinach, Parmesan cheese, and toasted pine nuts. Yield: 2 servings (serving size: 1 cup).

Calories 321 (23% from fat) **Protein** 12.8g **Fat** 8.1g (sat 2.0g) **Carbohydrate** 50.3g **Fiber** 2.7g **Cholesterol** 4mg **Iron** 3.9mg **Sodium** 289mg **Calcium** 114mg

COUSCOUS WITH CURRANTS

Currants look like small raisins and are usually found on the same shelf in the supermarket. If you can't find currants, use raisins; the two are interchangeable.

⅔	cup canned no-salt-added chicken broth, undiluted
⅓	cup couscous, uncooked
1	teaspoon olive oil
2	tablespoons sliced green onions
1	clove garlic, crushed
⅓	cup seeded, diced plum tomato
¼	cup drained canned chick-peas (garbanzo beans)
2	tablespoons currants or raisins
Dash of ground cumin	
2	tablespoons chopped fresh parsley
2	tablespoons lemon juice
¼	teaspoon pepper

Bring broth to a boil in a medium saucepan; stir in couscous. Remove from heat; cover and let stand 5

minutes or until couscous is tender and liquid is absorbed. Fluff with a fork; set aside.

Heat oil in a medium nonstick skillet over medium-high heat. Add green onions and garlic; sauté 1 minute. Add couscous, tomato, and next 3 ingredients; cook 2 minutes or until thoroughly heated. Remove from heat, and stir in parsley, lemon juice, and pepper. Serve warm. Yield: 2 servings (serving size: ¾ cup).

Calories 197 (17% from fat) **Protein** 6.7g **Fat** 3.8g (sat 0.6g) **Carbohydrate** 34.9g **Fiber** 1.6g **Cholesterol** 0mg **Iron** 1.9mg **Sodium** 180mg **Calcium** 44mg

WHAT'S AL DENTE?

Cooking times vary with the shape and thickness of the pasta. Check for doneness after the minimum recommended cooking time. Remove a piece of pasta from the water, and bite into it; perfectly cooked pasta will have a firm, tender consistency. This is called called *al dente*, Italian for "to the tooth."

Roasted Chicken and
Vegetables, page 110

LEAVE A CHICKEN OR TURKEY IN OUR TEST KITCHEN, AND YOU NEVER KNOW HOW IT WILL END UP. IT MAY BE DRESSED FOR THE GRILL, TIED TO BE BAKED, SLAPPED WITH HERB PASTE, BAKED IN A PIE, DRAPED IN SALSA, SIMPLY SAUTÉED, OR ROASTED FOR AN APPRECIATIVE AUDIENCE.

POULTRY

FOR LOW-FAT AND VERSATILE POULTRY, A CHANGE OF FLAVOR IS AS EASY AS OPENING THE PRODUCE DRAWER OR THE SPICE CABINET. KEEP GARLIC, HERBS, MESQUITE CHIPS, ONION, TOMATO, PEPPERS, AND A GOOD WINE ON HAND TO MAKE SURE YOU HAVE A WARDROBE OF FLAVORS TO MATCH ANY MOOD.

WHERE TO START? TRY THE PERSONAL POULTRY PICKS OF NATHALIE, JOHN, SUSAN, AND VANESSA: DEVILED CHICKEN BREASTS, UPTOWN CHICKEN AND REDEYE GRAVY, CHICKEN CUTLETS WITH PEPPERS AND MUSHROOMS, AND CHILES RELLENOS CASSEROLE.

Hawaiian Chicken

See page 218 for side dish suggestions to make an easy menu.

¼ cup unsweetened orange juice
2 tablespoons unsweetened pineapple juice
1 teaspoon minced fresh cilantro
¼ teaspoon salt
4 (4-ounce) skinned, boned chicken breast halves
¾ cup finely chopped fresh pineapple
1 tablespoon plus 1 teaspoon finely chopped sweet red pepper
1½ teaspoons minced fresh cilantro
1½ teaspoons white wine vinegar
1 teaspoon unsweetened orange juice
1 teaspoon seeded, finely chopped jalapeño pepper
Vegetable cooking spray
½ teaspoon pepper

Combine first 4 ingredients in a shallow dish, and stir well. Add chicken, turning to coat. Cover and marinate in refrigerator 2 hours, turning occasionally.

Combine pineapple and next 5 ingredients; stir well. Cover and let stand at room temperature 2 hours.

Remove chicken from marinade, reserving marinade. Place marinade in a small saucepan; bring to a boil. Remove from heat; set aside.

Coat grill rack with cooking spray; place on grill over medium-hot coals (350° to 400°). Sprinkle ½ teaspoon pepper over chicken. Place chicken on rack; grill, covered, 5 minutes on each side, basting with reserved marinade.

To serve, top each chicken breast with 3 tablespoons pineapple mixture. Yield: 4 servings (serving size: 1 chicken breast half and 3 tablespoons sauce).

Calories 175 (17% from fat) **Protein** 26.8g **Fat** 3.3g (sat 0.9g) **Carbohydrate** 8.3g **Fiber** 0.8g **Cholesterol** 72mg **Iron** 1.2mg **Sodium** 211mg **Calcium** 21mg

Boston Beach Jerk Chicken

Add oak, pecan, or hickory wood to a charcoal fire to add flavor and authenticity to jerk cooking.

1½ cups Wet Jerk Rub, divided
1 (3½-pound) broiler-fryer
Vegetable cooking spray
Fresh thyme sprigs (optional)
Lime wedges (optional)

Prepare Wet Jerk Rub; set aside. Remove and discard giblets from chicken. Rinse chicken under cold water, and pat dry. Remove skin, and trim excess fat; split chicken in half lengthwise. Place chicken in a large shallow dish, and spread 1¼ cups Wet Jerk Rub over both sides of chicken. Cover and marinate in refrigerator 1 to 4 hours.

Coat grill rack with cooking spray; place rack on grill over medium-hot coals (350° to 400°). Place chicken on rack, and grill 45 minutes or until done, turning occasionally and basting with remaining ¼ cup Wet Jerk Rub. If desired, garnish with thyme sprigs and lime wedges. Yield: 6 servings (serving size: 3 ounces chicken).

Calories 325 (41% from fat) **Protein** 38.8g **Fat** 14.7g (sat 3.6g) **Carbohydrate** 9.5g **Fiber** 2.6g **Cholesterol** 114mg **Iron** 3.6mg **Sodium** 904mg **Calcium** 103mg

WET JERK RUB:

4 cups (1-inch) pieces green onions
¼ cup fresh thyme leaves
3 tablespoons peeled, grated gingerroot
2 tablespoons fresh lime juice
2 tablespoons vegetable oil
1 tablespoon freshly ground pepper
1 tablespoon freshly ground coriander seeds
2 teaspoons salt
2 teaspoons freshly ground allspice
1 teaspoon freshly ground nutmeg
1 teaspoon ground cinnamon
5 cloves garlic, halved
3 bay leaves
1 to 2 fresh Scotch bonnet chiles, halved and seeded

Position knife blade in food processor bowl; add all ingredients.

Boston Beach Jerk Chicken

Process mixture until a thick paste forms, scraping sides of processor bowl once. Transfer jerk rub to a small bowl. Cover mixture, and store in refrigerator. Use jerk rub to marinate or baste chicken, turkey, or pork. Yield: 1½ cups (serving size: 1 tablespoon).

Note: Be sure to wear gloves when handling chiles to protect your skin from the hot oils in the chiles. You can substitute dried or fresh habaneros or 2 to 3 fresh serrano chiles for the Scotch bonnet chiles in this recipe, if desired. Order fresh habaneros from Frieda's Inc., P.O. Box 58488, Los Angeles, CA 90058 (800-241-1771).

Calories 21 (51% from fat) **Protein** 0.5g **Fat** 1.2g (sat 0.2g) **Carbohydrate** 2.3g **Fiber** 0.6g **Cholesterol** 0mg **Iron** 0.5mg **Sodium** 198mg **Calcium** 21mg

ALL ABOUT JERK

A jerk rub is the Jamaican form of barbecue sauce that's "packed" onto the chicken. For an authentic island meal, round out the menu with roasted sweet yams, plantains, or bananas; rice with beans; and cabbage with raisins.

MUSTARD- AND SAGE-GRILLED CHICKEN

Pesto is a pungent Italian herb sauce made with ground herbs, Parmesan, pine nuts, garlic, and olive oil. You can use commercially jarred pesto, but our Sage Pesto has about one-third the fat and calories.

¼ cup Sage Pesto
¼ cup minced fresh chives
¼ cup chopped fresh thyme
¼ cup Dijon mustard
½ teaspoon grated lemon rind
¼ cup fresh lemon juice
1 teaspoon extra-virgin olive oil
4 (6-ounce) skinned chicken breast halves
Vegetable cooking spray

Combine first 7 ingredients in a bowl, and stir well. Place chicken in a shallow dish; spread ½ cup pesto mixture over both sides of chicken. Cover and marinate in refrigerator 1 to 4 hours.

Coat grill rack with cooking spray; place on grill over medium-hot coals (350° to 400°). Place chicken, bone side up, on rack; grill, covered, 8 minutes on each side or until done, turning occasionally and basting with remaining pesto mixture. Yield: 4 servings (serving size: 1 chicken breast half).

Calories 286 (33% from fat) Protein 41.0g Fat 10.4g (sat 2.1g) Carbohydrate 4.6g Fiber 1.0g Cholesterol 110mg Iron 2.7mg Sodium 582mg Calcium 71mg

SAGE PESTO:

2 tablespoons pine nuts, toasted
2 large cloves garlic
2 cups torn spinach
2 cups fresh flat-leaf parsley leaves
¾ cup fresh sage leaves
2 tablespoons freshly grated Parmesan cheese
1 tablespoon plus 1 teaspoon lemon juice
⅛ teaspoon salt
3 tablespoons extra-virgin olive oil

Position knife blade in food processor bowl. Drop pine nuts and garlic through food chute with food processor running; process until minced. Add spinach and next 5 ingredients; process until finely minced. With processor running, slowly pour oil through food chute; process until well blended. Spoon into a heavy-duty, zip-top plastic bag; store in refrigerator. Yield: 1 cup (serving size: 1 tablespoon).

Calories 39 (81% from fat) Protein 1.1g Fat 3.5g (sat 0.6g) Carbohydrate 1.5g Fiber 0.8g Cholesterol 1mg Iron 0.9mg Sodium 42mg Calcium 38mg

LIME-GRILLED CHICKEN WITH BLACK BEAN SAUCE

QUICK & EASY

3 tablespoons fresh lime juice
2 tablespoons vegetable oil
¼ teaspoon ground red pepper
4 cloves garlic, crushed
4 (4-ounce) skinned, boned chicken breast halves
Vegetable cooking spray
2 cups water
½ cup diced sweet red pepper
1 tablespoon chopped purple onion
1 cup drained canned black beans
½ cup unsweetened orange juice
2 tablespoons balsamic vinegar
¼ teaspoon salt
⅛ teaspoon freshly ground black pepper
2 cloves garlic, crushed

Combine first 4 ingredients in a large heavy-duty, zip-top plastic bag.

Add chicken; seal bag, and marinate in refrigerator 8 hours, turning bag occasionally.

Remove chicken from bag, reserving marinade. Place marinade in a small saucepan; bring to a boil. Remove from heat; set aside.

Coat grill rack with cooking spray; place on grill over medium-hot coals (350° to 400°). Place chicken on rack, and grill, covered, 10 minutes on each side or until chicken is done, basting chicken occasionally with reserved marinade. Set aside, and keep warm.

Bring water to a boil in a small saucepan; add sweet red pepper and onion. Cook 30 seconds; drain. Plunge into ice water; drain well, and set aside.

Position knife blade in food processor bowl; add beans and remaining 5 ingredients. Process until smooth. Pour mixture into a saucepan; cook over medium heat until heated.

Spoon bean sauce evenly onto 4 serving plates. Place chicken breast halves on sauce; top evenly with diced pepper mixture. Yield: 4 servings (serving size: ¼ cup plus 1 tablespoon bean sauce, 1 chicken breast half, and 2 tablespoons diced pepper mixture).

Calories 263 (27% from fat) **Protein** 30.7g **Fat** 7.8g (sat 1.8g) **Carbohydrate** 16.3g **Fiber** 2.3g **Cholesterol** 72mg **Iron** 2.2mg **Sodium** 349mg **Calcium** 36mg

Balsamic Vinegar Chicken With Almond Peppers

Many regions of Italy have a version of almond peppers—a sweet-and-sour vegetable dish delicious hot or cold. When paired with a Parmesan-dusted chicken breast, it becomes a light lunch.

2   large sweet red peppers (about ¾ pound)
2   large green peppers (about ¾ pound)
2   teaspoons olive oil
⅓   cup raisins
¼   cup balsamic vinegar
1½ teaspoons sugar
¼   teaspoon salt
⅛   teaspoon pepper
¼   cup slivered almonds, toasted
6   (4-ounce) skinned, boned chicken breast halves
3   tablespoons fine, dry breadcrumbs
3   tablespoons grated Parmesan cheese
¼   cup all-purpose flour
2   egg whites, lightly beaten
2   teaspoons olive oil
2   tablespoons balsamic vinegar
2   tablespoons water

Cut peppers into 2½- x 2-inch strips. Heat 2 teaspoons oil in a large nonstick skillet over medium-high heat. Add pepper strips; sauté 8 minutes. Add raisins; sauté 1 minute. Add ¼ cup vinegar and next 3 ingredients; cook 1 minute. Remove from heat; stir in almonds. Set aside, and keep warm.

Place each piece of chicken between 2 sheets of heavy-duty plastic wrap, and flatten to ¼-inch thickness, using a meat mallet or rolling pin. Combine breadcrumbs and cheese in a shallow dish. Place flour in a shallow dish. Dredge each piece of chicken in flour, dip in egg whites, and dredge in breadcrumb mixture.

Heat 2 teaspoons olive oil in a large nonstick skillet over medium-high heat. Add chicken, and cook 3 minutes on each side or until done. Remove from heat. Place chicken and pepper mixture on a serving platter; set aside, and keep warm.

Add 2 tablespoons vinegar and water to skillet; stir with a wooden spoon to loosen browned bits. Spoon mixture over chicken and pepper mixture. Yield: 6 servings (serving size: 1 chicken breast half and ½ cup pepper mixture).

Calories 288 (30% from fat) **Protein** 31.3g **Fat** 9.5g (sat 2.0g) **Carbohydrate** 19.4g **Fiber** 2.6g **Cholesterol** 74mg **Iron** 2.8mg **Sodium** 253mg **Calcium** 73mg

"My family loves this recipe. I love the fact that it's easy enough to make often for weekday dinners and still looks elegant enough to serve to dinner guests, too."

———Nathalie Dearing,
Managing Editor

DEVILED CHICKEN BREASTS

QUICK & EASY

2   tablespoons Italian-seasoned breadcrumbs
4   (4-ounce) skinned, boned chicken breast halves
1   tablespoon olive oil
½   cup dry white wine
½   teaspoon dried savory, crushed
¼   teaspoon salt
¼   teaspoon coarsely ground pepper
1   (4-ounce) jar whole mushrooms, drained
1   tablespoon lemon juice
1   tablespoon honey mustard

Place crumbs in a heavy-duty, zip-top plastic bag; add chicken. Seal bag; shake until well coated. Heat oil in a nonstick skillet over medium heat. Add chicken; cook 3 minutes on each side or until browned. Add wine and next 4 ingredients; cover, reduce heat, and simmer 15 minutes or until chicken is done. Remove chicken and mushrooms with a slotted spoon; place on a serving platter. Add juice and mustard to skillet; stir. Cook 1 minute or until heated; serve with chicken. Yield: 4 servings (serving size: 1 chicken breast half and 1 tablespoon sauce).

Calories 215 (21% from fat) **Protein** 27.8g **Fat** 5.0g (sat 0.9g) **Carbohydrate** 8.4g **Fiber** 0.3g **Cholesterol** 66mg **Iron** 1.5mg **Sodium** 548mg **Calcium** 29mg

LEMON-BASIL CHICKEN

QUICK & EASY

1¼   cups fresh whole wheat breadcrumbs
1½   tablespoons minced fresh parsley
1½   teaspoons grated lemon rind
1   teaspoon dried basil
½   teaspoon salt
½   teaspoon pepper
3   tablespoons nonfat buttermilk
¾   teaspoon lemon juice
6   (6-ounce) skinned chicken breast halves
Vegetable cooking spray

Combine first 6 ingredients in a heavy-duty, zip-top plastic bag. Seal bag; shake well. Combine buttermilk and juice; brush over chicken. Place chicken in bag with crumb mixture. Seal bag; shake until coated. Place chicken on rack of a broiler pan coated with cooking spray; sprinkle with any remaining breadcrumbs. Bake, uncovered, at 400° for 40 to 45 minutes or until done.

Yield: 6 servings (serving size: 1 chicken breast half).

Calories 401 (17% from fat) **Protein** 58.1g **Fat** 7.6g (sat 2.0g) **Carbohydrate** 23.3g **Fiber** 1.8g **Cholesterol** 146mg **Iron** 2.9mg **Sodium** 579mg **Calcium** 88mg

"This recipe was a good, tasty introduction to Southern cuisine when I first moved to Alabama from Minnesota. Now I serve it to my fellow Yankees when they come to visit."

———John Kirkpatrick,
Test Kitchens Staff

UPTOWN CHICKEN AND REDEYE GRAVY

QUICK & EASY

1½   tablespoons all-purpose flour
½   teaspoon paprika
¼   teaspoon salt
⅛   teaspoon pepper
4   (4-ounce) skinned, boned chicken breast halves
Vegetable cooking spray
2   teaspoons margarine
½   cup chopped lean country ham (about 2 ounces)
½   cup strongly brewed coffee
¼   cup water
1   tablespoon brown sugar
8   (½-inch-thick) portobello mushroom slices
1   tablespoon all-purpose flour
1   tablespoon water

Combine first 4 ingredients in a large heavy-duty, zip-top plastic bag. Add chicken; seal bag, and shake to coat chicken.

Coat a large nonstick skillet with cooking spray; melt margarine in skillet over medium-high heat. Add chicken, and cook 2 minutes on each side or until golden. Combine ham and next 3 ingredients; pour over chicken. Bring to a boil; cover, reduce heat, and simmer 3 minutes. Add mushroom slices; cover and simmer 5 minutes or until chicken is done and mushroom slices are tender. Remove chicken and mushroom slices with a slotted spoon; place on a serving platter. Set aside, and keep warm.

Combine 1 tablespoon flour and 1 tablespoon water in a bowl; stir with a wire whisk. Add to cooking liquid in skillet. Bring to a boil; cook, stirring constantly with a wire whisk, 1 minute or until thickened. Spoon over chicken and mushrooms. Yield: 4 servings (serving size: 1 chicken breast half, 2 mushroom slices, and 2 tablespoons gravy).

Note: Portobello mushrooms are very large, dark mushrooms that boast an almost meatlike flavor and texture. You can substitute large button mushrooms if portobellos are not available.

Calories 209 (22% from fat) **Protein** 30.0g **Fat** 5.2g (sat 1.3g) **Carbohydrate** 9.2g **Fiber** 0.7g **Cholesterol** 74mg **Iron** 1.9mg **Sodium** 433mg **Calcium** 22mg

"I like this recipe because it's a different way to prepare chicken—it's colorful and has great flavor. I serve it at family birthday dinners, and everyone loves it, including my children."
——Susan M. McIntosh, editor of the first "Cooking Light" column in *Southern Living*

CHICKEN CUTLETS WITH PEPPERS AND MUSHROOMS

QUICK & EASY

Find a complete menu featuring this recipe, along with a photograph, on page 220.

2	(4-ounce) skinned, boned chicken breast halves
1	tablespoon seasoned breadcrumbs
	Vegetable cooking spray
½	teaspoon olive oil
1	cup sliced fresh mushrooms
½	cup plus 3 tablespoons canned low-sodium chicken broth, undiluted and divided
8	(3- x ¼-inch) strips sweet red pepper
2	teaspoons lemon juice
¼	teaspoon dried Italian seasoning
⅛	teaspoon salt
⅛	teaspoon dried crushed red pepper
1	clove garlic, minced
1	teaspoon cornstarch

Place each piece of chicken between 2 sheets of heavy-duty plastic wrap; flatten to ¼-inch thickness, using a meat mallet or rolling pin. Place breadcrumbs in a shallow dish; dredge chicken in breadcrumbs.

Coat a nonstick skillet with cooking spray, and add oil. Place skillet over medium heat until hot. Add chicken, and cook 3 minutes on each side or until done. Remove chicken from skillet; set aside, and keep warm.

Add mushrooms, 1 tablespoon chicken broth, and pepper strips to skillet; sauté 3 minutes. Add ½ cup chicken broth, lemon juice, and next 4 ingredients; bring to a boil. Cover, reduce heat, and simmer 10 minutes.

Combine remaining 2 tablespoons chicken broth and cornstarch; stir well, and add to skillet. Bring to a boil, and cook, stirring constantly, 1 minute. Serve sauce over chicken. Yield: 2 servings (serving size: 1 chicken breast half and 2½ tablespoons sauce).

Calories 211 (24% from fat) **Protein** 28.9g **Fat** 5.7g (sat 1.3g) **Carbohydrate** 9.6g **Fiber** 1.8g **Cholesterol** 72mg **Iron** 2.6mg **Sodium** 285mg **Calcium** 37mg

CHICKEN WITH ONIONS

You may remember this robust recipe from the Kwanzaa menu featured in our November/December 1994 issue. During the Kwanzaa festival, African-Americans reflect on their ancestry, family, and community. The ingredients in this recipe are true to the African-American food experience and are low in fat, salt, cholesterol, and calories.

1   teaspoon salt
1   teaspoon dried crushed red pepper
⅛   teaspoon black pepper
½   cup fresh lime juice
8   cups thinly sliced onion (about 4 large)
5   cloves garlic, minced
8   (4-ounce) skinned, boned chicken breast halves
Vegetable cooking spray
1   tablespoon olive oil, divided
4   cups cooked long-grain rice (cooked without salt or fat)

Combine first 6 ingredients in a large heavy-duty, zip-top plastic bag; add chicken. Seal bag, and shake until chicken is well coated. Marinate in refrigerator 2 hours, turning bag occasionally. Remove chicken and onion from marinade, discarding marinade. Set aside.

Coat an ovenproof Dutch oven with cooking spray; add 1½ teaspoons oil, and place over medium-high heat until hot. Add 4 chicken breast halves to Dutch oven; cook 2 minutes on each side or until browned. Remove chicken from Dutch oven; set aside, and keep warm. Repeat procedure with remaining 1½ teaspoons oil and 4 chicken breast halves.

Remove Dutch oven from heat; add marinated onion slices. Return chicken breasts to Dutch oven, nestling them into onion slices. Bake, uncovered, at 450° for 20 minutes. Remove chicken from Dutch oven; stir onion slices, scraping bottom of Dutch oven to loosen browned bits. Return chicken to Dutch oven; reduce oven temperature to 375°, and bake 15 additional minutes.

Spoon rice evenly onto individual serving plates, and top evenly with chicken and onion mixture. Yield: 8 servings (serving size: 1 chicken breast half, ½ cup rice, and ½ cup onion mixture).

Calories 303 (10% from fat) **Protein** 29.8g **Fat** 3.5g (sat 0.6g) **Carbohydrate** 36.9g **Fiber** 2.7g **Cholesterol** 66mg **Iron** 2.0mg **Sodium** 371mg **Calcium** 53mg

ROASTED CHICKEN AND VEGETABLES

QUICK & EASY

Split-roasted chicken served with fries is found on virtually every French bistro menu. Our rendition, cooked in one skillet, is made with seasoned skinless chicken breasts roasted with potatoes, fennel, and olives.

¾   cup coarsely chopped sweet red pepper
½   cup slivered fennel bulb
2   tablespoons chopped ripe olives
2   teaspoons chopped fresh rosemary
1½ teaspoons olive oil
12 small round red potatoes, quartered
3   large shallots, peeled and halved lengthwise
2   cloves garlic, crushed
2   teaspoons minced fresh sage
½   teaspoon coarsely ground pepper
¼   teaspoon salt
¼   teaspoon paprika
2   (4-ounce) skinned, boned chicken breast halves
Vegetable cooking spray
1½ teaspoons olive oil
⅔   cup canned low-sodium chicken broth, undiluted
Fresh rosemary sprigs (optional)

Combine first 8 ingredients in a bowl; toss well, and set aside.

Combine sage and next 3 ingredients, and rub over both sides of chicken breasts. Coat a large oven-proof skillet with cooking spray; add 1½ teaspoons oil, and place over medium-high heat until hot. Add chicken breasts; cook 1 minute on each side or until browned. Remove chicken from skillet, and set aside.

Remove skillet from heat. Add vegetable mixture to skillet; stir well. Return chicken breasts to skillet, nestling them into vegetables; bake, uncovered, at 450° for 20 minutes. Remove chicken breasts from skillet; stir vegetables, scraping bottom of skillet to loosen browned bits. Return chicken breasts to skillet; reduce oven temperature to 375°, and bake 15 additional minutes.

Spoon vegetable mixture evenly onto 2 serving plates, and place a chicken breast half on each plate. Add chicken broth to skillet; bring to a boil over high heat, and cook 1 minute, scraping bottom of skillet to loosen browned bits. Spoon sauce evenly over chicken. Garnish with rosemary sprigs, if desired. Yield: 2 servings (serving size: 1 chicken breast half, 1⅓ cups vegetables, and 3 tablespoons sauce).

Calories 403 (24% from fat) **Protein** 33.6g **Fat** 10.6g (sat 1.6g) **Carbohydrate** 45.0g **Fiber** 5.0g **Cholesterol** 66mg **Iron** 6.1mg **Sodium** 490mg **Calcium** 107mg

ROASTED COQ AU VIN SUPPER

For a quicker version of classic coq au vin (French for "chicken with wine"), skin the chicken and prep the vegetables early in the day. Use a bulb baster to baste the chicken and vegetables with the pan juices.

⅓   cup all-purpose flour
1   teaspoon paprika
½   teaspoon salt
½   teaspoon freshly ground pepper
3   (8-ounce) chicken breast halves, skinned (about 1½ pounds)
3   chicken thighs, skinned (about 1 pound)
3   chicken drumsticks, skinned (about ¾ pound)
1   tablespoon olive oil, divided
1   cup canned low-sodium chicken broth, undiluted
½   cup dry white vermouth
1   teaspoon dried thyme
1   teaspoon dried rosemary
¼   pound small shallots, peeled (about 12 shallots)
8   cloves garlic
1   (16-ounce) package fresh whole baby carrots
¾   pound small round red potatoes (about 6), quartered
1   (8-ounce) package fresh crimini or button mushrooms, stems removed
¼   teaspoon salt

Combine first 4 ingredients in a large heavy-duty, zip-top plastic bag.

Add chicken pieces to bag; seal bag, and shake to coat.

Heat 1½ teaspoons oil in a large nonstick skillet over medium heat. Add half of chicken pieces, shaking off excess flour. Cook 5 minutes on each side or until browned. Remove chicken from skillet; place in a shallow roasting pan. Repeat procedure with remaining 1½ teaspoons oil and chicken pieces; set aside.

Add broth and next 5 ingredients to skillet; cook over medium heat 1 minute, scraping bottom of skillet with a wooden spoon to loosen browned bits. Remove from heat; set aside.

Arrange carrots, potato, and mushrooms around chicken in roasting pan; sprinkle vegetables with ¼ teaspoon salt. Pour broth mixture over chicken and vegetables.

Bake, uncovered, at 400° for 1 hour and 5 minutes or until chicken is done and vegetables are tender, basting occasionally with juices in pan. Yield: 6 servings (serving size: 3 ounces chicken and 1 cup vegetables).

Calories 289 (19% from fat) **Protein** 29.0g **Fat** 6.2g (sat 1.2g) **Carbohydrate** 29.5g **Fiber** 4.4g **Cholesterol** 78mg **Iron** 3.7mg **Sodium** 428mg **Calcium** 69mg

FETA-STUFFED CHICKEN

QUICK & EASY

4 (4-ounce) skinned, boned chicken breast halves
¼ cup dry breadcrumbs
¼ cup (1 ounce) crumbled feta cheese with basil and tomato
Vegetable cooking spray
1½ teaspoons margarine, melted
3 cups torn spinach
½ cup chopped fresh basil
1 tablespoon balsamic vinegar
1 teaspoon olive oil
⅛ teaspoon pepper

Place each chicken breast half between 2 sheets of heavy-duty plastic wrap; flatten to ¼-inch thickness, using a meat mallet or rolling pin. Dredge chicken in breadcrumbs. Spoon 1 tablespoon cheese onto each piece of chicken; fold chicken in half.

Place folded breast halves in an 8-inch square baking dish coated with cooking spray. Drizzle melted margarine over chicken. Bake, uncovered, at 400° for 25 minutes or until chicken is done.

Combine spinach and basil in a bowl; drizzle with vinegar and oil. Sprinkle pepper over salad; toss well. Serve chicken over salad. Yield: 4 servings (serving size: 1 chicken breast half and ¾ cup salad).

Calories 207 (27% from fat) **Protein** 29.6g **Fat** 6.2g (sat 1.9g) **Carbohydrate** 7.0g **Fiber** 2.0g **Cholesterol** 71mg **Iron** 2.4mg **Sodium** 237mg **Calcium** 114mg

CHICKEN POT PIE

9 cups water
1 tablespoon black peppercorns
2½ pounds chicken pieces, skinned
3 stalks celery, each cut into 4 pieces
1 small onion, quartered
1 bay leaf
1 (16-ounce) package frozen mixed vegetables
1½ cups peeled, diced potato
1 cup sliced fresh mushrooms
1 clove garlic, minced
¼ cup plus 2 tablespoons all-purpose flour
1 teaspoon poultry seasoning
¾ teaspoon salt
¼ teaspoon pepper
1 cup 1% low-fat milk
Vegetable cooking spray
Biscuit Topping

Combine first 6 ingredients in a Dutch oven; bring to a boil. Reduce heat, and simmer, uncovered, 1 hour. Remove chicken from broth, reserving chicken broth. Let chicken cool. Bone chicken, and coarsely chop; set aside.

Pour chicken broth through a wire-mesh strainer lined with a layer of cheesecloth into a bowl; discard vegetables and bay leaf remaining in strainer. Skim fat from chicken broth; set aside 4½ cups broth. Reserve remaining chicken broth for another use.

Combine reserved 4½ cups chicken broth, mixed vegetables, and next

3 ingredients in Dutch oven. Bring mixture to a boil; cover, reduce heat, and simmer 15 minutes or until vegetables are tender.

Combine flour and next 3 ingredients in a bowl; add milk, stirring with a wire whisk until smooth. Add flour mixture to vegetable mixture; cook over medium heat, stirring constantly, 5 minutes or until mixture is thickened and bubbly. Stir in chopped chicken. Spoon chicken mixture into a 13- x 9- x 2-inch baking dish coated with cooking spray.

Prepare Biscuit Topping; drop heaping tablespoons of topping dough over chicken mixture, forming 16 biscuits. Bake at 400° for 25 minutes or until biscuits are golden. Yield: 8 servings.

BISCUIT TOPPING:

2 cups all-purpose flour
2 teaspoons baking powder
½ teaspoon salt
¼ teaspoon sugar
⅛ teaspoon garlic powder
1 cup 1% low-fat milk
1½ tablespoons margarine, melted

Combine first 5 ingredients; stir well. Add milk and margarine, stirring mixture just until dry ingredients are moistened. Yield: dough for 16 biscuits.

Calories 448 (23% from fat) **Protein** 38.9g **Fat** 11.3g (sat 3.1g) **Carbohydrate** 46.1g **Fiber** 4.7g **Cholesterol** 94mg **Iron** 5.1mg **Sodium** 560mg **Calcium** 206mg

CHICKEN AND HAM TETRAZZINI

This easy make-ahead casserole was a hit with our readers and our staff.

1   (7-ounce) package spaghetti, uncooked
1   tablespoon reduced-calorie margarine
1   cup sliced fresh mushrooms
1   cup chopped onion
1   cup chopped green pepper
2   cloves garlic, minced
¼   cup all-purpose flour
½   teaspoon poultry seasoning
½   teaspoon pepper
1¼ cups 1% low-fat milk
¾   cup (3 ounces) shredded reduced-fat sharp Cheddar cheese, divided
1½ cups skinned, shredded roasted chicken breast (about 5 ounces)
¾   cup finely chopped extra-lean ham (about ¼ pound)
⅔   cup grated Parmesan cheese, divided
¼   cup dry sherry
1   (10¾-ounce) can reduced-fat, reduced-sodium cream of mushroom soup, undiluted
1   (4-ounce) jar diced pimiento, drained
Vegetable cooking spray
1   teaspoon paprika
2   tablespoons sliced almonds

Cook spaghetti according to package directions, omitting salt and fat;

Chicken and Ham Tetrazzini

drain well. Rinse under cold running water; drain well, and set aside.

Melt margarine in a large nonstick skillet over medium-high heat. Add mushrooms and next 3 ingredients; sauté 4 minutes or until tender. Stir in flour, poultry seasoning, and ½ teaspoon pepper; cook, stirring constantly, 30 seconds. Gradually add milk, and cook, stirring constantly, 1½ minutes or until thickened. Remove from heat, and stir in ¼ cup Cheddar cheese, stirring until cheese melts. Add chicken, ham, ⅓ cup Parmesan, and next 3 ingredients; stir well.

Combine spaghetti and chicken mixture in a large bowl; stir well. Spoon mixture into a 13- x 9- x 2-inch baking dish coated with cooking spray.

Combine remaining ⅓ cup Parmesan cheese and paprika, and stir well. Sprinkle Parmesan cheese mixture, remaining ½ cup Cheddar cheese, and almonds in alternating diagonal rows across top of casserole. Bake, uncovered, at 350° for 20 minutes or until bubbly. Yield: 6 servings (serving size: 2 cups).

Note: To assemble casserole up to four hours ahead, just omit cheese-almond topping; cover and chill. Add topping just before baking.

Calories 397 (27% from fat) Protein 27.5g Fat 11.6g (sat 4.8g) Carbohydrate 42.2g Fiber 2.4g Cholesterol 51mg Iron 3.4mg Sodium 775mg Calcium 341mg

CREAMY CHICKEN AND RICE CASSEROLE

QUICK & EASY

For the quickest and easiest way to cut raw chicken, use your kitchen shears.

1   (6.9-ounce) package one-third-less-salt chicken-flavored rice-and-vermicelli mix with chicken broth and herbs
1   tablespoon margarine
2¼ cups hot water
Vegetable cooking spray
1½ pounds skinned, boned chicken breast halves, cut into bite-size pieces
1   cup sliced fresh mushrooms
½   teaspoon garlic powder
¾   cup nonfat sour cream
¼   teaspoon pepper
1   (10¾-ounce) can reduced-fat, reduced-sodium cream of mushroom soup, undiluted
¼   cup crushed multigrain crackers (about 6 crackers)
1   tablespoon margarine, melted
½   teaspoon poppy seeds

Cook rice mix in a large nonstick skillet according to package directions, using 1 tablespoon margarine and 2¼ cups hot water. Remove mixture from skillet; set aside. Wipe skillet with a paper towel.

Coat skillet with cooking spray; place over high heat until hot. Add chicken, mushrooms, and garlic powder; sauté 6 minutes or until chicken is done.

Combine rice mixture, chicken mixture, sour cream, pepper, and soup in a bowl; stir well. Spoon mixture into a 2-quart casserole coated with cooking spray.

Combine cracker crumbs, melted margarine, and poppy seeds; stir well, and sprinkle over chicken mixture. Bake, uncovered, at 350° for 35 minutes or until thoroughly heated. Yield: 6 servings (serving size: 1⅓ cups).

Note: If desired, assemble this casserole ahead, omitting the cracker-crumb mixture; then just cover and chill or freeze (thaw frozen casserole overnight in refrigerator). Let stand at room temperature 30 minutes; top with cracker-crumb mixture, and bake as directed.

Calories 334 (18% from fat) Protein 32.2g Fat 6.8g (sat 1.6g) Carbohydrate 30.0g Fiber 0.2g Cholesterol 68mg Iron 2.0mg Sodium 687mg Calcium 19mg

CHICKEN DIVAN

QUICK & EASY

To get 3 cups chopped cooked chicken, start with about 1½ pounds uncooked boneless, skinless chicken breasts.

2   (10-ounce) packages frozen broccoli spears, thawed
3   cups chopped cooked chicken breast (skinned before cooking and cooked without salt)
½   cup (2 ounces) shredded reduced-fat sharp Cheddar cheese
1¼ cups skim milk
1   teaspoon lemon juice
½   teaspoon curry powder
⅛   teaspoon pepper
1   (10¾-ounce) can reduced-fat cream of mushroom soup, undiluted
3   tablespoons all-purpose flour
3   tablespoons water
½   cup finely crushed onion-flavored Melba toast rounds (about 18)
1   tablespoon margarine, melted

Arrange broccoli spears in 2 rows, with stalks toward center, in a 13- x 9- x 2-inch baking dish. Spoon chicken on top of stalk ends, and top chicken with cheese. Set aside.

Combine milk and next 4 ingredients in a heavy saucepan; stir well. Combine flour and water in a small bowl, and stir well. Add to soup mixture, stirring well. Bring to a boil over medium heat, stirring constantly with a wire whisk. Cook, stirring constantly, 8 minutes or until thickened and bubbly. Pour over chicken.

Combine Melba toast crumbs and margarine in a bowl; sprinkle over soup mixture. Cover and bake at 350° for 20 minutes. Uncover and bake 15 additional minutes or until thoroughly heated. Let stand 10 minutes. Yield: 6 servings.

Calories 355 (26% from fat) Protein 44.5g Fat 10.2g (sat 2.7g) Carbohydrate 20.8g Fiber 2.3g Cholesterol 104mg Iron 2.9mg Sodium 691mg Calcium 192mg

SHORTCUTS TO CASSEROLES

• Instead of chopping fresh onions and green peppers, buy them already chopped and frozen in plastic bags. You don't have to defrost them; just measure the amount you need right out of the bag. Spoon the remainder into a plastic freezer storage bag.
• Use jarred and canned sliced or chopped mushrooms in place of fresh mushrooms.
• In recipes calling for cooked chicken, we tried a frozen product—fully cooked, ready-to-eat roasted chicken breast—and found it worked just fine. Or you can substitute cut-up leftover turkey.

CHICKEN PARMIGIANA

With 3 cups of chopped tomato in this recipe, you'll get a hefty helping of vitamins A and C, potassium, and fiber. Find photographed instructions for seeding tomatoes on page 182.

1½ cups finely chopped onion
3   cloves garlic, minced
Vegetable cooking spray
3   cups peeled, seeded, and chopped tomato (about 2 pounds)
1½ teaspoons dried oregano
1   teaspoon dried basil
½   teaspoon ground pepper
¼   teaspoon salt
4   (4-ounce) skinned, boned chicken breast halves
¼   cup all-purpose flour
¼   cup grated Parmesan cheese
1   egg white, lightly beaten
1   tablespoon olive oil
1   cup (4 ounces) shredded part-skim mozzarella cheese

Place chopped onion and garlic in a medium saucepan coated with cooking spray; cover and cook over low heat 15 minutes or until tender. Add tomato and next 4 ingredients; simmer, uncovered, 45 minutes. Set mixture aside.

Place each chicken breast half between 2 sheets of heavy-duty plastic wrap. Flatten chicken to ⅛-inch thickness, using a meat mallet or rolling pin.

Combine flour and Parmesan cheese in a shallow dish. Dip each piece of chicken in egg white; dredge in flour mixture. Heat olive oil in a large nonstick skillet over medium-high heat. Add chicken; cook 2 minutes on each side or until browned.

Arrange chicken in an 11- x 7- x 2-inch baking dish or in individual gratin dishes coated with cooking spray. Pour tomato mixture evenly over chicken, and sprinkle with mozzarella cheese. Bake, uncovered, at 350° for 20 minutes or until thoroughly heated. Yield: 4 servings (serving size: 1 chicken breast half and ½ cup sauce).

Calories 342 (31% from fat) Protein 38.9g Fat 11.8g (sat 4.8g) Carbohydrate 19.7g Fiber 3.4g Cholesterol 86mg Iron 2.5mg Sodium 474mg Calcium 306mg

"There are a lot of pluses to this recipe: It's an easy one-dish meal for the cook, children love it, and it freezes well. I serve it for family dinners and informal company meals; all I add is a salad and bread."

——Vanessa Johnson, former Assistant Test Kitchens Director

CHILES RELLENOS CASSEROLE

½   pound ground turkey or chicken
1   cup chopped onion
1¾   teaspoons ground cumin
1½   teaspoons dried oregano
½   teaspoon garlic powder
¼   teaspoon salt
¼   teaspoon pepper
1   (16-ounce) can fat-free refried beans
2   (4-ounce) cans whole green chiles, drained and cut lengthwise into quarters
Vegetable cooking spray
1   cup (4 ounces) shredded colby-Monterey Jack cheese blend
1   cup frozen whole kernel corn, thawed and drained
⅓   cup all-purpose flour
¼   teaspoon salt
1⅓   cups skim milk
⅛   teaspoon hot sauce
2   eggs, lightly beaten
2   egg whites

Cook ground turkey and onion in a nonstick skillet over medium-high heat until turkey is browned, stirring until it crumbles. Remove from heat; add cumin and next 5 ingredients to skillet. Stir well, and set mixture aside.

Arrange half of green chile quarters in an 11- x 7- x 1½-inch baking dish coated with cooking spray; top with half of cheese. Spoon bean mixture in mounds onto cheese, and spread gently, leaving a ¼-inch border around edge of dish; top with corn. Arrange remaining chile strips over corn; top with remaining cheese. Set aside.

Combine flour and ¼ teaspoon salt in a bowl; gradually add milk and hot sauce, stirring with a wire whisk until blended. Stir in eggs and egg whites; pour over casserole. Bake, uncovered, at 350° for 1 hour and 5 minutes or until set; let stand 5 minutes. Cut into squares to serve. Yield: 6 servings (serving size: 1 square).

Calories 340 (26% from fat) **Protein** 26.1g **Fat** 9.8g (sat 4.8g) **Carbohydrate** 38.0g **Fiber** 5.4g **Cholesterol** 117mg **Iron** 3.9mg **Sodium** 890mg **Calcium** 232mg

TURKEY-TORTILLA CASSEROLE

1   tablespoon plus ¼ teaspoon vegetable oil, divided
¾   pound oven-roasted turkey breast, cut into 2- x ¼-inch strips (about 2½ cups)
1   teaspoon dried oregano, divided
¼   teaspoon salt
¾   teaspoon ground cumin, divided
⅛   teaspoon pepper
2   large cloves garlic, minced
¾   cup fresh corn kernels, divided
¾   cup sliced green onions
⅓   cup chopped fresh cilantro
1   large clove garlic, minced
3   tablespoons all-purpose flour
2¼   teaspoons chili powder
⅛   teaspoon ground cinnamon
1   cup water
1   (10½-ounce) can low-sodium chicken broth
5   (6-inch) corn tortillas, cut in half
Vegetable cooking spray
½   cup (2 ounces) shredded reduced-fat extra-sharp Cheddar cheese
¼   cup nonfat sour cream
Cilantro sprigs (optional)
Cherry tomato slices (optional)

Heat ¾ teaspoon oil in a medium nonstick skillet over medium-high heat. Add turkey; sauté 1 minute. Add ¾ teaspoon oregano, salt, ¼ teaspoon cumin, pepper, and 2

Turkey-Tortilla Casserole

cloves garlic; sauté 1 minute. Add ½ cup corn and onions, and sauté 1 minute. Spoon into a bowl; stir in chopped cilantro. Set aside.

Heat 1½ teaspoons oil in skillet over medium heat. Add remaining ¼ teaspoon oregano, remaining ½ teaspoon cumin, and 1 clove garlic; sauté 1 minute. Add flour, chili powder, and cinnamon; cook, stirring constantly with a wire whisk, 1 minute. Gradually add water and broth to mixture, and cook, stirring constantly with whisk, 5 minutes or until mixture is thickened and

bubbly. Pour sauce into a bowl; cover and set aside.

Brush remaining 1 teaspoon oil evenly over both sides of tortilla halves. Place a nonstick skillet over medium-high heat until hot. Add 5 tortilla halves, and cook 30 seconds on each side or until softened. Remove from skillet; set aside, and keep warm. Repeat procedure with remaining tortilla halves.

Arrange 5 tortilla halves in an 8-inch square baking dish coated with cooking spray. Spread ⅓ cup sauce over tortillas, and top with turkey

mixture. Spoon ⅔ cup sauce over turkey mixture; top with remaining 5 tortilla halves. Spread remaining ⅔ cup sauce over tortillas; top with cheese and remaining ¼ cup corn. Bake at 450° for 15 minutes or until bubbly. Cut into squares; serve with sour cream. If desired, garnish with cilantro sprigs and tomato. Yield: 4 servings (serving size: 1 square and 1 tablespoon sour cream).

Calories 377 (28% from fat) **Protein** 35.7g **Fat** 11.6g (sat 3.4g) **Carbohydrate** 33.1g **Fiber** 4.3g **Cholesterol** 68mg **Iron** 3.8mg **Sodium** 424mg **Calcium** 248mg

CURRIED TURKEY BALLOTTINE

Although this recipe requires extra effort, it's well worth it for an impressive entrée. Save some time by having the butcher bone the turkey breast for you.

1	(5-pound) whole turkey breast, skinned and boned
2¾	cups plus 3 tablespoons water, divided
¼	cup raisins
¼	cup dried apricots
1	tablespoon olive oil, divided
1	cup diced onion
½	cup diced sweet red pepper
½	cup diced green pepper
½	cup diced celery
3	cloves garlic, crushed
½	cup couscous, uncooked
2	teaspoons caraway seeds
1½	teaspoons ground cumin
1½	teaspoons ground coriander
½	teaspoon salt
¼	teaspoon pepper
⅛	teaspoon hot sauce
1	cup sliced carrot
1	cup dry white vermouth
1	cup canned low-sodium chicken broth, undiluted
½	cup sliced onion
½	cup sliced celery
Watercress	
1	teaspoon curry powder
2	teaspoons cornstarch
¼	teaspoon salt
⅛	teaspoon pepper

Trim fat from turkey breast; remove tendons. Place outer side of

Curried Turkey Ballottine

turkey breast on heavy-duty plastic wrap. Starting from center, slice horizontally through thickest portion of each side of breast almost to, but not through, outer edges. Flip cut pieces over to enlarge breast. Place heavy-duty plastic wrap over turkey, and pound turkey to a more even thickness, using a meat mallet or rolling pin.

Combine 2 cups water, raisins, and apricots in a small saucepan;

bring mixture to a boil. Cover, reduce heat, and simmer 5 minutes or until apricots are tender. Drain mixture, and set aside.

Heat 2 teaspoons olive oil in a medium saucepan over medium heat. Add diced onion, and cook 10 minutes, stirring occasionally. Add diced red pepper and next 3 ingredients; sauté 1 minute. Add raisin mixture to onion mixture, and set aside.

Bring ¾ cup water to a boil in a small saucepan. Remove from heat. Add couscous; cover and let stand 5 minutes or until couscous is tender and liquid is absorbed. Fluff couscous with a fork.

Combine onion mixture, couscous, caraway seeds, and next 5 ingredients, and toss well. Spread mixture over turkey breast to within 2 inches of edges; roll up turkey breast, jellyroll fashion, starting with short side. Tie securely at 2-inch intervals with heavy string.

Heat remaining 1 teaspoon oil in a large roasting pan over medium-high heat. Add turkey, and brown on all sides. Add carrot and next 4 ingredients to pan. Insert meat thermometer into thickest portion of turkey roll. Cover and bake at 350° for 1½ hours or until meat thermometer registers 170°.

Transfer turkey roll to a large serving platter lined with watercress, reserving pan drippings and vegetables. Let turkey roll stand 10 minutes. Remove string; cut turkey roll into 13 slices.

Strain pan drippings and vegetables; discard vegetables. Pour liquid into a saucepan; bring to a boil over medium-high heat. Cook 8 minutes or until liquid is reduced to 1½ cups; set aside.

Place curry powder in a small saucepan over medium-high heat. Cook, stirring constantly, 45 seconds. Add reserved 1½ cups cooking liquid to saucepan.

Combine cornstarch and remaining 3 tablespoons water, and stir well. Add to cooking liquid in saucepan, and stir well. Bring to a boil, and cook, stirring constantly, 1 minute. Stir in ¼ teaspoon salt and ⅛ teaspoon pepper. Serve sauce with turkey roll. Yield: 13 servings (serving size: 3 ounces turkey and 2 tablespoons sauce).

Calories 238 (20% from fat) **Protein** 36.9g **Fat** 5.3g (sat 1.4g) **Carbohydrate** 8.7g **Fiber** 1.4g **Cholesterol** 83mg **Iron** 2.5mg **Sodium** 236mg **Calcium** 45mg

TECHNIQUE

For Rolling a Boneless Turkey Breast

1. Roll up the turkey breast, jellyroll fashion, starting with short side of turkey.

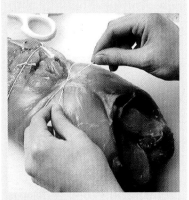

2. Tie turkey securely at 2-inch intervals with heavy string.

Turkey   119

Fresh Tomato-Squash
Salad, page 126

SALADS

Imagine. Fresh pineapple in Alaska. Eight types of lettuce in a grocery store near you. The availability of fresher, tastier produce of any kind, from anywhere, has revolutionized the way we think about, serve, and savor salad. So now the decision is not whether to douse iceberg lettuce with

&

DRESSINGS

fat-free Ranch or Italian dressing, but whether to go with an earthy lentil salad or a bitter greens combo. Whether to toss in Asiago cheese or to crumble feta over the top. Whether to dress a salad with balsamic vinegar or garlic-wine vinegar. Or whether to stick to the good ol' basics like Creamy Potato Salad.

TECHNIQUE

For Sectioning Grapefruit

This technique gives you perfect citrus fruit slices every time.

1. Cut the top and bottom from the grapefruit. Holding the fruit with one hand, cut away the rind and bitter white pith.

2. Gently slide the knife between the membrane and the grapefruit section on both sides, and lift out the citrus section.

GRAPEFRUIT SALAD WITH CHAMPAGNE DRESSING

It's okay to substitute any other dry champagne (one that isn't sweet) for the brut in this recipe.

¼	cup plus 2 tablespoons brut champagne
2	tablespoons raspberry vinegar
2	tablespoons honey
1	tablespoon vegetable oil
2	teaspoons Dijon mustard
4	cups tightly packed torn romaine lettuce
3	cups fresh grapefruit sections (about 3 medium grapefruit)
2	cups halved fresh strawberries
½	cup vertically sliced purple onion

Combine first 5 ingredients in a small bowl; stir with a wire whisk until blended. Cover and chill.

Combine lettuce and remaining 3 ingredients in a large bowl, and toss gently. Pour dressing over lettuce mixture; toss gently. Serve immediately. Yield: 6 servings (serving size: 1½ cups).

Calories 109 (22% from fat) **Protein** 1.6g **Fat** 2.7g (sat 0.4g) **Carbohydrate** 19.0g **Fiber** 2.6g **Cholesterol** 0mg **Iron** 0.8mg **Sodium** 54mg **Calcium** 33mg

CITRUS, FIG, AND PROSCIUTTO SALAD

QUICK & EASY

3	medium oranges
3	cups tightly packed torn romaine lettuce
3	cups tightly packed torn curly leaf lettuce
1	pound fresh figs, each cut into 4 wedges
4	ounces chopped lean prosciutto
½	teaspoon grated orange rind
⅓	cup fresh orange juice
2	tablespoons white wine vinegar
2	tablespoons water
1½	tablespoons vegetable oil
1	tablespoon honey
¼	teaspoon salt
⅛	teaspoon hot pepper sauce

Peel oranges; cut crosswise into ¼-inch-thick slices. Cut each orange slice in half. Combine orange slices, romaine, and next 3 ingredients in a large bowl; toss gently.

Combine grated orange rind and remaining 7 ingredients in a jar. Cover jar tightly, and shake mixture vigorously. Drizzle orange juice mixture over salad, and toss salad gently to coat. Yield: 6 servings (serving size: 2 cups).

Calories 174 (29% from fat) **Protein** 6.3g **Fat** 5.6g (sat 1.3g) **Carbohydrate** 27.7g **Fiber** 6.2g **Cholesterol** 11mg **Iron** 1.0mg **Sodium** 398mg **Calcium** 64mg

LAYERED CRANBERRY-APPLESAUCE SALAD

2   envelopes unflavored gelatin
1¾   cups cold water
½   cup sugar
1   (12-ounce) can frozen cranberry juice concentrate, thawed and undiluted
1¼   cups sliced fresh strawberries
1¼   cups unsweetened applesauce
1   cup low-fat sour cream
¼   cup chopped walnuts
2   tablespoons powdered sugar

Sprinkle gelatin over cold water in a medium saucepan; let stand 1 minute. Stir in ½ cup sugar. Cook over medium heat, stirring until gelatin and sugar dissolve, about 2 minutes. Remove from heat. Reserve 2 teaspoons concentrate; add remaining concentrate to gelatin mixture. Stir in berries and applesauce. Pour half of mixture into an 11- x 7- x 1½-inch dish. Cover and chill until firm. Reserve remaining half of gelatin mixture; do not chill.

Combine reserved 2 teaspoons concentrate, sour cream, walnuts, and powdered sugar; stir well. Spread sour cream mixture over firm gelatin layer. Gradually pour reserved gelatin mixture over sour cream mixture. Cover; chill until firm. Cut into squares. Yield: 15 servings (one 2-inch square piece).

Calories 120 (24% from fat) **Protein** 2.2g **Fat** 3.2g (sat 1.3g) **Carbohydrate** 21.8g **Fiber** 0.8g **Cholesterol** 6mg **Iron** 0.3mg **Sodium** 9mg **Calcium** 29mg

Five-Fruit Salad

FIVE-FRUIT SALAD

QUICK & EASY

For a sweet springtime salad, substitute fresh cherries for blackberries.

1   tablespoon grated orange rind
1   cup fresh orange sections
1   cup fresh blackberries
1   cup fresh strawberries, hulled and halved
1   cup seedless green grapes, halved
1   cup cubed fresh pear
¼   cup firmly packed brown sugar
⅛   teaspoon ground cloves
Fresh mint sprigs (optional)

Combine first 8 ingredients in a medium bowl; stir mixture well. Cover and chill at least 2 hours. Garnish with fresh mint sprigs, if desired. Yield: 8 servings (serving size: ½ cup).

Calories 81 (4% from fat) **Protein** 0.7g **Fat** 0.4g (sat 0.1g) **Carbohydrate** 20.7g **Fiber** 3.8g **Cholesterol** 0mg **Iron** 0.4mg **Sodium** 3mg **Calcium** 31mg

Tangy Marinated Coleslaw

4   cups coarsely shredded green
    cabbage
1½ cups seeded, thinly sliced
    cucumber (about 1 medium
    cucumber)
1   cup coarsely shredded carrot
½   cup diced purple onion
½   cup diced green pepper
¼   cup cider vinegar
1   tablespoon sugar
1   tablespoon Dijon mustard
1   tablespoon vegetable oil
2   teaspoons prepared
    horseradish
½   teaspoon pepper
¼   teaspoon salt

Combine first 5 ingredients in a
large bowl; toss well.

Combine vinegar and remaining
6 ingredients in a jar. Cover tightly,
and shake vigorously. Pour over vegetable mixture; toss gently. Cover
and chill 8 hours. Serve chilled or at
room temperature. Yield: 6 servings
(serving size: 1 cup).

Calories 64 (38% from fat) Protein 1.3g
Fat 2.7g (sat 0.5g) Carbohydrate 9.8g
Fiber 2.5g Cholesterol 0mg Iron 0.8mg
Sodium 189mg Calcium 39mg

Mediterranean Lentil Salad

1   cup dried lentils
4   cups water
3   large sweet red peppers
    (about 1½ pounds)
¼   cup balsamic vinegar
¼   cup canned low-sodium
    chicken broth, undiluted
1   tablespoon olive oil
1   teaspoon dried whole
    basil
¼   teaspoon salt
¼   teaspoon pepper
1   clove garlic, minced
8   romaine lettuce leaves
¼   cup (1 ounce) crumbled
    goat cheese

Combine lentils and 4 cups water
in a saucepan. Bring mixture to a
boil; cover, reduce heat, and simmer
30 to 35 minutes or until tender.
Drain; rinse under cold water, and
set aside.

Cut peppers in half lengthwise;
remove and discard seeds and membrane. Place peppers, skin side up,
on a baking sheet; flatten with palm
of hand. Broil 5½ inches from heat
(with electric oven door partially
opened) 15 to 20 minutes or until
charred. Place in ice water until
cool; peel and discard skins. Cut
peppers into 2- x ½-inch strips.

Combine lentils, pepper strips,
vinegar, and next 6 ingredients in a
large bowl; toss mixture gently.
Cover and chill 2 hours. Arrange
lettuce leaves on individual salad
plates. Top lettuce leaves evenly with
lentil mixture, and sprinkle with
goat cheese. Yield: 4 servings (serving size: 2 lettuce leaves, 1 cup salad,
and 1 tablespoon cheese).

Calories 254 (22% from fat) Protein 16.3g
Fat 6.1g (sat 1.7g) Carbohydrate 36.3g
Fiber 8.1g Cholesterol 6mg Iron 6.6mg
Sodium 242mg Calcium 86mg

Gazpacho Salad

3   cups seeded, chopped
    tomato
1   cup peeled, chopped
    cucumber
1   cup chopped green pepper
¼   cup thinly sliced green
    onions
¼   cup chopped purple onion
2   tablespoons minced fresh
    basil
2½ tablespoons red wine
    vinegar
1   teaspoon olive oil
1   teaspoon Dijon mustard
⅛   teaspoon salt
⅛   teaspoon pepper
2   cloves garlic, minced

Combine first 5 ingredients in a
large bowl; set aside. Combine basil
and remaining 6 ingredients; stir
with a wire whisk until blended.
Pour vinaigrette mixture over tomato mixture, and toss gently. Cover
and chill 1 hour. Yield: 5 servings
(serving size: 1 cup).

Calories 51 (26% from fat) Protein 1.6g
Fat 1.5g (sat 0.2g) Carbohydrate 9.4g
Fiber 2.3g Cholesterol 0mg Iron 1.1mg
Sodium 100mg Calcium 20mg

"This salad is my favorite recipe to take to cookouts and potluck dinners. People always ooh and aah over its rich, creamy taste—especially after they find out it's light. It's quick to make because there's not a lot of chopping. I even mix the dressing ahead of time to have on hand; it'll keep for a week in the refrigerator."

——Ellen Templeton Carroll, Senior Editor–Projects

CREAMY POTATO SALAD

6	medium-size round red potatoes (about 2 pounds)
¼	cup chopped green onions
1	(2-ounce) jar diced pimiento, drained
½	cup nonfat mayonnaise
¼	cup plain low-fat yogurt
¼	cup low-fat sour cream
1	tablespoon sugar
2	tablespoons prepared mustard
1	tablespoon white wine vinegar
½	teaspoon salt
½	teaspoon celery seeds
¼	teaspoon pepper
⅛	teaspoon garlic powder

Green onion fan (optional)

Cut potatoes into ½-inch pieces; place in a medium saucepan. Add water to cover. Bring to a boil; cover, reduce heat, and simmer 15 to 20 minutes or until tender. Drain and cool. Combine potato, chopped green onions, and pimiento in a large bowl; toss gently.

Combine mayonnaise and next 9 ingredients; stir well. Add to potato mixture, tossing gently to coat.

Cover and chill. Garnish with a green onion fan, if desired. Yield: 8 servings (serving size: ¾ cup).

Calories 88 (14% from fat) **Protein** 3.1g **Fat** 1.4g (sat 0.7g) **Carbohydrate** 16.8g **Fiber** 1.6g **Cholesterol** 3mg **Iron** 3.1mg **Sodium** 405mg **Calcium** 54mg

Creamy Potato Salad

Sliced Tomato and Onion Salad

¼ cup balsamic vinegar
3   tablespoons water
1   teaspoon olive oil
1   teaspoon Dijon mustard
¼   teaspoon coarsely ground
    pepper
⅛   teaspoon salt
5   medium tomatoes
    (about 2½ pounds)
1   large purple onion, thinly
    sliced and separated into
    rings
2   teaspoons minced fresh
    oregano

Combine first 6 ingredients in a jar; cover tightly, and shake vigorously. Set aside.

Core tomatoes; cut into ½-inch-thick slices. Layer tomato and onion slices in a shallow dish, and sprinkle with oregano. Pour vinegar mixture over tomato and onion slices; cover and marinate in refrigerator 3 hours. Yield: 12 servings.

Calories 34 (21% from fat) Protein 1.1g Fat 0.8g (sat 0.1g) Carbohydrate 6.8g Fiber 1.7g Cholesterol 0mg Iron 0.6mg Sodium 45mg Calcium 14mg

Fresh Tomato-Squash Salad

QUICK & EASY

Turn to page 220 for a menu that includes this recipe.

3½ cups diagonally sliced small
    yellow squash (about 1
    pound)
¾   pound small tomatoes, cut
    into ½-inch-thick wedges
½   cup vertically sliced purple
    onion
¼   cup packed small fresh basil
    leaves
¼   cup white wine vinegar
1½ teaspoons olive oil
⅛   teaspoon salt
Dash of pepper
1   clove garlic, minced

Arrange squash in a steamer basket over boiling water. Cover and steam 1 minute; drain. Plunge squash into ice water; drain well. Combine squash, tomato wedges, onion, and basil in a large bowl; set aside.

Combine vinegar and remaining 4 ingredients; stir well. Pour over vegetables; toss gently. Serve at room temperature or chilled on individual salad plates. Yield: 6 servings (serving size: 1 cup).

Calories 41 (33% from fat) Protein 1.4g Fat 1.5g (sat 0.2g) Carbohydrate 6.6g Fiber 2.1g Cholesterol 0mg Iron 0.6mg Sodium 55mg Calcium 22mg

Tossed Salad Supremo

QUICK & EASY

Make the salad and the dressing up to four hours before serving, and chill them in separate containers. Packages of bitter greens may be available premixed in your supermarket. If not, you can substitute a mixture of arugula, curly endive, radicchio, and watercress.

6   cups tightly packed bitter
    greens
⅓   cup (1¼ ounces) crumbled
    feta cheese
¼   cup chopped fresh basil
3   plum tomatoes, quartered
    lengthwise
3   tablespoons canned
    low-sodium chicken broth,
    undiluted
2   tablespoons balsamic vinegar
1½ teaspoons olive oil
¼   teaspoon sugar
¼   teaspoon salt
¼   teaspoon freshly ground
    pepper
1   clove garlic, minced

Combine first 4 ingredients in a large bowl, and toss gently.

Combine broth and remaining 6 ingredients; stir well. Pour over greens mixture; toss gently. Yield: 6 servings (serving size: 2 cups).

Calories 57 (46% from fat) Protein 3.2g Fat 2.9g (sat 1.1g) Carbohydrate 5.7g Fiber 2.5g Cholesterol 5mg Iron 1.6mg Sodium 182mg Calcium 78mg

SPINACH SALAD WITH ASIAGO CHEESE AND CROUTONS

Use a vegetable peeler or a cheese plane to shave thin slices of Asiago. Like Parmesan and Romano, Asiago is a hard cheese.

6	(¾-ounce) slices French bread, cut into ¾-inch cubes
1	teaspoon dried whole oregano
1	clove garlic, crushed
6	cups loosely packed torn fresh spinach
3	cups loosely packed torn radicchio
⅓	cup balsamic vinegar
1½	tablespoons water
1	teaspoon sugar
¼	teaspoon pepper
2	cloves garlic, minced
2	teaspoons extra-virgin olive oil
1½	ounces shaved Asiago cheese

Combine first 3 ingredients in a large heavy-duty, zip-top plastic bag. Seal bag; shake to coat bread cubes. Turn bread cube mixture out onto a 15- x 10- x 1-inch jellyroll pan; arrange bread cubes in a single layer. Bake at 350° for 15 minutes or until toasted. Set aside.

Combine spinach and radicchio in a large bowl, and toss gently. Set salad aside.

Combine vinegar and next 4 ingredients in a small saucepan; bring to a boil. Reduce heat, and simmer, uncovered, 2 minutes.

Remove from heat; add oil, stirring constantly with a wire whisk.

Immediately pour vinegar mixture over salad; toss well. Spoon onto a serving platter; top with bread cube mixture and cheese. Serve immediately. Yield: 6 servings (serving size: 1½ cups).

Calories 128 (29% from fat) **Protein** 6.6g **Fat** .4.1g (sat 1.5g) **Carbohydrate** 16.8g **Fiber** 2.8g **Cholesterol** 5mg **Iron** 2.3mg **Sodium** 288mg **Calcium** 161mg

FETA, PEAR, AND WATERCRESS SALAD

QUICK & EASY

The sharp, tangy flavor of feta paired with ripe pears or apples seems to make the fruit taste even sweeter.

1½	cups tightly packed torn red leaf lettuce
½	cup tightly packed trimmed watercress
½	cup thinly sliced red pear
2	tablespoons crumbled feta cheese
1	tablespoon balsamic vinegar
1	teaspoon water
1	teaspoon walnut oil or vegetable oil
1	teaspoon Dijon mustard
Dash of garlic powder	
Dash of dried oregano	

Arrange first 3 ingredients on 2 salad plates; sprinkle with cheese. Combine vinegar and remaining 5 ingredients, and stir well. Drizzle evenly over salads. Yield: 2 servings (serving size: 1½ cups salad and 2 tablespoons dressing).

Calories 75 (50% from fat) **Protein** 2.0g **Fat** 4.2g (sat 1.4g) **Carbohydrate** 8.1g **Fiber** 1.9g **Cholesterol** 6mg **Iron** 0.7mg **Sodium** 158mg **Calcium** 55mg

GREAT GREEN FLAVOR

Change the flavor of salad by varying the leafy greens you use. Watercress and arugula have peppery flavors. Boston and butterhead lettuce are sweet and succulent. Kale tastes much like cabbage. Beet greens taste like beets. Bitter greens have a bite and include curly endive; escarole; romaine lettuce; radicchio; and dandelion, turnip, and collard greens.

GUIDE TO GREENS

RedLeaf Lettuce

Dandelion Greens

Escarole

Endive

Romaine Lettuce

Butterhead Lettuce

Radicchio

Kale

Watercress

Arugula

Boston Lettuce

Beet Greens

CREAMY CAESAR SALAD WITH SPICY CROUTONS

We ran this recipe with a menu depicting regional California cuisine back in July/August 1995. We suggested serving it with Grilled Seafood Cioppino (page 192) and sourdough bread.

1	clove garlic, halved
½	cup nonfat mayonnaise
2	tablespoons red wine vinegar
2	teaspoons Dijon mustard
2	teaspoons white wine Worcestershire sauce
1	teaspoon anchovy paste
¼	teaspoon pepper
2	teaspoons olive oil
¾	teaspoon Cajun seasoning
1	clove garlic, minced
2	cups (¾-inch) sourdough bread cubes
18	cups torn romaine lettuce (about 2 large heads)
⅓	cup freshly grated Parmesan cheese

Drop garlic halves through opening of an electric blender lid with blender running; process until minced. Add mayonnaise and next 5 ingredients to blender; cover and process until well blended. Cover and chill at least 1 hour.

Combine olive oil, Cajun seasoning, and 1 clove minced garlic in a medium microwave-safe bowl. Microwave at HIGH for 20 seconds. Add bread cubes, and toss gently to coat. Spread bread cubes in a single layer on a baking sheet; bake at 400° for 15 minutes or until croutons are golden.

Place lettuce in a large bowl. Add chilled dressing; toss gently to coat. Sprinkle with cheese, and top with croutons. Yield: 6 servings.

Calories 137 (27% from fat) **Protein** 7.7g **Fat** 4.1g (sat 1.3g) **Carbohydrate** 18.2g **Fiber** 4.1g **Cholesterol** 4mg **Iron** 3.0mg **Sodium** 836mg **Calcium** 176mg

STEP BY STEP

Creamy Caesar Salad With Spicy Croutons

If you prepare the dressing ahead and keep it in the refrigerator, you can make this restaurant specialty in just 20 minutes. Our eggless version of Caesar salad dressing is a safe alternative to the traditional one, which has a coddled egg.

1. An easy way to mince garlic for the dressing is to drop it through the blender lid with the blender running.

2. Add mayonnaise and the remaining dressing ingredients to the blender; process until smooth. Chill the mixture to blend the flavors.

3. Coat bread cubes with a garlic-spice mixture; bake at 400° for 15 minutes. (Tip: stale bread works well for croutons.)

4. Toss romaine and dressing gently. Don't be surprised when the volume of lettuce decreases. Top with cheese and croutons.

BULGUR-BROCCOLI SALAD WITH SOY WALNUTS

Bulgur is actually dried, cracked wheat kernels. It has a nutty flavor and a chewy texture.

1½ cups boiling water
¾ cup bulgur (cracked wheat), uncooked
2 cups chopped fresh broccoli
½ cup finely chopped carrot
¼ cup finely chopped purple onion
¼ cup chopped walnuts
1 tablespoon low-sodium soy sauce
½ teaspoon sugar
⅛ teaspoon freshly ground pepper
½ teaspoon grated lemon rind
3 tablespoons fresh lemon juice
1 tablespoon water
1 teaspoon vegetable oil
1 clove garlic, crushed

Combine boiling water and bulgur in a large bowl; stir well. Let stand 20 minutes or until bulgur is tender and liquid is absorbed. Fluff with a fork; set aside.

Arrange broccoli in a steamer basket over boiling water. Cover and steam 3 minutes or until broccoli is crisp-tender. Add broccoli, carrot, and onion to bulgur; stir well.

Place a small nonstick skillet over medium-high heat until hot. Add walnuts; cook, stirring constantly, 3 minutes. Add soy sauce, stirring constantly until sauce is absorbed. Remove walnuts from skillet, and set aside.

Combine sugar and remaining 6 ingredients; stir well with a wire whisk. Add to bulgur mixture; toss well. Top with soy walnuts. Yield: 4 servings (serving size: 1 cup).

Calories 178 (31% from fat) **Protein** 7.0g **Fat** 6.1g (sat 0.6g) **Carbohydrate** 27.6g **Fiber** 7.4g **Cholesterol** 0mg **Iron** 1.5mg **Sodium** 143mg **Calcium** 44mg

Bulgur-Broccoli Salad With Soy Walnuts

SOUTHWESTERN TURKEY AND BLACK BEAN SALAD

To cut attractive orange slices, see the step-by-step instructions for sectioning citrus fruits on page 122. Find a picture of this salad with a complete menu on page 221.

¾ teaspoon ground cumin
¾ teaspoon chili powder
⅛ teaspoon salt
⅛ teaspoon ground red pepper
1 pound turkey breast cutlets, cut into ½-inch-wide strips
Vegetable cooking spray
1½ cups tightly packed torn curly endive
1½ cups tightly packed torn romaine lettuce
1 cup fresh orange sections (about 2 oranges)
¼ cup chopped purple onion
1 (15-ounce) can seasoned black beans, rinsed and drained
⅓ cup chopped fresh cilantro
¼ cup fresh lime juice
2 tablespoons fresh orange juice
2 teaspoons vegetable oil
⅛ teaspoon salt
Dash of ground red pepper
1 small clove garlic, minced

Combine first 4 ingredients in a large heavy-duty, zip-top plastic bag. Add turkey; seal bag, and shake to coat turkey.

Coat a large nonstick skillet with cooking spray; place over medium-high heat until hot. Add turkey, and sauté 4 minutes or until lightly browned. Spoon into a large bowl; add endive and next 4 ingredients.

Combine cilantro and remaining 6 ingredients in a bowl; stir with a wire whisk. Add to turkey mixture, tossing gently to coat. Serve at room temperature. Yield: 4 servings (serving size: 2¼ cups).

Calories 287 (12% from fat) **Protein** 33.8g **Fat** 3.9g (sat 0.7g) **Carbohydrate** 30.2g **Fiber** 9.3g **Cholesterol** 71mg **Iron** 4.5mg **Sodium** 560mg **Calcium** 99mg

CHUTNEY CHICKEN SALAD

QUICK & EASY

If you can't find mango chutney in your supermarket, substitute another fruit chutney.

2 tablespoons chopped almonds
Vegetable cooking spray
1½ pounds skinned, boned chicken breasts
1 cup diagonally sliced celery
½ cup sliced green onions
1 (9-ounce) jar mango chutney
6 cups loosely packed sliced romaine lettuce

Place chopped almonds on a baking sheet. Bake at 350° for 8 minutes or until toasted; set aside.

Coat a large nonstick skillet with cooking spray; place over medium heat until hot. Add chicken; cook 7 minutes on each side or until done. Remove chicken from skillet; cut across grain into thin slices.

Combine almonds, chicken, celery, green onions, and mango chutney in a large bowl; toss well. Arrange green lettuce on individual salad plates; spoon chicken mixture evenly over lettuce. Yield: 6 servings (serving size: ⅔ cup chicken mixture and 1 cup lettuce).

Calories 259 (16% from fat) **Protein** 28.6g **Fat** 4.7g (sat 1.0g) **Carbohydrate** 25.5g **Fiber** 2.3g **Cholesterol** 72mg **Iron** 2.2mg **Sodium** 159mg **Calcium** 65mg

CHOOSE CHUTNEY FOR FLAVOR

Chutney is a fruit condiment that looks much like thick fruit preserves. Unlike fruit preserves, it contains vinegar, spices, and sometimes nuts. It can taste sweet to tart, and mild to spicy hot.

Chutney is traditionally served as a condiment with Indian curries, but it's also a great source of flavor for many recipes. Serve it with cheese or as a spread for bread; stir it into salads, soups, or sandwich fillings; or serve it with poultry and meats for extra flavor.

If you want to try making your own chutney, find recipes for Fresh Pumpkin Chutney and Fresh Mango Chutney on page 156.

BLACKENED CHICKEN SALAD

3   tablespoons Spicy Seasoning
3   cups chopped tomato
¾   cup diced sweet yellow pepper
¼   cup finely chopped purple onion
1   tablespoon sugar
3   tablespoons cider vinegar
¼   teaspoon salt
⅛   teaspoon pepper
¼   cup lemon juice
¼   cup Dijon mustard
3   tablespoons water
1   tablespoon honey
4   (4-ounce) skinned, boned chicken breast halves
Vegetable cooking spray
1   pound Sugar Snap peas, trimmed
8   cups torn romaine lettuce
Flat-leaf parsley sprigs (optional)

Prepare Spicy Seasoning; set aside. Combine tomato and next 6 ingredients in a bowl, and toss well. Cover and chill.

Combine lemon juice and next 3 ingredients in a large bowl; stir well with a wire whisk. Cover and chill.

Rub chicken with 3 tablespoons Spicy Seasoning. Coat a large heavy skillet with cooking spray, and place over medium-high heat until hot. Add chicken, and cook 7 minutes on each side or until chicken is done. Remove chicken from skillet, and let cool. Cut chicken across grain into thin slices, and set aside.

Blackened Chicken Salad

Arrange peas in a steamer basket over boiling water. Cover; steam 2 minutes. Rinse under cold water; drain. Add peas and lettuce to lemon juice mixture; toss well. Arrange lettuce mixture in 4 large salad bowls; top each serving with 1 cup tomato mixture and 1 sliced chicken breast half. Garnish with parsley, if desired. Yield: 4 servings.

Calories 298 (16% from fat) **Protein** 32.1g **Fat** 5.4g (sat 1.0g) **Carbohydrate** 31.0g **Fiber** 6.6g **Cholesterol** 72mg **Iron** 5.7mg **Sodium** 1205mg **Calcium** 113mg

SPICY SEASONING:

2½ tablespoons paprika
2   tablespoons garlic powder
1   tablespoon salt
1   tablespoon onion powder
1   tablespoon dried thyme
1   tablespoon ground red pepper
1   tablespoon black pepper

Combine all ingredients in a small mixing bowl, and stir well. Store mixture in an airtight container. Use

to season fish, poultry, meats, or assorted vegetables. Yield: ½ cup plus 1½ tablespoons (analysis per 1 teaspoon).

Note: You may substitute a commercial spice mix for Spicy Seasoning and still produce chicken with a blackened flavor. Just remember that commercial spice mixes are often high in sodium.

Calories 18 (15% from fat) **Protein** 0.9g **Fat** 0.3g (sat 0.1g) **Carbohydrate** 3.9g **Fiber** 0.9g **Cholesterol** 0mg **Iron** 1.2mg **Sodium** 759mg **Calcium** 21mg

GRILLED TUNA SALAD WITH CITRUS VINAIGRETTE

1¾   cups Citrus Vinaigrette, divided
1½   pounds tuna steaks
Vegetable cooking spray
4   cups loosely packed torn Boston lettuce
2   cups loosely packed torn fresh spinach leaves
1   cup thinly sliced radicchio
1   cup loosely packed torn curly endive
1   cup sliced mushrooms
1   cup cherry tomato halves
1   large sweet red pepper, seeded and cut into thin strips
½   cup alfalfa sprouts
½   cup (1-inch) slices green onions

Prepare Citrus Vinaigrette. Place tuna in a nonmetal dish; drizzle with 1 cup Citrus Vinaigrette. Cover and marinate in vinaigrette in refrigerator 1 hour, turning tuna once. Drain, reserving vinaigrette marinade. Place vinaigrette marinade in a small saucepan; bring to a boil. Remove from heat; set aside.

Coat grill rack with cooking spray; place on grill over medium-hot coals (350° to 400°). Place tuna on rack; grill, covered, 5 minutes on each side or until fish flakes easily when tested with a fork, basting often with reserved marinade. Discard skin from tuna. Cut tuna into bite-size pieces, and set aside.

Combine Boston lettuce and remaining 8 ingredients in a large bowl. Drizzle with remaining ¾ cup Citrus Vinaigrette; toss well. Add tuna, and toss gently. Yield: 6 servings (serving size: 2 cups).

Calories 287 (31% from fat) **Protein** 29.8g **Fat** 9.8g (sat 2.0g) **Carbohydrate** 20.6g **Fiber** 2.4g **Cholesterol** 44mg **Iron** 2.6mg **Sodium** 155mg **Calcium** 47mg

CITRUS VINAIGRETTE:

Here's a tip for chopping lots of basil or any other leafy herb: Pack the leaves in a measuring cup, and snip with kitchen shears until they're finely chopped.

¾   cup frozen orange juice concentrate, thawed and undiluted
½   cup water
¼   cup plus 2 tablespoons fresh lime juice
¼   cup minced fresh basil
1½   tablespoons olive oil
1½   teaspoons minced fresh tarragon
1½   teaspoons Dijon mustard
⅛   teaspoon salt

Combine all ingredients, and stir mixture well with a wire whisk. Serve chilled or at room temperature over mixed salad greens, fruit, or seafood. Yield: 1¾ cups (serving size: 1 tablespoon).

Calories 20 (36% from fat) **Protein** 0.2g **Fat** 0.8g (sat 0.1g) **Carbohydrate** 3.2g **Fiber** 0.1g **Cholesterol** 0mg **Iron** 0.0mg **Sodium** 18mg **Calcium** 3mg

FAT FACTS FOR DRESSINGS

When you want to know which of our dressing recipes has the lowest amount of fat, check out the number of fat grams, *not* the percentage of fat from calories. Because you eat dressing *with* salad greens, the total fat percentage of the salad will be in keeping with a low-fat diet. We consider about 1 tablespoon of dressing to be an adequate amount for a single salad serving.

THOUSAND ISLAND DRESSING

½   cup plain low-fat yogurt
½   cup reduced-calorie mayonnaise
¼   cup reduced-calorie chili sauce
2   tablespoons sweet pickle relish
1   tablespoon minced onion
1   tablespoon finely chopped celery
1   teaspoon lemon juice
⅛   teaspoon pepper

Combine all ingredients. Cover and chill. Serve dressing over salad greens. Yield: 1½ cups (serving size: 1 tablespoon).

Calories 20 (63% from fat) **Protein** 0.3g **Fat** 1.4g (sat 0.3g) **Carbohydrate** 1.6g **Fiber** 0.0g **Cholesterol** 2mg **Iron** 0.0mg **Sodium** 53mg **Calcium** 9mg

Parmesan-Green Peppercorn Dressing

PARMESAN-GREEN PEPPERCORN DRESSING

1   cup nonfat buttermilk
¼   cup grated Parmesan cheese
¼   cup nonfat sour cream
¼   cup reduced-calorie mayonnaise
2   tablespoons lemon juice
2   teaspoons dried whole green peppercorns, crushed
¼   teaspoon pepper
⅛   teaspoon salt

Combine all ingredients in a small bowl; stir mixture well with a wire whisk. Cover dressing, and chill. Serve over assorted salad greens. Yield: 1¾ cups (serving size: 1 tablespoon).

Calories 14 (51% from fat) **Protein** 0.8g **Fat** 0.8g (sat 0.3g) **Carbohydrate** 0.9g **Fiber** 0.0g **Cholesterol** 2mg **Iron** 0.1mg **Sodium** 50mg **Calcium** 21mg

CREAMY CELERY SEED DRESSING

¼ cup plus 2 tablespoons reduced-calorie mayonnaise
¼ cup plus 2 tablespoons plain nonfat yogurt
2 tablespoons sugar
2 tablespoons white vinegar
1 tablespoon prepared mustard
¼ teaspoon celery seeds
⅛ teaspoon salt
⅛ teaspoon pepper

Combine all ingredients. Cover; chill. Serve over fresh spinach. Yield: 1 cup (serving size: 1 tablespoon).

Calories 25 (58% from fat) Protein 0.4g Fat 1.6g (sat 0.2g) Carbohydrate 2.5g Fiber 0.0g Cholesterol 2mg Iron 0.0mg Sodium 76mg Calcium 12mg

CREAMY CUCUMBER DRESSING

Find this pictured on page 218.

1 cup plain low-fat yogurt
⅓ cup peeled, seeded, and finely chopped cucumber
¼ cup reduced-calorie mayonnaise
2 tablespoons chopped green onions
2 tablespoons lemon juice
¼ teaspoon salt
¼ teaspoon dried dillweed
⅛ teaspoon pepper

Combine all ingredients; stir well. Cover and chill. Serve over salad greens. Yield: 1¾ cups (serving size: 1 tablespoon).

Calories 12 (53% from fat) Protein 0.5g Fat 0.7g (sat 0.2g) Carbohydrate 0.9g Fiber 0.0g Cholesterol 1mg Iron 0.0mg Sodium 43mg Calcium 16mg

ORANGE-POPPY SEED DRESSING

⅔ cup unsweetened orange juice
3 tablespoons water
2 tablespoons white wine vinegar
2 teaspoons cornstarch
2 teaspoons sweet-hot mustard
2 teaspoons honey
¾ teaspoon poppy seeds

Combine first 6 ingredients in a medium saucepan; stir well. Bring to a boil over medium heat. Cook, stirring constantly, 1 minute or until thickened and bubbly. Stir in poppy seeds. Cover and chill thoroughly. Serve over salad greens or fruit. Yield: ¾ cup plus 2 tablespoons (serving size: 1 tablespoon).

Calories 12 (8% from fat) Protein 0.2g Fat 0.1g (sat 0.0g) Carbohydrate 2.5g Fiber 0.0g Cholesterol 0mg Iron 0.0mg Sodium 7mg Calcium 3mg

RED WINE VINAIGRETTE

QUICK & EASY

¼ cup dry red wine
¼ cup red wine vinegar
¼ cup tomato juice
2 tablespoons water
2 tablespoons olive oil
½ teaspoon minced fresh thyme
½ teaspoon minced fresh oregano
½ teaspoon minced fresh tarragon
½ teaspoon pepper
1 clove garlic, minced

Combine all ingredients in a jar; cover tightly, and shake mixture vigorously. Serve vinaigrette over salad greens. Yield: 1 cup (serving size: 1 tablespoon).

Calories 22 (70% from fat) Protein 0.1g Fat 1.7g (sat 0.2g) Carbohydrate 0.5g Fiber 0.0g Cholesterol 0mg Iron 0.1mg Sodium 14mg Calcium 2mg

VERSATILE VINAIGRETTES

Don't save flavorful vinaigrettes for just salads. They also make great marinades for meats, poultry, seafood, and fresh vegetables. Or, for a delicious, light snack, brush a little vinaigrette on top of French or Italian bread slices, and bake until toasted.

Grilled New Yorker, page 139

Lucky for us, sandwiches these days are much more than greasy grilled cheese sandwiches or all-the-way hamburgers. In fact, if you've given up the classic fat-filled kind, you'll never look back once you've sampled the numerous light options throughout this chapter.

SANDWICHES

We've redefined the sandwich, starting with the bread. Our flavorful fillings are encased in pita pockets or calzone pastries, rolled up in flour tortillas, or hidden in low-fat cranberry biscuits. Our fillings include roasted vegetables, feta cheese, and spicy ground pork. But if you get nostalgic for the old-fashioned kind, check out our Chicken Club, the Sloppy Joes, or our absolute favorite—the Grilled New Yorker.

Sloppy Joes

2 pounds lean ground round
1½ cups chopped onion
½ cup chopped green pepper
2 cloves garlic, minced
⅔ cup water
½ cup no-salt-added ketchup
2 tablespoons prepared mustard
2 teaspoons chili powder
1½ teaspoons ground cumin
½ teaspoon salt
¼ teaspoon pepper
2 (8-ounce) cans no-salt-added tomato sauce
1 (15-ounce) can black beans, drained
1 (14½-ounce) can no-salt-added whole tomatoes, drained and chopped
1 (6-ounce) can tomato paste
13 (1½-ounce) hamburger buns

Cook first 4 ingredients in a Dutch oven over medium heat until meat is browned, stirring until meat crumbles; drain meat mixture. Wipe drippings from Dutch oven with a paper towel.

Return meat mixture to Dutch oven. Add water and next 10 ingredients; stir well. Bring to a boil; cover, reduce heat, and simmer 30 minutes, stirring occasionally. Serve on hamburger buns. Yield: 13 servings (serving size: 1 bun and ⅔ cup meat mixture).

Calories 320 (24% from fat) **Protein** 21.5g
Fat 8.4g (sat 2.1g) **Carbohydrate** 39.4g
Fiber 2.0g **Cholesterol** 57mg **Iron** 3.7mg
Sodium 347mg **Calcium** 52mg

Open-Face Sesame-Beef Subs

QUICK & EASY

1 teaspoon sesame seeds
¾ pound lean boneless beef sirloin steak
½ cup canned no-salt-added beef broth, undiluted
1 tablespoon cornstarch
1 tablespoon rice vinegar
1 tablespoon reduced-sodium soy sauce
¼ teaspoon sugar
¼ teaspoon dark sesame oil
¼ pound fresh snow pea pods
Vegetable cooking spray
1 teaspoon vegetable oil
1 small onion, sliced
1 clove garlic, minced
1 (1-inch) piece peeled gingerroot
4 (1-ounce) diagonally cut slices French bread (about 1 inch thick), toasted

Spread sesame seeds in a thin layer in an ungreased shallow pan. Bake at 350° for 10 to 15 minutes, stirring occasionally. Remove from oven, and set aside.

Trim fat from steak. Slice steak diagonally across grain into ¼-inch-wide strips. Set aside.

Combine broth and next 5 ingredients in a medium bowl; stir well, and set aside. Wash snow peas; trim ends, remove strings, and set aside.

Coat a wok or large nonstick skillet with cooking spray; drizzle vegetable oil around top of wok, coating sides. Heat at medium-high (375°) until hot. Add onion, garlic, and gingerroot; stir-fry 5 minutes or until onion is tender. Add steak strips, and stir-fry 3 minutes or to desired degree of doneness. Add snow peas, and stir-fry 30 seconds. Add broth mixture; cook, stirring constantly, 1 minute or until mixture is thickened. Remove and discard gingerroot.

Spoon beef mixture evenly over bread slices. Sprinkle evenly with sesame seeds. Yield: 4 servings (serving size: 1 sandwich).

Calories 266 (25% from fat) **Protein** 22.4g
Fat 7.3g (sat 2.1g) **Carbohydrate** 25.4g
Fiber 1.7g **Cholesterol** 53mg **Iron** 3.7mg
Sodium 342mg **Calcium** 39mg

Slim Slicing

For tender strips of meat, slice steak diagonally across the grain into ¼-inch-wide strips.

MEDITERRANEAN PITA PIZZAS

Pizza for two is a cinch with ready-made "crusts" and imaginative toppings. This recipe pairs pitas with lamb, eggplant, and feta for a taste of the Middle East.

Vegetable cooking spray
6   ounces lean ground lamb
2½   cups peeled, cubed eggplant (about ½ pound)
⅓   cup water
½   teaspoon dried oregano
½   teaspoon lemon juice
¼   teaspoon garlic powder
⅓   cup Italian-style tomato paste
2   (8-inch) pita bread rounds, toasted
3   tablespoons (1 ounce) crumbled feta cheese

Coat a large skillet with cooking spray; place skillet over medium-high heat until hot. Add ground lamb, and cook until meat is browned, stirring until it crumbles. Drain meat, and set aside. Wipe drippings from skillet with a paper towel.

Add eggplant to skillet; cook eggplant over medium-high heat, stirring constantly, 2 minutes. Add water and next 3 ingredients; stir well. Cover, reduce heat, and cook 5 minutes. Uncover and cook over high heat 1 additional minute. Add cooked lamb and tomato paste; cook until thoroughly heated, stirring occasionally.

Place pita rounds on a baking sheet. Spread lamb mixture evenly over pita rounds, and top with cheese. Broil 5½ inches from heat (with electric oven door partially opened) 2 minutes or until cheese softens. Yield: 2 servings (serving size: 1 pizza).

Calories 386 (25% from fat) **Protein** 25.5g **Fat** 10.7g (sat 4.2g) **Carbohydrate** 45.6g **Fiber** 9.1g **Cholesterol** 68mg **Iron** 5.1mg **Sodium** 456mg **Calcium** 195mg

GRILLED NEW YORKER

QUICK & EASY

1   tablespoon reduced-calorie mayonnaise
1   teaspoon Dijon mustard
4   (1-ounce) slices rye bread
2   (¾-ounce) nonfat process Swiss cheese slices
4   ounces thinly sliced lean, lower-salt smoked ham
1   cup thinly sliced green cabbage
Vegetable cooking spray

Combine mayonnaise and mustard in a bowl; stir well. Spread mayonnaise mixture on 2 bread slices; top each with 1 cheese slice, 1 ounce ham, ½ cup cabbage, and 1 ounce ham. Top with remaining 2 bread slices.

Coat a nonstick skillet with cooking spray, and place over medium heat until hot. Add sandwiches, and cook 3 minutes on each side or until golden. Yield: 2 servings (serving size: 1 sandwich).

Calories 276 (20% from fat) **Protein** 20.4g **Fat** 6.0g (sat 2.0g) **Carbohydrate** 36.2g **Fiber** 4.4g **Cholesterol** 35mg **Iron** 1.1mg **Sodium** 1183mg **Calcium** 209mg

WATCHING SODIUM

Contrary to what you might think, the sandwich's greatest enemy is sodium, not fat. The pillars of sandwich making—bread, lunchmeats, cheese, mustard, and mayonnaise—really pile on the sodium. Fat-free cheese and reduced-calorie condiments help slash fat and calories, but not salt. As a result, these sandwiches are often higher in sodium than normal.

If you're watching your sodium intake, check the nutritional information for each recipe, and add low-sodium accompaniments like carrot and celery sticks rather than potato chips or pickles.

Spicy Pork Calzones With Chutney Sauce

Using commercial bread dough is easier than making pizza dough for these calzones, and it also gives the calzones a chewier, more breadlike texture.

1¼   pounds lean ground pork
½   cup chopped onion
½   cup finely chopped pitted prunes
2   tablespoons seeded, minced jalapeño pepper
½   teaspoon ground cumin
¼   teaspoon salt
¼   teaspoon ground nutmeg
⅛   teaspoon ground cinnamon
⅔   cup water
1   tablespoon plus 1 teaspoon cornstarch
1   (1-pound) loaf frozen white bread dough, thawed
Vegetable cooking spray
⅓   cup hot mango chutney
⅔   cup plain low-fat yogurt

Spicy Pork Calzones With Chutney Sauce

Cook pork and onion in a large nonstick skillet over medium heat until pork is browned, stirring until it crumbles; drain. Wipe drippings from skillet with a paper towel.

Return pork mixture to skillet. Add prunes and next 5 ingredients; stir well. Combine ⅔ cup water and cornstarch; stir well. Add to pork mixture. Cook, stirring constantly, 1 minute; remove from heat.

Divide dough into 8 equal portions. Working with 1 portion at a time (cover remaining dough to keep from drying out), roll each portion to ⅛-inch thickness. Place on a large baking sheet coated with cooking spray, and pat each portion into a 6-inch circle. Spoon about ⅓ cup pork mixture onto half of each circle; moisten edges of dough with water. Fold dough over filling; press edges together with a fork to seal. Lightly coat with cooking spray.

Bake at 375° for 20 minutes or until golden. Remove from oven, and lightly coat again with cooking spray. Keep calzones warm.

Place chutney in container of an electric blender; cover and process until smooth. Combine chutney and yogurt; stir well. Serve sauce with calzones. Yield: 8 servings (serving size: 1 calzone and 2 tablespoons sauce).

Calories 362 (25% from fat) **Protein** 20.5g **Fat** 10.1g (sat 3.3g) **Carbohydrate** 47.6g **Fiber** 1.3g **Cholesterol** 49mg **Iron** 1.3mg **Sodium** 428mg **Calcium** 93mg

CHICKEN CLUB

2 tablespoons no-salt-added tomato juice
2 tablespoons balsamic vinegar
2 (4-ounce) skinned, boned chicken breast halves
Vegetable cooking spray
Dash of pepper
4 slices turkey bacon
6 (¾-ounce) slices light sourdough bread, toasted
1 tablespoon reduced-calorie mayonnaise
2 cups loosely packed torn romaine lettuce
8 (¼-inch-thick) slices tomato (about 2 medium)

Combine tomato juice and balsamic vinegar in a shallow dish; set mixture aside.

Place each piece of chicken between 2 sheets of heavy-duty plastic wrap, and flatten to ¼-inch thickness, using a meat mallet or rolling pin. Add chicken to vinegar mixture. Cover and marinate in refrigerator at least 1 hour, turning chicken occasionally.

Remove chicken from marinade, discarding marinade. Coat a large nonstick skillet with cooking spray, and place skillet over medium heat until hot. Add chicken; cook 2 minutes on each side or until done. Remove from skillet, and sprinkle with pepper; set chicken aside, and keep warm.

Cook turkey bacon in a microwave oven according to package directions. Cut each bacon slice in half crosswise; set bacon slices aside, and keep warm.

Spread 1 side of each of 2 slices of bread with ¾ teaspoon mayonnaise. Top each with ½ cup lettuce, 2 tomato slices, and 1 chicken breast half; cover with another slice of bread. Top each with ½ cup lettuce, 2 tomato slices and 4 half-slices of bacon. Spread 1 side of each remaining slice of bread with ¾ teaspoon mayonnaise; place on top of sandwiches. Cut each sandwich in half, and secure with wooden picks. Yield: 2 servings (serving size: 1 sandwich).

Calories 370 (26% from fat) Protein 38.9g Fat 10.5g (sat 2.3g) Carbohydrate 32.9g Fiber 7.9g Cholesterol 95mg Iron 1.8mg Sodium 931mg Calcium 37mg

A CHANGE OF TASTE

The easiest way to change the personality of a sandwich is to change the type of bread you use to make it. Try pita or "pocket" bread for sandwich fillings like salads or meat mixtures. If it's a creamy spread, roll it up in a flour tortilla. And for sliced bread sandwiches, vary the bread with distinctly flavored breads like sourdough, rye, or dark pumpernickel. Whole wheat tastes almost sweet and a bit nutlike. Just make sure the bread complements the filling flavor.

TURKEY ROLL-UPS

QUICK & EASY

This easy pickup is great for grab-and-go nibbling.

¼ cup plus 2 tablespoons (1½ ounces) shredded reduced-fat sharp Cheddar cheese
1 tablespoon thinly sliced green onions
2 teaspoons Dijon mustard
1 (8-ounce) tub nonfat process cream cheese, softened
6 (8-inch) flour tortillas
12 (1-ounce) slices cooked deli turkey breast
12 large fresh spinach leaves or curly leaf lettuce leaves
24 (⅛-inch-thick) slices cucumber

Combine first 4 ingredients; stir well. Spread 3 tablespoons cheese mixture over each tortilla. Top each with 2 slices turkey, 2 spinach leaves, and 4 cucumber slices; roll up. Yield: 6 servings (serving size: 1 roll-up).

Calories 257 (20% from fat) Protein 22.1g Fat 5.6g (sat 1.6g) Carbohydrate 25.6g Fiber 1.9g Cholesterol 11mg Iron 1.8mg Sodium 983mg Calcium 231mg

CRANBERRY BISCUITS WITH SMOKED TURKEY

You may remember these little sandwiches from the wedding reception menu we featured in April 1995. The biscuits are a breeze to make in the food processor; you can also make them by hand.

Spicy Mustard (optional)
2 cups bread flour
1 teaspoon baking powder
¼ teaspoon salt
2 tablespoons vegetable shortening
3 tablespoons sugar
1 package active dry yeast
⅔ cup warm nonfat buttermilk (105° to 115°)
2 tablespoons warm water (105° to 115°)
½ cup dried cranberries
Vegetable cooking spray
1 pound thinly sliced cooked smoked turkey breast

Prepare Spicy Mustard, if desired. Set aside.

Position knife blade in food processor bowl; combine flour, baking powder, and salt in processor bowl, and pulse 2 times or until blended. Add shortening, and process 10 seconds or until blended.

Combine sugar and next 3 ingredients in a small bowl; let stand 5 minutes. Slowly pour yeast mixture through food chute with processor running; process until dough leaves sides of bowl and forms a ball.

Turn dough out onto a lightly floured surface, and knead in cranberries. Roll dough to ½-inch thickness; cut with a 2-inch biscuit cutter into 20 biscuits. Place on a baking sheet coated with cooking spray. Let rise, uncovered, in a warm place (85°), free from drafts, 20 minutes or until puffy.

Bake at 425° for 8 minutes or until golden. Split biscuits, and fill each with ¾ ounce turkey. Serve with Spicy Mustard, if desired. Yield: 10 servings (serving size: 2 biscuits).

Calories 201 (17% from fat) Protein 12.7g Fat 3.7g (sat 0.9g) Carbohydrate 27.8g Fiber 0.7g Cholesterol 1mg Iron 1.5mg Sodium 452mg Calcium 53mg

SPICY MUSTARD:

½ cup sugar
½ cup dry mustard
½ cup malt vinegar
2 egg whites, lightly beaten

Combine all ingredients in a medium saucepan. Cook mixture over medium-low heat, stirring constantly, 5 minutes or until thickened. Yield: 1 cup (serving size: 1 tablespoon).

Calories 41 (22% from fat) Protein 1.1g Fat 1.0g (sat 0.1g) Carbohydrate 7.1g Fiber 0.0g Cholesterol 0mg Iron 0.2mg Sodium 7mg Calcium 7mg

TUNA BURGERS

QUICK & EASY

Fat content of albacore tuna can vary greatly. It depends on the fish's diet and the depth and temperature of the water in which the fish was caught. To get the lowest fat tuna available, read the can's nutrition label carefully.

2 tablespoons nonfat mayonnaise
2 tablespoons creamy mustard-mayonnaise blend
1 egg white
2 (6-ounce) cans albacore tuna in water, drained and flaked
½ cup dry breadcrumbs, divided
¼ cup chopped green onions
Vegetable cooking spray
¼ cup nonfat mayonnaise
4 (1½-ounce) hamburger buns, split
4 lettuce leaves
4 slices tomato
4 slices sweet onion

Combine first 3 ingredients in a medium bowl, and stir well. Add tuna, ¼ cup breadcrumbs, and green onions; stir well. Divide mixture into 4 equal portions, shaping each into a 4-inch patty. Press remaining ¼ cup breadcrumbs evenly onto both sides of patties.

Coat a large nonstick skillet with cooking spray; place over medium-high heat until hot. Add patties; cover and cook 3 minutes. Carefully turn patties; cook, uncovered, 3 minutes or until patties are golden.

Spread ¼ cup mayonnaise evenly on split sides of buns. Place lettuce, tomato, onion, and tuna patties on bottom halves of buns. Place bun tops on sandwiches. Yield: 4 servings (serving size: 1 sandwich).

Calories 335 (20% from fat) **Protein** 23.5g **Fat** 7.6g (sat 1.2g) **Carbohydrate** 41.8g **Fiber** 1.4g **Cholesterol** 41mg **Iron** 2.0mg **Sodium** 869mg **Calcium** 48mg

Tuna Burgers

OPEN-FACE PEPPER AND CHEESE MELTS

QUICK & EASY

Vegetable cooking spray
1   cup green pepper strips
1   tablespoon minced fresh basil
1   clove garlic, minced
1   medium onion, sliced and separated into rings
1   tablespoon plus 1 teaspoon stone-ground mustard
4   (1-ounce) slices rye bread, toasted
8   (¼-inch-thick) slices tomato (about 2 medium)
4   (1-ounce) slices part-skim mozzarella cheese, each cut lengthwise into 4 strips

Coat a nonstick skillet with cooking spray; place over medium heat until hot. Add pepper strips and next 3 ingredients, and sauté 8 minutes or until tender. Set aside, and keep warm.

Spread 1 teaspoon mustard over each bread slice; place on a baking sheet. Top each bread slice with 2 slices tomato and 4 strips cheese. Broil 5½ inches from heat (with electric oven door partially opened) 2 minutes or until cheese melts. Top each sandwich with about ⅓ cup pepper mixture. Yield: 4 servings (serving size: 1 sandwich).

Calories 205 (33% from fat) **Protein** 10.2g **Fat** 7.4g (sat 3.8g) **Carbohydrate** 26.6g **Fiber** 3.5g **Cholesterol** 22mg **Iron** 1.5mg **Sodium** 346mg **Calcium** 187mg

GRILLED CHEESE WITH ARTICHOKES

QUICK & EASY

Looking for a good source of vitamins A and C, calcium, iron, and potassium? You'll find it in this healthy grilled cheese topped with artichokes and tomatoes.

2   teaspoons Dijon mustard
4   (2-ounce) sandwich rolls,
    split and toasted
8   (¾-ounce) nonfat process
    American cheese slices
1   cup sliced canned artichoke
    hearts, drained
8   (¼-inch-thick) slices tomato
    (about 2 medium)
2   tablespoons oil-free Italian
    dressing

Spread ½ teaspoon mustard on split side of top half of each roll, and set aside.

Place bottom halves of rolls on a baking sheet. Top each half with 2 American cheese slices, ¼ cup sliced artichoke, and 2 tomato slices; drizzle each half with 1½ teaspoons dressing.

Broil sandwich halves 5½ inches from heat (with electric oven door partially opened) 2 minutes or until cheese melts. Cover with tops of rolls. Yield: 4 servings (serving size: 1 sandwich).

Calories 283 (19% from fat) **Protein** 17.8g
Fat 6.0g (sat 1.2g) **Carbohydrate** 39.9g
Fiber 0.9g **Cholesterol** 34mg **Iron** 1.8mg
Sodium 778mg **Calcium** 343mg

ROASTED VEGETABLE AND FETA CALZONES

Use your oven to add more flavor to vegetables. Roasting eggplant, onions, peppers, zucchini, asparagus, or tomatoes, for example, makes the water in the vegetables evaporate. This process concentrates their natural sugars, yielding a rich, sweet taste and soft texture.

3   cups peeled, chopped
      eggplant
2   cups chopped yellow
      onion
1½   cups diced mushrooms
1½   cups diced zucchini
1   cup diced sweet red pepper
1   tablespoon olive oil
½   teaspoon pepper
¼   teaspoon salt
1   cup (4 ounces) crumbled
      feta cheese
½   cup chopped fresh basil
1   (1-pound) loaf frozen white
      bread dough, thawed
Vegetable cooking spray
1   egg white
1   tablespoon water

Combine first 8 ingredients on a 15- x 10- x 1-inch jellyroll pan; stir well, and spread evenly. Bake at 425° for 45 minutes, stirring every 15 minutes. Spoon vegetables into a bowl; stir in cheese and basil.

Divide dough into 8 equal portions. Working with 1 portion at a time (cover remaining dough to keep from drying out), roll each portion into a 7-inch circle on a lightly floured surface. Spoon ½ cup vegetable mixture onto half of each circle; moisten edges of dough with water. Fold dough over filling; press edges together with a fork to seal. Place calzones on a baking sheet coated with cooking spray.

Combine egg white and water; brush over calzones. Bake at 375° for 20 minutes or until golden. Let cool on a wire rack. Serve warm or at room temperature. Yield: 8 servings (serving size: 1 calzone).

Calories 313 (23% from fat) **Protein** 11.7g
Fat 8.0g (sat 3.1g) **Carbohydrate** 49.5g
Fiber 1.9g **Cholesterol** 13mg **Iron** 2.8mg
Sodium 683mg **Calcium** 147mg

ROASTING VEGETABLES IN FLAVOR

Roasting vegetables is simple when you follow these tips:
• Use a shallow roasting pan or baking sheet that is large enough to hold the vegetables without crowding them. Roast at dry, high temperatures (425°).
• Cut vegetables roughly the same size for even cooking.
• Coat each piece with cooking spray; arrange pieces in a single layer to roast.
• Bake root vegetables (carrots, potatoes, parsnips, turnips, onions, and garlic) 15 to 20 minutes, stirring occasionally; bake other vegetables 10 to 15 minutes, stirring occasionally.

ROASTED VEGETABLE PITAS

- 1   (1-pound) eggplant
- 1   tablespoon chopped parsley
- 2   tablespoons fresh lemon juice
- 1   teaspoon olive oil
- ¼   teaspoon salt
- ⅛   teaspoon pepper
- 1   large clove garlic, crushed
- 1   medium-size sweet red pepper (about 7 ounces)
- ½   cup drained canned cannellini beans
- ½   teaspoon ground cumin
- 2   (6-inch) onion pita bread rounds
- ¼   cup plain low-fat yogurt
- 2   tablespoons chopped green onions

Coarsely ground pepper

Pierce eggplant several times with a fork; place on a baking sheet. Broil 5½ inches from heat (with electric oven door partially opened) 30 minutes or until very tender, turning often. Let cool; peel and coarsely chop. Combine eggplant, parsley, and next 5 ingredients in a bowl; stir well, and set aside.

Cut sweet red pepper in half lengthwise; remove and discard seeds and membrane. Place red pepper halves, skin side up, on a baking sheet, and flatten with palm of hand. Broil 5½ inches from heat (with electric oven door partially opened) 10 minutes or until pepper halves are charred. Place in ice water until cool; peel and discard skin.

Roasted Vegetable Pitas

Cut pepper halves lengthwise into thin strips.

Combine beans and cumin; stir. Top pitas evenly with eggplant mixture, pepper strips, bean mixture, yogurt, and green onions. Sprinkle with ground pepper. Yield: 2 servings (serving size: 1 sandwich).

Calories 294 (15% from fat) **Protein** 11.6g
Fat 5.0g (sat 1.0g) **Carbohydrate** 53.8g
Fiber 6.1g **Cholesterol** 3mg **Iron** 4.7mg
Sodium 543mg **Calcium** 194mg

Grapefruit-Cranberry
Marmalade, page 157

SAUCES

These are the recipes that make people beg. They want to know where you bought that delicious barbecue sauce basted on the meat? Or just where you found that divine orange syrup on top of the pancakes? You alone decide whether to be evasive or to share your secret.

& CONDIMENTS

Then, during the holidays, you can astound the crowd when you tell them that the thick, rich-tasting gravy you served with the turkey was low in fat. If they get over the shock, serve them light pound cake drizzled with our three-star Caramel Sauce. Your reputation will never be the same.

Step by Step

For Caramel Sauce

1. Cook sugar and water in a heavy saucepan over medium-low heat until sugar completely dissolves. It's crucial that the sugar dissolve completely; run a spoon through the mixture—you should not feel any sugar or grit. Cover the saucepan, increase the heat to medium, and boil 1 minute to dissolve any sugar crystals clinging to the sides of the pan. Undissolved sugar can make the entire mixture clump.

2. Continue to boil, uncovered, over medium heat. It will take about 8 minutes for any color change to occur. Do not stir—it can cause the sugar to crystallize. After about 10 minutes, watch the syrup closely because it can darken quickly.

3. Remove the pan from heat; let stand 1 minute. Stir in margarine, using a long-handled spoon. Be careful—it's hot and may bubble and spatter. Carefully add milk, stirring vigorously. Don't panic when caramel hardens and clumps on the spoon; this is normal.

4. Place the saucepan over medium heat, and cook mixture, stirring constantly, until the caramel sauce is smooth.

CARAMEL SAUCE

This thin sauce becomes thicker when chilled, but it's still pourable and perfect over low-fat ice cream.

1	cup sugar
¼	cup water
1	tablespoon margarine
¾	cup evaporated skimmed milk
½	teaspoon vanilla extract

Dash of salt

Combine sugar and water in a heavy saucepan, and place over medium-low heat. Cook 13 minutes or until sugar dissolves. (Do not stir.) Cover, increase heat to medium, and boil 1 minute. (This will dissolve any sugar crystals clinging to sides of pan.) Uncover and boil 10 additional minutes or until amber or golden. (Do not stir.)

Remove from heat; let stand 1 minute. Carefully add margarine, stirring until it melts. Gradually add milk, stirring constantly. (Caramel will harden and stick to spoon.) Place pan over medium heat, and cook, stirring constantly, 3 minutes or until caramel melts and mixture is smooth. Remove from heat; stir in vanilla and salt. Pour sauce into a bowl; serve warm or chilled. Store in an airtight container in the refrigerator. Yield: 1¼ cups (analysis per 1 tablespoon).

Calories 52 (10% from fat) **Protein** 0.7g **Fat** 0.6g (sat 0.1g) **Carbohydrate** 11.1g **Fiber** 0.0g **Cholesterol** 0mg **Iron** 0.0mg **Sodium** 32mg **Calcium** 28mg

MAPLE-WALNUT SAUCE

QUICK & EASY

¼ cup firmly packed brown sugar
1 tablespoon cornstarch
1 teaspoon unsweetened cocoa
⅛ teaspoon salt
¾ cup water
⅓ cup 2% low-fat milk
⅓ cup finely chopped walnuts
2 teaspoons imitation maple flavoring
½ teaspoon imitation butter flavoring
½ teaspoon vanilla extract

Combine first 4 ingredients in a 1-quart glass measure; stir well. Gradually add water and milk to dry ingredients, stirring with a wire whisk until blended. Stir in walnuts. Microwave at HIGH 4 minutes or until thickened and bubbly, stirring with wire whisk every 2 minutes. Stir in maple and butter flavorings and vanilla. Serve warm or at room temperature over pancakes or low-fat vanilla ice cream. Store in an airtight container in the refrigerator. Yield: 1 cup plus 3 tablespoons (analysis per 1 tablespoon).

Conventional Directions: Combine first 4 ingredients in a small saucepan; stir well. Gradually stir in water and milk, stirring until blended; stir in walnuts. Cook over medium heat, stirring constantly, 10 minutes or until thickened. Remove from heat; stir in maple and butter flavorings and vanilla.

Calories 30 (42% from fat) **Protein** 0.7g **Fat** 1.4g (sat 0.1g) **Carbohydrate** 3.7g **Fiber** 0.1g **Cholesterol** 0mg **Iron** 0.1mg **Sodium** 18mg **Calcium** 9mg

BITTERSWEET CHOCOLATE SAUCE

QUICK & EASY

Use Dutch process cocoa in this recipe because it dissolves easily to make a smooth sauce.

⅔ cup Dutch process cocoa
½ cup firmly packed brown sugar
⅔ cup skim milk
1 tablespoon plus 1 teaspoon vanilla extract

Combine cocoa and brown sugar in a medium saucepan; add milk. Stir well with a wire whisk. Bring mixture to a boil over medium-high heat, stirring constantly. Reduce heat to medium-low, and cook, stirring constantly, 7 minutes or until thickened.

Remove from heat; stir in vanilla. Serve warm over fresh fruit, angel food cake, or low-fat ice cream. Store sauce in an airtight container in the refrigerator. Yield: 1 cup (analysis per 1 tablespoon).

Calories 48 (9% from fat) **Protein** 1.4g **Fat** 0.5g (sat 0.3g) **Carbohydrate** 9.1g **Fiber** 0.0g **Cholesterol** 0mg **Iron** 0.8mg **Sodium** 10mg **Calcium** 24mg

TART LEMON CURD

Traditional lemon curd gets its richness from butter and egg yolks. Our low-fat version tastes just as creamy and rich, and it's very tart—you don't need much sauce for the flavor to go a long way. Try it over blueberries.

⅔ cup sugar
1 tablespoon grated lemon rind
2 teaspoons cornstarch
2 tablespoons margarine
⅔ cup fresh lemon juice
1 egg, lightly beaten

Combine first 3 ingredients in a bowl; stir well. Melt margarine in a small, heavy nonaluminum saucepan over low heat. Add cornstarch mixture to margarine, stirring well. Stir in lemon juice. Bring to a boil over medium heat, stirring constantly; cook 1 minute. Gradually stir about one-fourth of hot mixture into egg; add to remaining hot mixture, stirring constantly. Cook, stirring constantly, 3 minutes or until thickened.

Pour mixture into a small bowl; cover and chill. Serve over fresh fruit, reduced-fat scones, angel food cake, or low-fat ice cream. Store in an airtight container in the refrigerator. Yield: 1¼ cups (analysis per 1 tablespoon).

Calories 43 (29% from fat) **Protein** 0.4g **Fat** 1.4g (sat 0.3g) **Carbohydrate** 7.7g **Fiber** 0.0g **Cholesterol** 11mg **Iron** 0.0mg **Sodium** 17mg **Calcium** 3mg

FRESH ORANGE PANCAKE SYRUP

Serve this syrup over Buttermilk Pancakes (as pictured on page 27) or as a dessert sauce over angel food cake. For the secret to sectioning citrus, see page 122.

1   cup sugar
1⅓ cups unsweetened orange juice
1⅓ cups fresh orange sections (about 4 medium oranges)

Combine sugar and orange juice in a large nonaluminum saucepan. Bring to a boil over medium heat; cook 20 to 25 minutes or until reduced to 1 cup, stirring occasionally. Remove from heat; stir in orange sections. Serve warm or chilled with pancakes or over angel food cake. Store in an airtight container in the refrigerator. Yield: 2 cups (analysis per 1 tablespoon).

Calories 33 (0% from fat) Protein 0.1g Fat 0.0g (sat 0.0g) Carbohydrate 8.3g Fiber 0.4g Cholesterol 0mg Iron 0.0mg Sodium 0mg Calcium 4mg

FIERY-SWEET BARBECUE SAUCE

QUICK & EASY

1   cup low-sugar orange marmalade
1   cup reduced-calorie ketchup
¼   cup cider vinegar
1   tablespoon low-sodium soy sauce
¾   teaspoon celery seeds
½   teaspoon ground red pepper

Combine all ingredients in a 1-quart glass measure, and stir well. Cover with wax paper. Microwave at HIGH 6 minutes or until mixture comes to a boil, stirring after 3 minutes. Use for basting chicken, beef, or pork while cooking. Store sauce in an airtight container in the refrigerator. Yield: 2½ cups (analysis per 1 tablespoon).

Calories 5 (0% from fat) Protein 0.0g Fat 0.0g (sat 0.0g) Carbohydrate 0.9g Fiber 0.0g Cholesterol 0mg Iron 0.0mg Sodium 12mg Calcium 3mg

CRANBERRY JEZEBEL SAUCE

QUICK & EASY

When you sample this hot fruit sauce, you may feel as shameless as the biblical Jezebel it's named after. But don't worry—it's low in calories, fat, cholesterol, and sodium.

1   cup water
½   cup sugar
½   cup firmly packed brown sugar
1   (12-ounce) bag fresh or frozen cranberries
3   tablespoons prepared horseradish
1   tablespoon Dijon mustard

Combine first 3 ingredients in a medium saucepan; stir well. Bring to a boil over medium heat; add cranberries. Return to a boil, and cook 10 minutes, stirring occasionally. Spoon into a bowl; let cool to room temperature. Stir in horseradish and mustard; cover and chill. Serve with beef or pork; or pour over cream cheese, and serve with crackers. Store in an airtight container in the refrigerator. Yield: 2½ cups (serving size: ¼ cup).

Calories 86 (2% from fat) Protein 0.2g Fat 0.2g (sat 0.0g) Carbohydrate 21.9g Fiber 0.4g Cholesterol 0mg Iron 0.2mg Sodium 52mg Calcium 11mg

CHARRED MANGO SALSA

In our July/August 1993 issue, we featured great chefs and their favorite salsas. This memorable salsa, from Chef Tony Ruppe of Houston, goes well with game, fish, chicken, and beef.

2   (6-inch) Anaheim chiles
Vegetable cooking spray
1   cup (½-inch-thick) onion slices (about 1 medium onion)
2   cups (½-inch-thick) mango wedges (about 2 medium mangos)
¼   cup fresh lime juice
¼   cup coarsely chopped fresh cilantro
2   tablespoons seeded, minced serrano chiles
2   tablespoons rice vinegar
¼   teaspoon freshly ground pepper
⅛   teaspoon salt

Place Anaheim chiles on a baking sheet. Broil 5½ inches from heat (with electric oven door partially opened) 15 minutes or until charred, turning once. Place in ice water until cool; peel and discard skins. Cut chiles in half lengthwise; discard seeds and membranes. Coarsely chop chiles; set aside.

Coat a large skillet with cooking spray, and place over medium-high heat until hot. Place onion slices in a single layer in skillet, and cook 5 minutes on each side. Remove onion slices, and set aside. Coat skillet with cooking spray; place mango wedges in a single layer in skillet, and cook 4 minutes.

Chop mango wedges. Combine Anaheim chile, onion, and mango in a bowl; stir in lime juice and remaining ingredients. Serve at room temperature or chilled with roasted game or grilled chicken, fish, or beef. Store salsa in an airtight container in the refrigerator. Yield: 2 cups (serving size: ¼ cup).

Calories 44 (8% from fat) **Protein** 0.8g **Fat** 0.4g (sat 0.0g) **Carbohydrate** 10.8g **Fiber** 1.3g **Cholesterol** 0mg **Iron** 0.4mg **Sodium** 39mg **Calcium** 14mg

ROASTED RED PEPPER SAUCE

1½   pounds sweet red peppers (about 4 medium)
2   cups canned low-sodium chicken broth, undiluted
1½   teaspoons olive oil
1   cup chopped onion
¾   cup chopped carrot
½   cup chopped celery
½   teaspoon dried whole thyme
¼   teaspoon salt
¼   teaspoon freshly ground pepper
1   (14½-ounce) can no-salt-added whole tomatoes, undrained and chopped
2   cloves garlic, minced

Cut peppers in half lengthwise; remove and discard seeds and membranes. Place peppers, skin side up, on a baking sheet; flatten with palm of hand. Broil 5½ inches from heat (with electric oven door partially opened) 15 to 20 minutes or until charred. Place peppers in ice water until cool; peel and discard skins. Chop peppers; set aside.

Combine broth and oil in a large nonstick skillet, and bring to a simmer over medium heat. Add onion, carrot, and celery, and cook 10 minutes or until tender, stirring occasionally. Add chopped pepper, thyme, and remaining ingredients; cover and cook 5 minutes. Reduce heat, and simmer, uncovered, 25 minutes or until thickened.

Position knife blade in food processor bowl; add roasted pepper mixture. Process 30 seconds or until smooth, scraping sides of processor bowl once.

Serve sauce with tortilla chips, grilled fish, poultry, or pasta. Store in an airtight container in the refrigerator up to 1 week. Yield: 3⅓ cups (serving size: ⅓ cup).

Calories 46 (25% from fat) **Protein** 1.6g **Fat** 1.3g (sat 0.2g) **Carbohydrate** 8.1g **Fiber** 1.6g **Cholesterol** 0mg **Iron** 1.3mg **Sodium** 90mg **Calcium** 28mg

FRESH TOMATO SAUCE

This sauce is also great with grilled poultry or steak, as a pizza topping, or spooned over polenta or eggs. For tips on seeding tomatoes, see page 182.

Vegetable cooking spray
1   tablespoon olive oil
1   cup finely chopped onion
3   cloves garlic, minced
5½ cups seeded, chopped
    tomato (about 3 pounds)
¼   cup chopped fresh basil
½   teaspoon salt
¼   teaspoon pepper

Coat a large nonstick skillet with cooking spray. Add oil, and place over medium heat until hot. Add onion and garlic; sauté 3 minutes or until tender. Add tomato and remaining ingredients; stir well, and bring to a boil. Reduce heat to medium-low, and cook, uncovered, 10 minutes or until reduced to 4 cups, stirring occasionally. Serve over pasta. Store sauce in an airtight container in the refrigerator. Yield: 4 cups (serving size: ½ cup).

Calories 42 (24% from fat) Protein 1.4g Fat 1.1g (sat 0.1g) Carbohydrate 8.0g Fiber 2.0g Cholesterol 0mg Iron 0.6mg Sodium 159mg Calcium 15mg

SELECTING SAVORY TOMATOES

If you aren't picking them right off the vine, use these tips:
• Choose well-shaped tomatoes that are heavy for their size.
• Look for tomatoes that are slightly soft when squeezed.
• Once ripe, tomatoes will keep in the refrigerator one or two days.

MARINARA SAUCE

QUICK & EASY

When fresh tomatoes aren't in season, you can make this in a matter of minutes—it's made with canned tomatoes. Serve it with pasta or as dipping sauce for breadsticks.

1   tablespoon olive oil
¾   cup chopped onion
1   teaspoon dried rosemary,
    crushed
4   cloves garlic, crushed
½   teaspoon sugar
¼   teaspoon salt
¼   teaspoon pepper
1   (14½-ounce) can no-salt-
    added whole tomatoes,
    undrained and chopped
¼   cup finely chopped fresh
    basil

Heat olive oil in a medium saucepan over medium heat. Add onion, rosemary, and garlic; sauté

3 minutes. Add sugar and next 3 ingredients; cook, uncovered, over medium heat 10 minutes, stirring often. Remove from heat, and stir in basil. Serve with pasta or breadsticks. Store sauce in an airtight container in the refrigerator. Yield: 1¾ cups (serving size: ¼ cup).

Calories 40 (45% from fat) Protein 0.8g Fat 2.0g (sat 0.3g) Carbohydrate 5.2g Fiber 0.4g Cholesterol 0mg Iron 0.4mg Sodium 92mg Calcium 29mg

BLACK-EYED PEA AND TOMATO SALSA

QUICK & EASY

Serve this salsa over grilled pork or boneless chicken breasts. Save any extra to serve as a dip with baked tortilla chips.

Vegetable cooking spray
1   cup chopped onion
½   cup chopped lean
    Canadian-style bacon
2   cloves garlic, minced
¼   teaspoon ground cumin
¼   teaspoon pepper
1   (15-ounce) can black-eyed
    peas, drained
1   (14½-ounce) can no-salt-
    added whole tomatoes,
    undrained and chopped
⅓   cup minced fresh cilantro
1   tablespoon seeded, finely
    chopped jalapeño pepper

Coat a large nonstick skillet with cooking spray; place over medium

Black-Eyed Pea and
Tomato Salsa

heat until hot. Add onion, bacon, and garlic, and sauté 5 minutes. Stir in cumin and next 3 ingredients; bring to a boil. Remove from heat, and stir in cilantro and jalapeño. Spoon salsa into a bowl; cover and chill 1 to 8 hours.

Serve at room temperature with pork or chicken or as a dip with Italian bread or no-oil-baked tortilla chips. Store in an airtight container in the refrigerator. Yield: 3½ cups (serving size: ¼ cup).

Calories 42 (13% from fat) Protein 3.2g Fat 0.6g (sat 0.2g) Carbohydrate 6.5g Fiber 0.7g Cholesterol 3mg Iron 0.6mg Sodium 147mg Calcium 22mg

SALSA DEFINED

Although most traditional salsas consist of chiles, onions, and tomatoes, many of today's salsas are made with uncooked fruits or vegetables. Consistency ranges from thick sauces to relishlike chopped mixtures.

SUN-DRIED TOMATO-AVOCADO SALSA

½   ounce sun-dried tomatoes, packed without oil (about 6)
1   cup boiling water
1¼   cups diced plum tomato
¾   cup peeled, diced avocado (about 1 large)
¼   cup finely chopped purple onion
2   tablespoons chopped fresh basil
1   tablespoon seeded, finely chopped jalapeño pepper
2   tablespoons orange juice
2   teaspoons grated lemon rind
¼   teaspoon salt
¼   teaspoon pepper
1   clove garlic, crushed

Combine sun-dried tomatoes and boiling water in a small bowl; let stand 30 minutes. Drain and chop.

Combine chopped sun-dried tomato, plum tomato, and remaining ingredients in a bowl; stir well. Serve at room temperature with pork or chicken. Yield: 2½ cups (serving size: ¼ cup).

Calories 28 (58% from fat) **Protein** 0.6g **Fat** 1.8g (sat 0.3g) **Carbohydrate** 3.1g **Fiber** 0.7g **Cholesterol** 0mg **Iron** 0.3mg **Sodium** 92mg **Calcium** 6mg

MADEIRA-MUSHROOM SAUCE

Even though this sauce is made with turkey drippings, the gravy tastes great served with beef. One taste and you'll never go back to cream gravy. Be sure to follow the directions (at right) for degreasing turkey drippings. The drippings give the gravy its flavor, but degreasing is the key to making it low fat.

1½   teaspoons margarine
½   cup sliced fresh mushrooms
½   teaspoon dried thyme
1¼   cups degreased turkey drippings
½   cup Madeira
1   teaspoon lemon juice
¼   teaspoon salt
2   tablespoons cornstarch
2   tablespoons water

Melt margarine in a heavy saucepan over medium-high heat. Add mushrooms and thyme, and sauté 3 minutes or until tender. Add drippings, Madeira, lemon juice, and salt; bring mixture to a boil. Combine cornstarch and water, stirring with a wire whisk; add to sauce. Bring to a boil, and cook, stirring constantly, 1 minute or until slightly thickened. Serve with beef or poultry. Yield: 2 cups (serving size: ⅓ cup).

Calories 57 (38% from fat) **Protein** 4.3g **Fat** 2.4g (sat 0.6g) **Carbohydrate** 4.6g **Fiber** 0.3g **Cholesterol** 9mg **Iron** 0.8mg **Sodium** 132mg **Calcium** 9mg

HOW TO DEGREASE TURKEY DRIPPINGS

It's easier than you think to remove the fat from the drippings left in the roasting pan after roasting a turkey. The simplest way is to chill the drippings overnight and then to lift off the solidified fat. But here's a quicker way to do it:

Place the drippings in a large heavy-duty, zip-top plastic bag (the fat will rise to the top). Carefully snip off one corner of the bag. Begin draining the drippings into a 4-cup measure or large bowl, stopping before the fat layer reaches the opening. Cover; refrigerate the drippings.

TURKEY GRAVY

Be sure to follow the directions above to degrease the drippings.

1   tablespoon margarine
3   tablespoons all-purpose flour
1   cup canned low-sodium chicken broth, undiluted
1   cup degreased turkey drippings
¼   cup dry white wine
¼   teaspoon salt

Melt margarine in a medium-size heavy saucepan over medium heat. Stir in all-purpose flour, and cook,

Turkey Gravy

APPLE BUTTER

Any good cooking apple can be used in place of Winesap.

4   large Winesap apples, peeled, cored, and each cut into 8 wedges
1   cup unsweetened apple juice
½   cup firmly packed brown sugar
1   teaspoon ground cinnamon
¼   teaspoon salt
¼   teaspoon ground cloves
⅛   teaspoon ground allspice

Combine apple wedges and juice in a large saucepan; bring to a boil. Cover, reduce heat, and simmer 12 minutes or until apple wedges are tender, stirring occasionally. Drain apple wedges, discarding liquid.

Position knife blade in food processor bowl; add apple wedges. Process 1 minute or until smooth. Return to saucepan; add brown sugar and remaining ingredients, stirring well.

Cook, uncovered, over medium heat 20 minutes or until mixture is very thick, stirring often. Spoon into hot sterilized jars, filling to ¼-inch from top; wipe jar rims. Cover at once with metal lids, and screw on bands. Store in refrigerator up to 3 weeks. Serve with pancakes, bagels, or low-fat biscuits. Yield: 2½ cups (analysis per 1 tablespoon).

stirring constantly with a wire whisk, 1 minute. Gradually add chicken broth and remaining ingredients, stirring constantly.

Bring mixture to a boil, stirring constantly. Reduce heat; simmer, uncovered, until mixture is slightly thickened. Serve gravy with poultry, dressing, or mashed potatoes. Yield: 2⅓ cups (serving size: ⅓ cup).

Calories 57 (44% from fat) **Protein** 3.3g **Fat** 2.8g (sat 0.6g) **Carbohydrate** 3.2g **Fiber** 0.1g **Cholesterol** 6mg **Iron** 0.6mg **Sodium** 128mg **Calcium** 4mg

Calories 25 (4% from fat) **Protein** 0.0g **Fat** 0.1g (sat 0.0g) **Carbohydrate** 6.4g **Fiber** 0.6g **Cholesterol** 0mg **Iron** 0.1mg **Sodium** 16mg **Calcium** 4mg

How to Cook a Pumpkin

For the best flavor, use a small cooking pumpkin. A 4-pound pumpkin will yield about 4½ cups cubed, cooked pumpkin or 4 cups mashed cooked pumpkin.

To cook fresh pumpkin, here's all you do: Cut the pumpkin in half vertically, and then discard the seeds and stringy pulp. Place the pumpkin, cut side down, in a large shallow baking dish. Add water to a depth of ½ inch. Bake at 350° for 1 hour or until the pumpkin is crisp-tender when pierced with a fork; cool. (The pumpkin should be tender enough to mash, yet firm enough to handle when cut into cubes.) Cut each half into wedges, and peel. You can substitute acorn or butternut squash for pumpkin in most recipes.

Fresh Pumpkin Chutney

¾   cup apple juice
½   cup dry white wine
½   cup cider vinegar
¼   cup firmly packed brown sugar
1   teaspoon grated orange rind
¼   teaspoon ground cinnamon
⅛   teaspoon ground nutmeg
¼   cup dried currants
2½   cups cooked, diced fresh pumpkin

Combine first 7 ingredients in a large saucepan; bring to a boil over medium-high heat. Add currants; reduce heat, and simmer 5 minutes. Add pumpkin; cook 15 additional minutes, stirring occasionally. Spoon mixture into a bowl; let cool to room temperature. Serve with chicken or pork. Store chutney in an airtight container in the refrigerator up to 2 weeks. Yield: 2½ cups (serving size: ¼ cup).

Calories 50 (4% from fat) **Protein** 0.5g **Fat** 0.2g (sat 0.0g) **Carbohydrate** 12.8g **Fiber** 0.4g **Cholesterol** 0mg **Iron** 0.6mg **Sodium** 5mg **Calcium** 18mg

Fresh Mango Chutney

6   whole cloves
4   whole allspice
4   whole cardamom
1   (3-inch) stick cinnamon, broken
1½   cups peeled, diced ripe mango
¾   cup cider vinegar
½   cup coarsely chopped onion
⅓   cup firmly packed brown sugar
¼   cup golden raisins
1½   teaspoons peeled, minced gingerroot
1   jalapeño pepper
1   clove garlic, minced

Place first 4 ingredients on a square of cheesecloth; tie with string.

Combine diced mango and remaining 7 ingredients in a saucepan. Add spice bag to pan. Bring mixture to a boil; reduce heat, and simmer, uncovered, 45 minutes or until mixture is thickened, stirring often. Remove spice bag and jalapeño pepper from saucepan, and discard.

Serve with pork, ham, lamb, or chicken. Store chutney in an airtight container in the refrigerator up to 2 weeks. Yield: 1½ cups (analysis per 1 tablespoon).

Calories 28 (3% from fat) **Protein** 0.2g **Fat** 0.1g (sat 0.0g) **Carbohydrate** 7.3g **Fiber** 0.3g **Cholesterol** 0mg **Iron** 0.2mg **Sodium** 2mg **Calcium** 6mg

GRAPEFRUIT-CRANBERRY MARMALADE

Make this marmalade in winter when grapefruit is in season. Store grapefruit in a plastic bag in the vegetable drawer of the refrigerator, and it will keep up to two weeks. For tips on sectioning the grapefruit, see our step-by-step instructions on page 122.

4	medium grapefruit (about 4 pounds)
1½	cups water
2½	cups fresh cranberries
3	cups sugar

Using a vegetable peeler, carefully remove rind from grapefruit; discard bitter white pith. Cut grapefruit rind into julienne strips. Peel and section grapefruit.

Combine grapefruit rind, sections, and water in a large saucepan; bring mixture to a boil. Reduce heat to medium, and simmer 15 minutes, stirring occasionally. Add cranberries, and cook 10 minutes. Stir in sugar; cook 30 minutes or until mixture is slightly thickened, stirring occasionally. Pour into decorative jars or airtight containers. Store in refrigerator up to 3 weeks. Serve with bagels, scones, or low-fat biscuits. Yield: 5¼ cups (serving size: 2 tablespoons).

Calories 65 (0% from fat) Protein 0.2g Fat 0.0g (sat 0.0g) Carbohydrate 16.8g Fiber 0.2g Cholesterol 0mg Iron 0.0mg Sodium 0mg Calcium 3mg

Easy Refrigerator Pickles

EASY REFRIGERATOR PICKLES

Traditional bread and butter pickles have 50% more sugar and seven times as much salt as these.

6	cups thinly sliced cucumber (about 2 pounds)
2	cups thinly sliced onion
1½	cups white vinegar
1	cup sugar
½	teaspoon salt
½	teaspoon mustard seeds
½	teaspoon celery seeds
½	teaspoon ground turmeric

Place half of cucumber in a large glass bowl; top with half of onion.

Repeat layering procedure with remaining cucumber and onion.

Combine vinegar and remaining 5 ingredients in a saucepan; stir well. Bring to a boil; boil 1 minute.

Pour vinegar mixture over cucumber and onion; let mixture cool. Cover and marinate pickles in refrigerator 4 days. Store in refrigerator up to 1 month. Yield: 6½ cups (serving size: ¼ cup).

Calories 40 (2% from fat) Protein 0.4g Fat 0.1g (sat 0.0g) Carbohydrate 10.3g Fiber 0.5g Cholesterol 0mg Iron 0.2mg Sodium 46mg Calcium 8mg

Gratin Dauphinois,
page 168

JUST BECAUSE IT'S SERVED ON THE SIDE DOESN'T MEAN A RECIPE SHOULDN'T GET STAR BILLING. BESIDES, YOU KNOW THAT FRUITS, VEGETABLES, AND GRAINS ARE GOOD FOR YOU.

BUT NO MATTER HOW HEALTHY RICE, BARLEY, GRITS, OR ANY FOOD MAY BE,

SIDES

YOU'LL ONLY SERVE IT AGAIN AND AGAIN IF IT TASTES GOOD. FORTUNATELY, WE'VE DISCOVERED LOW-FAT COOKING TECHNIQUES LIKE GRILL-SMOKING AND OVEN ROASTING, AND FLAVOR ENHANCERS LIKE FRESH HERBS AND SEASONINGS THAT MAKE ANY SIDE SENSATIONAL.

SPEAKING OF SENSATIONAL, BE SURE YOU TRY GRATIN DAUPHINOIS. CALL IT BY ITS FRENCH NAME FOR DINNER GUESTS, BUT TELL THE KIDS IT'S SCALLOPED POTATOES AND CHEESE.

CARIBBEAN BANANAS

QUICK & EASY

2   medium-size firm, ripe
     bananas (about ¾ pound)
1   tablespoon reduced-calorie
     margarine
½   teaspoon curry powder
⅛   teaspoon ground ginger
⅛   teaspoon chili powder

Peel bananas. Cut each in half crosswise; then cut in half lengthwise. Set aside.

Melt margarine in a large nonstick skillet over medium-high heat. Add curry powder, ginger, and chili powder to skillet, and cook 30 seconds. Add bananas; cook 1 minute. Turn bananas; cook 1 additional minute. Yield: 2 servings (serving size: 4 banana pieces).

Calories 184 (18% from fat) **Protein** 1.8g **Fat** 3.7g (sat 0.8g) **Carbohydrate** 40.3g **Fiber** 5.2g **Cholesterol** 0mg **Iron** 0.7mg **Sodium** 73mg **Calcium** 15mg

CITRUS AND DRIED FRUIT COMPOTE

If you can't find dried tart cherries in your supermarket, substitute another dried fruit, or order them by mail from The Wooden Spoon Catalog (800-431-2207) or Melissa's/World Variety Produce Inc. (800-468-7111).

1   cup water
⅔   cup sugar
¾   cup dried apricot halves
⅓   cup dried tart cherries
¼   cup golden raisins
2   cups pink grapefruit sections
     (about 2 large grapefruit)
2   cups orange sections (about
     3 large oranges)
1   teaspoon chopped fresh
     mint

Combine water and sugar in a saucepan; bring to a boil. Add apricot halves, cherries, and raisins; stir well. Cover, reduce heat, and simmer 10 minutes. Pour mixture into a bowl; cool. Stir in grapefruit sections, orange sections, and chopped mint. Serve chilled or at room temperature. Yield: 10 servings (serving size: ½ cup).

Calories 143 (2% from fat) **Protein** 1.4g **Fat** 0.3g (sat 0.0g) **Carbohydrate** 36.8g **Fiber** 2.7g **Cholesterol** 0mg **Iron** 0.8mg **Sodium** 9mg **Calcium** 32mg

CHILLED ASPARAGUS WITH FETA VINAIGRETTE

QUICK & EASY

You can also serve this dressing over salmon or salad greens.

1¼   pounds asparagus
2   tablespoons crumbled
     reduced-fat feta cheese
2½   tablespoons lemon juice
1½   tablespoons orange juice
1   tablespoon water
2   teaspoons Dijon mustard
1   teaspoon vegetable oil
2   drops hot sauce
½   cup diced sweet red pepper

Snap off tough ends of asparagus. Remove scales from stalks with a knife or vegetable peeler, if desired. Arrange asparagus spoke-fashion on a 12-inch round glass platter, stem ends out. Cover with heavy-duty plastic wrap, and vent. Microwave at HIGH 4 minutes or until crisp-tender, rotating platter a half-turn after 2 minutes. Let stand, covered, 2 minutes. Cover and chill.

Combine cheese and next 6 ingredients, and stir with a wire whisk. Arrange asparagus evenly on 4 individual serving plates; top each serving with 2 tablespoons feta cheese dressing and 2 tablespoons diced pepper. Yield: 4 servings.

Calories 69 (35% from fat) **Protein** 4.6g **Fat** 2.7g (sat 0.9g) **Carbohydrate** 8.9g **Fiber** 3.2g **Cholesterol** 3mg **Iron** 1.4mg **Sodium** 171mg **Calcium** 32mg

ASPARAGUS AND CHEESE SOUFFLÉ

2   cups water
¾   cup chopped fresh asparagus
1   cup skim milk
1   tablespoon cornstarch
2   egg yolks, lightly beaten
¼   cup (1 ounce) shredded reduced-fat sharp Cheddar cheese
¼   teaspoon salt
¼   teaspoon dried whole dillweed
⅛   teaspoon coarsely ground pepper
4   egg whites
Vegetable cooking spray

Bring water to a boil in a small saucepan; add asparagus. Cook 3 minutes; drain and set aside.

Combine milk and cornstarch in a saucepan, and stir well. Bring to a boil over medium heat, and cook, stirring constantly, 2 minutes.

Gradually stir about one-fourth of hot milk mixture into 2 beaten egg yolks; add to remaining hot mixture, stirring constantly. Cook, stirring constantly, 1 minute or until thickened. Add cheese and next 3 ingredients, stirring until cheese melts. Stir in asparagus.

Beat 4 egg whites at high speed of an electric mixer until stiff peaks form. Stir one-fourth of beaten egg whites into asparagus mixture, and fold remaining egg whites into asparagus mixture.

Spoon mixture into a 2-quart soufflé dish coated with cooking spray. Place on middle rack of a 400° oven; immediately reduce temperature to 375°, and bake 40 minutes. Serve immediately. Yield: 6 servings (serving size: ¾ cup).

Calories 72 (36% from fat) **Protein** 6.6g **Fat** 2.9g (sat 1.1g) **Carbohydrate** 4.7g **Fiber** 0.3g **Cholesterol** 77mg **Iron** 0.4mg **Sodium** 194mg **Calcium** 107mg

BAKED BEANS

3   cups dried Great Northern beans
8   cups water
1¼   cups chopped onion
1   cup barbecue sauce
¾   cup firmly packed brown sugar
¼   cup molasses
1   tablespoon prepared mustard
½   teaspoon salt
¼   teaspoon pepper
⅛   teaspoon garlic powder
4   slices turkey bacon, cut crosswise into ¼-inch strips

Sort and wash beans; place in an ovenproof Dutch oven. Cover with water to a depth of 2 inches above beans, and bring to a boil; cook 2 minutes. Remove from heat; cover and let stand 1 hour.

Drain beans, and return to Dutch oven. Add 8 cups water and onion; bring to a boil. Cover, reduce heat, and simmer 2 hours or until tender.

Drain bean mixture; return to Dutch oven. Add barbecue sauce and remaining ingredients, and stir well. Cover and bake at 350° for 1 hour. Yield: 16 servings (serving size: ½ cup).

Calories 198 (11% from fat) **Protein** 9.6g **Fat** 2.5g (sat 0.6g) **Carbohydrate** 34.4g **Fiber** 13.9g **Cholesterol** 9mg **Iron** 2.4mg **Sodium** 400mg **Calcium** 82mg

GREEN BEANS WITH ONION AND SAVORY

QUICK & EASY

Both summer and winter savory varieties taste like a cross between thyme and mint. Summer savory is slightly milder than the winter savory; use both with discretion.

1¼   pounds fresh green beans
2   tablespoons chopped fresh savory
½   cup vertically sliced purple onion
2   teaspoons olive oil
¼   teaspoon salt
Dash of freshly ground pepper

Wash beans; trim ends, and remove strings. Arrange beans in a vegetable steamer over boiling water; sprinkle savory over beans. Cover and steam 20 minutes or until crisp-tender. Combine bean mixture and onion in a bowl. Combine olive oil, salt, and pepper; add to bean mixture. Toss gently. Serve warm. Yield: 5 servings (serving size: 1 cup).

Calories 55 (33% from fat) **Protein** 2.1g **Fat** 2.0g (sat 0.3g) **Carbohydrate** 9.1g **Fiber** 2.6g **Cholesterol** 0mg **Iron** 1.3mg **Sodium** 124mg **Calcium** 56mg

Green Bean Casserole

GREEN BEAN CASSEROLE

Vegetable cooking spray
¼ cup finely chopped onion
2 tablespoons all-purpose flour
1 cup skim milk
½ cup (2 ounces) shredded reduced-sodium, reduced-fat Swiss cheese
½ cup low-fat sour cream
1 teaspoon sugar
½ teaspoon salt
2 (9-ounce) packages frozen French-style green beans, thawed and drained
1 egg white, lightly beaten
1½ cups herb-seasoned stuffing mix
2 teaspoons margarine, melted

Coat a medium saucepan with cooking spray; place over medium heat until hot. Add onion to pan; sauté 5 minutes or until onion is tender. Add flour, and cook, stirring constantly, 1 minute. Gradually add milk, stirring until blended. Stir in Swiss cheese, sour cream, sugar, and salt; cook, stirring constantly, 5 minutes or until mixture is thickened and bubbly.

Place green beans in an 8-inch square baking dish, and pour Swiss cheese sauce over beans. Combine egg white, stuffing mix, and margarine in a medium bowl. Stir mixture well, and sprinkle over green bean mixture. Bake at 350° for 25 minutes or until casserole is thoroughly heated. Yield: 8 servings (serving size: ½ cup).

Calories 139 (30% from fat) **Protein** 6.9g **Fat** 4.7g (sat 2.1g) **Carbohydrate** 18.7g **Fiber** 2.1g **Cholesterol** 11mg **Iron** 0.8mg **Sodium** 382mg **Calcium** 169mg

BROCCOLI WITH DIJON VINAIGRETTE

QUICK & EASY

2¼ pounds fresh broccoli
2 teaspoons olive oil
¼ cup finely chopped green onions
½ teaspoon dried tarragon
½ teaspoon dry mustard
3 cloves garlic, minced
2 tablespoons red wine vinegar
2 tablespoons water
1 tablespoon Dijon mustard
⅛ teaspoon salt
¼ teaspoon pepper

Remove broccoli leaves, and cut off tough ends of stalks; discard. Wash broccoli, and cut into spears. Arrange broccoli in a steamer basket over boiling water. Cover and steam

6 minutes or until crisp-tender. Place in a serving bowl; keep warm.

Heat oil in a small saucepan over medium heat. Add green onions and next 3 ingredients, and sauté 3 minutes. Remove from heat; add vinegar and remaining 4 ingredients, stirring with a wire whisk until blended. Drizzle over broccoli, tossing gently to coat. Yield: 8 servings.

Calories 52 (29% from fat) Protein 4.0g Fat 1.7g (sat 0.2g) Carbohydrate 7.6g Fiber 4.1g Cholesterol 0mg Iron 1.2mg Sodium 126mg Calcium 67mg

BROCCOLI-RICE CASSEROLE

2   (10-ounce) packages frozen chopped broccoli, thawed and drained
1   tablespoon plus 2 teaspoons margarine, divided
¼   cup chopped onion
3   tablespoons all-purpose flour
½   teaspoon dry mustard
1¼ cups skim milk
½   teaspoon salt
⅛   teaspoon pepper
1¾ cups cooked long-grain rice (cooked without salt or fat)
1   cup (4 ounces) shredded reduced-fat sharp Cheddar cheese
¼   cup nonfat mayonnaise
Vegetable cooking spray
⅓   cup crushed unsalted whole grain Melba toast (about 5)

Cook broccoli in boiling water to cover 3 minutes; drain and set aside.

Melt 1 tablespoon plus 1 teaspoon margarine in a medium saucepan over medium heat; add onion. Cook, stirring constantly, 3 minutes or until onion is tender. Add flour and mustard; cook, stirring constantly with a wire whisk, 1 minute. Gradually add milk, stirring constantly. Cook, stirring constantly, 2 additional minutes or until mixture is thickened and bubbly. Remove from heat, and stir in salt and pepper. Combine broccoli, milk mixture, rice, cheese, and mayonnaise in a large bowl; stir well. Spoon into a shallow 2-quart casserole coated with cooking spray.

Melt remaining 1 teaspoon margarine; combine melted margarine and Melba toast crumbs, stirring well. Sprinkle crumb mixture over broccoli mixture. Bake, uncovered, at 350° for 25 minutes or until thoroughly heated. Yield: 6 servings (serving size: ¾ cup).

Calories 214 (31% from fat) Protein 9.9g Fat 7.3g (sat 2.8g) Carbohydrate 48.2g Fiber 1.8g Cholesterol 14mg Iron 1.1mg Sodium 530mg Calcium 258mg

GARLIC-MARINATED CARROTS

QUICK & EASY

To save time, buy preshredded carrots, or shred your own in a food processor.

2   tablespoons white wine vinegar
1   tablespoon olive oil
¼   teaspoon salt
¼   teaspoon pepper
5   cups coarsely shredded carrot (about 1½ pounds)
4   cloves garlic, thinly sliced or crushed
1   bay leaf

Combine first 4 ingredients in a large bowl; stir well with a wire whisk. Add carrot, garlic, and bay leaf; toss well to coat. Cover and chill at least 8 hours. Discard bay leaf before serving. Yield: 5 servings (serving size: 1 cup).

Calories 76 (34% from fat) Protein 1.3g Fat 2.9g (sat 0.4g) Carbohydrate 12.2g Fiber 3.6g Cholesterol 0mg Iron 0.7mg Sodium 157mg Calcium 37mg

MARBLED CARROTS AND PARSNIPS

3   cups sliced carrot (about 1 pound)
4   cups water, divided
3   cups sliced parsnip (about 1 pound)
1   cup skim milk, divided
1   tablespoon plus 1 teaspoon reduced-calorie margarine, divided
½   teaspoon vanilla extract
2   teaspoons sugar
¼   teaspoon salt

Combine carrot slices and 2 cups water in a medium saucepan. Bring to a boil; cover, reduce heat, and simmer 35 minutes or until very tender. Drain well; set carrot aside.

Combine parsnip and remaining 2 cups water in a medium saucepan. Bring to a boil; cover, reduce heat, and simmer 20 minutes or until very tender. Drain well, and set parsnip aside.

Position knife blade in food processor bowl. Place carrot, ½ cup milk, 2 teaspoons margarine, and vanilla in processor bowl; process until smooth. Place mixture in a saucepan; cook over medium-low heat 5 minutes or until thoroughly heated, stirring occasionally. Set mixture aside.

Rinse and dry processor bowl and knife blade. Position knife blade in processor bowl. Place parsnip slices, remaining ½ cup milk, remaining 2 teaspoons margarine, sugar, and salt in processor bowl; process until smooth. Place mixture in a saucepan; cook over medium-low heat 5 minutes or until heated.

Spoon carrot mixture into 1 side of a small serving bowl; spoon parsnip mixture into other side. Pull a small rubber spatula through mixtures to create a marbled pattern. Yield: 4 servings (serving size: 1 cup).

Calories 169 (13% from fat) **Protein** 4.3g **Fat** 2.4g (sat 0.4g) **Carbohydrate** 34.0g **Fiber** 4.9g **Cholesterol** 1mg **Iron** 1.1mg **Sodium** 265mg **Calcium** 140mg

HONEY-BAKED ROOT VEGETABLES

Rutabagas look like large turnips with thin, pale yellow skin. Although the flesh is slightly sweet, you can substitute rutabagas for turnips in any recipe.

2   tablespoons honey
1   tablespoon margarine, melted
¼   teaspoon salt
1   pound carrots, cut into 4- x ½-inch sticks
1   small rutabaga (about 1 pound), cut into 4- x ½-inch sticks
Vegetable cooking spray

Combine first 3 ingredients in a large bowl; stir well. Add carrot and rutabaga; toss to coat vegetables.

Arrange carrot and rutabaga sticks in a single layer in a 15- x 10- x 1-inch jellyroll pan coated with cooking spray. Bake at 375° for 1 hour or until vegetables are tender, stirring occasionally. Yield: 4 servings (serving size: 1 cup).

Calories 149 (21% from fat) **Protein** 2.6g **Fat** 3.4g (sat 0.6g) **Carbohydrate** 29.5g **Fiber** 4.9g **Cholesterol** 0mg **Iron** 1.2mg **Sodium** 243mg **Calcium** 87mg

CREAMED CORN

4   ears fresh corn
2   cups 2% low-fat milk, divided
¾   cup coarsely chopped onion
½   teaspoon black peppercorns
¼   cup all-purpose flour
½   teaspoon salt

Cut off tops of corn kernels; scrape milk and remaining pulp from cobs, using the dull side of a knife blade. Set corn pulp aside, and reserve 1 cob. (Discard remaining 3 cobs.)

Cut reserved cob in half. Combine cob halves, 1¾ cups milk, onion, and peppercorns in a medium saucepan; bring to a boil. Reduce heat, and simmer, uncovered, 5 minutes, stirring occasionally. Strain mixture; discard cob halves, onion, and peppercorns.

Combine ¼ cup flour and remaining ¼ cup milk in a medium saucepan, stirring with a wire whisk until blended. Stir in warm milk mixture. Cook over low heat, stirring constantly, 3 minutes or until thickened. Add corn pulp and salt, and stir well. Cook over medium-low heat 15 minutes or until corn is tender, stirring often. Yield: 6 servings (serving size: ½ cup).

Calories 114 (17% from fat) **Protein** 4.8g **Fat** 2.2g (sat 1.1g) **Carbohydrate** 20.4g **Fiber** 2.0g **Cholesterol** 7mg **Iron** 0.6mg **Sodium** 245mg **Calcium** 102mg

BRAISED LEEKS WITH TOMATOES

QUICK & EASY

3	cups chopped leek (about 4 medium)
¾	cup canned low-sodium chicken broth, undiluted
½	teaspoon dried basil
½	teaspoon dried chervil
¼	teaspoon salt
⅛	teaspoon pepper
2	cloves garlic, crushed
¼	cup dry white wine
1	tablespoon cornstarch
1	(14½-ounce) can no-salt-added whole tomatoes, drained and chopped

Combine first 7 ingredients in a 2-quart casserole. Cover; microwave at HIGH 6 minutes, stirring after 3 minutes. Combine wine and cornstarch; stir until blended. Add to leek mixture. Stir in tomatoes. Microwave, uncovered, at HIGH 6 minutes or until thickened and bubbly, stirring after 3 minutes. Yield: 5 servings (serving size: ½ cup).

Calories 62 (6% from fat) **Protein** 1.8g **Fat** 0.4g (sat 0.0g) **Carbohydrate** 13.6g **Fiber** 0.8g **Cholesterol** 0mg **Iron** 1.8mg **Sodium** 149mg **Calcium** 61mg

TECHNIQUE

For Preparing Leeks

1. Remove any tough outer leaves. Trim roots from base. Run cold water between the leaves to thoroughly wash away dirt.

2. Cut tops and dark green stems off leek.

3. Cut leek vertically down the middle.

4. Turn leek horizontally, and chop into small pieces.

UPSIDE-DOWN ONION TART

1   large baking potato (about 1 pound)
2   tablespoons olive oil
⅛   teaspoon salt
⅛   teaspoon pepper
Vegetable cooking spray
1   teaspoon olive oil
3   cups thinly sliced leek
3   tablespoons Neufchâtel or lite ricotta cheese
3   tablespoons freshly grated Romano cheese
3   tablespoons freshly grated Parmesan cheese
½   teaspoon dried thyme
1   tablespoon butter
1   tablespoon sugar
3   medium Vidalia onions (about 1¾ pounds), peeled and halved
2   medium purple onions (about 1 pound), peeled and quartered
2   small onions, peeled and halved
3   tablespoons rice vinegar
1   tablespoon peeled, grated gingerroot
2   large cloves garlic, sliced
Freshly ground pepper
Fresh thyme sprigs

Scrub potato, and pat dry with a paper towel. Cut potato lengthwise into ⅛-inch-thick slices. Combine potato slices, 2 tablespoons oil, salt, and ⅛ teaspoon pepper; toss gently. Coat a large baking sheet with cooking spray; using your finger, trace a

Grilled Eggplant With Sesame Marinade, facing page

12-inch circle on baking sheet; arrange potato slices spoke-fashion on circle, overlapping slices. Bake at 400° for 15 minutes or until tender; set potato crust aside.

Wrap handle of a 10-inch skillet with aluminum foil. Coat skillet with cooking spray; add 1 teaspoon oil, and place over medium heat until hot. Add leek; sauté 5 minutes or until tender. Remove leek from skillet; toss with cheeses and dried thyme, and set aside.

Melt butter in skillet over medium heat; sprinkle sugar over butter. Arrange onion halves and quarters, cut sides up, in skillet; top with leek mixture. Sprinkle vinegar, gingerroot, and sliced garlic over onion mixture. Cover; cook over medium-low heat 20 minutes, shaking skillet

occasionally to loosen onion from skillet bottom. Uncover and cook 8 additional minutes. Bake, uncovered, at 350° for 20 minutes or until onion is tender. Remove from oven; shake skillet to loosen onion from bottom of skillet.

Place potato crust (in sections) on onion mixture in skillet. Bake at 375° for 30 minutes or until potato is lightly browned. Remove from oven; let stand 10 minutes. Shake tart to loosen from skillet; invert tart onto a serving platter. Sprinkle with freshly ground pepper, and garnish with fresh thyme, if desired. Yield: 8 servings (serving size: 1 wedge).

Calories 185 (36% from fat) **Protein** 5.5g **Fat** 7.5g (sat 2.6g) **Carbohydrate** 25.7g **Fiber** 3.1g **Cholesterol** 10mg **Iron** 1.8mg **Sodium** 151mg **Calcium** 125mg

GRILLED EGGPLANT WITH SESAME MARINADE

QUICK & EASY

To toast sesame seeds, spread them in a shallow pan, and bake at 350° for 5 minutes. Stir at least once so they'll toast evenly.

1   (1-pound) eggplant, cut diagonally into 1-inch slices
½   teaspoon salt
1   tablespoon rice vinegar
1   teaspoon sesame seeds, toasted
2   teaspoons dark sesame oil
½   teaspoon lemon juice
⅛   teaspoon dried crushed red pepper
2   cloves garlic, crushed
Vegetable cooking spray

Place eggplant on several layers of paper towels; sprinkle salt over cut sides of eggplant. Let stand 15 minutes; blot dry with paper towels.

Combine rice vinegar and next 5 ingredients; stir well. Brush over eggplant; let stand 10 minutes. Coat grill rack with cooking spray; place on grill over medium-hot coals (350° to 400°). Place eggplant on rack; grill, uncovered, 5 minutes on each side, basting often with remaining sesame seed mixture. Yield: 4 servings (serving size: 1 slice).

Calories 58 (45% from fat) **Protein** 1.5g **Fat** 2.9g (sat 0.4g) **Carbohydrate** 8.1g **Fiber** 1.8g **Cholesterol** 0mg **Iron** 0.8mg **Sodium** 152mg **Calcium** 53mg

ROASTED PEPPERS

QUICK & EASY

Toss these peppers into a pasta dish, or serve them as a nonfat topping for grilled steaks or chicken breasts.

3   medium-size sweet red peppers (about 1¼ pounds)
3   medium-size yellow peppers (about 1¼ pounds)
2   tablespoons balsamic vinegar
¼   teaspoon salt

Cut peppers in half lengthwise; remove and discard seeds and membranes. Place peppers, skin side up, on a baking sheet; flatten with palm of hand. Broil 5½ inches from heat (with electric oven door partially opened) 15 to 20 minutes or until charred. Place in ice water until cool; peel and discard skins. Cut peppers into strips.

Combine roasted pepper strips, balsamic vinegar, and salt in a bowl, and toss well. Yield: 3 cups (serving size: ½ cup).

Calories 23 (16% from fat) **Protein** 0.8g **Fat** 0.4g (sat 0.1g) **Carbohydrate** 4.9g **Fiber** 1.5g **Cholesterol** 0mg **Iron** 1.2mg **Sodium** 101mg **Calcium** 6mg

STEP BY STEP

Roasted Peppers

1. Cut the peppers in half, and remove the seeds and membranes. Then place the peppers on a baking sheet, and press each with the palm of your hand to flatten them.

2. Broil the peppers 5½ inches from heat 15 to 20 minutes or until the skins are blackened. Immediately plunge the charred peppers into a bowl of ice water.

3. Peel the charred skins from the peppers, and discard the pepper skins. The soft, slippery roasted pepper flesh will be ready to use or to freeze.

"I have lots of favorites from the magazine, but this recipe is one I make at home all the time. It's quick, easy, and goes with anything. It's gourmet-in-a-flash and unbelievably decadent."

—Jill G. Melton,
Senior Food Editor

GRATIN DAUPHINOIS

QUICK & EASY

In this recipe, more commonly known as scalloped potatoes with cheese, the cheese mixture bubbles up in the dish while it cooks. Don't worry; it won't run over, but will result in golden, crispy edges.

1   clove garlic, halved
Butter-flavored vegetable cooking spray
6   medium-size red potatoes, peeled and cut into ⅛-inch-thick slices (about 2 pounds)
2   tablespoons margarine, melted
½   teaspoon salt
⅛   teaspoon pepper
½   cup (2 ounces) grated Gruyère cheese
1   cup skim milk

Rub inside of a 1½-quart casserole with cut sides of garlic. Discard garlic. Coat dish with cooking spray.
Arrange half of potato slices in casserole. Drizzle with 1 tablespoon margarine. Sprinkle with half of salt, half of pepper, and half of cheese. Repeat procedure with remaining potato slices, margarine, salt, pepper, and cheese.
Bring milk to a boil in a small saucepan over low heat. Pour milk over potato mixture.
Bake potato mixture, uncovered, at 425° for 40 minutes or until potato is tender. Let stand 10 minutes before serving. Yield: 7 servings (serving size: 1 cup).

Calories 165 (33% from fat) Protein 6.0g Fat 6.1g (sat 2.2g) Carbohydrate 22.2g Fiber 1.8g Cholesterol 10mg Iron 0.9mg Sodium 258mg Calcium 134mg

POTATO GRATIN

Vegetable cooking spray
1   cup chopped onion
1   clove garlic, halved
6   medium baking potatoes, peeled and cut into ⅛-inch-thick slices (about 2½ pounds)
¼   teaspoon salt
¼   teaspoon freshly ground pepper
¾   cup (3 ounces) shredded extra-sharp Cheddar cheese
¼   cup freshly grated Romano cheese
1¾   cups canned low-sodium chicken broth, undiluted
1   cup evaporated skimmed milk

Coat a small nonstick skillet with cooking spray; place over medium heat until hot. Add onion, and sauté 5 minutes or until tender; set aside.
Rub a shallow 3-quart baking dish with cut sides of garlic halves; discard garlic. Coat dish with cooking spray. Arrange one-third of potato slices in prepared baking dish, and sprinkle with ⅛ teaspoon salt and ⅛ teaspoon pepper. Top with half of sautéed onion and half of Cheddar and Romano cheeses. Repeat layers, ending with remaining potato slices.
Bring broth and milk to a boil over low heat in a small saucepan; pour over potato mixture. Bake, uncovered, at 425° for 50 minutes or until tender. Let stand 5 minutes before serving. Yield: 6 servings (serving size: 1 cup).

Calories 245 (25% from fat) Protein 12.2g Fat 6.9g (sat 4.0g) Carbohydrate 34.3g Fiber 2.9g Cholesterol 21mg Iron 1.7mg Sodium 323mg Calcium 294mg

SPUD FACTS

One medium potato (about 6 ounces) has about 180 calories and less than ¼ gram of fat. Besides providing 3 grams of fiber, a reasonable amount of niacin, riboflavin, and thiamine, and almost half of the adult requirement for vitamin C, a potato contains more potassium than bananas and has practically no sodium.

"I make these potatoes for company because they serve 10 people and are very impressive looking. The finished recipe looks like rocks cut open to expose their colorful minerals."

——John Stark, Senior Editor

INDIAN STUFFED POTATOES

1	cup grated fresh coconut or ½ cup flaked sweet coconut
⅛	teaspoon baking soda
2	cups chopped fresh cilantro
1	tablespoon all-purpose flour
1	teaspoon salt
1	teaspoon seeded, minced serrano chile
1	teaspoon peeled, grated gingerroot
20	small round red potatoes (about 1½ pounds)
2	tablespoons vegetable oil
5	whole cloves
1	(3-inch) cinnamon stick
1½	cups finely chopped onion
2	teaspoons ground cardamom
1	teaspoon ground ginger
¼	teaspoon chili powder
2	cups water
¼	cup plain nonfat yogurt

Combine coconut and baking soda in a medium bowl; toss well. Add 2 cups cilantro and next 4 ingredients; stir well. Set sauce aside.

Using a melon baller, scoop a hole out of center of each potato. Stuff center of each potato with coconut mixture, reserving any remaining coconut mixture.

Heat oil in a large nonstick skillet over medium-high heat. Add cloves and cinnamon stick; sauté 1 minute. Remove spices from oil with a slotted spoon, and discard. Add onion to skillet; sauté 3 minutes or until tender. Stir in cardamom, ground ginger, and chili powder. Add potatoes to skillet, stuffed sides up; sprinkle with reserved coconut mixture. Combine water and yogurt, and stir well. Pour mixture over potatoes; bring to a boil. Cover, reduce heat, and simmer 40 minutes or until tender; remove from heat. Cut potatoes in half horizontally, and serve with sauce. Yield: 10 servings (serving size: 4 potato halves and 3 tablespoons sauce).

Calories 147 (29% from fat) **Protein** 3.3g **Fat** 4.8g (sat 2.1g) **Carbohydrate** 24.0g **Fiber** 3.0g **Cholesterol** 0mg **Iron** 1.9mg **Sodium** 267mg **Calcium** 52mg

CREAMED PUMPKIN POTATOES

If you don't have fresh pumpkin, substitute 2¼ cups canned unsweetened pumpkin instead.

4	cups (1½-inch) peeled, cubed baking potato (about 1½ pounds)
3	cups cubed, cooked fresh pumpkin
¼	cup (1 ounce) shredded sharp Cheddar cheese
¼	cup sour cream (at room temperature)
½	teaspoon salt
⅛	teaspoon ground white pepper

Place potato in a large saucepan; add water to cover, and bring to a boil. Cover and cook 30 minutes or until tender; drain.

Combine potato, pumpkin, and remaining ingredients; beat at medium speed of an electric mixer until smooth. Yield: 5 servings (serving size: 1 cup).

Calories 161 (25% from fat) **Protein** 4.9g **Fat** 4.5g (sat 2.8g) **Carbohydrate** 26.7g **Fiber** 2.7g **Cholesterol** 11mg **Iron** 1.5mg **Sodium** 283mg **Calcium** 79mg

GRILLED POTATO AND PEPPER KABOBS

6 small round red potatoes, halved (about ½ pound)
2 tablespoons water
1 small sweet red pepper
¼ cup tomato juice
2 tablespoons chopped fresh basil
2 tablespoons finely chopped green onions
1 teaspoon olive oil
½ teaspoon Dijon mustard
⅛ teaspoon pepper
Vegetable cooking spray

Combine potato halves and water in a 1-quart casserole. Cover and microwave at HIGH 4 minutes or until crisp-tender; drain. Thread 6 potato halves onto each of 2 (10-inch) skewers; set aside.

Cut red pepper in half lengthwise; discard seeds and membranes. Cut each half into 6 (1-inch) squares. Thread squares onto a 10-inch skewer; set aside.

Combine tomato juice and next 5 ingredients. Reserve 2 tablespoons tomato juice mixture; set aside.

Coat grill rack with cooking spray; place on grill over medium-hot coals (350° to 400°). Place potato kabobs on rack; grill, covered, 2 minutes, basting often with tomato juice mixture. Add pepper kabobs to rack; grill, covered, 6 minutes, basting often with tomato juice mixture. Remove vegetables from skewers; toss with reserved 2 tablespoons tomato juice mixture. Yield:

2 servings (serving size: 6 potato halves and 6 pepper squares).

Calories 124 (21% from fat) Protein 3.2g Fat 2.9g (sat 0.4g) Carbohydrate 22.6g Fiber 2.9g Cholesterol 0mg Iron 2.3mg Sodium 157mg Calcium 27mg

TECHNIQUE

For Cooking Spaghetti Squash

1. Cut 1 (3-pound) spaghetti squash in half lengthwise with a heavy, sharp knife. Remove and discard seeds from squash using a large metal spoon.

Place squash, cut sides down, in a 13- x 9- x 2-inch baking dish, and add water to dish to a depth of ½ inch. (The water keeps the squash from drying out.) Bake at 350° for 45 minutes or until tender when pricked with a fork.

2. Remove strands of squash by scraping the cut sides of flesh with tines of a fork.

SQUASH CAKES WITH PEPPER SAUCE

Spaghetti squash is rich in fiber and low in calories.

2½ cups cooked spaghetti squash
⅓ cup chopped green onions
2 tablespoons all-purpose flour
½ teaspoon salt
¼ teaspoon dried dillweed
⅛ teaspoon pepper
1 egg white, lightly beaten
Vegetable cooking spray
2 teaspoons vegetable oil, divided
Sweet Red Pepper Sauce

Combine squash and green onions; toss well. Combine flour and next 3 ingredients; sprinkle over squash mixture, and toss well. Add egg white; stir well.

Coat a large nonstick skillet with cooking spray, and add 1 teaspoon oil; place over medium heat until hot. Spoon about ⅓ cup squash mixture per cake into skillet, spreading into 3-inch rounds. Cook 4 minutes on each side or until browned; repeat procedure with remaining 1 teaspoon oil and squash mixture. Serve with Sweet Red Pepper Sauce. Yield: 6 servings (serving size: 1 cake and about 3 tablespoons sauce).

Calories 71 (29% from fat) Protein 2.2g Fat 2.3g (sat 0.4g) Carbohydrate 11.5g Fiber 2.3g Cholesterol 0mg Iron 1.5mg Sodium 271mg Calcium 30mg

Vegetable cooking spray

2¾ cups chopped sweet red
pepper

¼ cup chopped green onions

1 small clove garlic, minced

¼ cup water

2 tablespoons no-salt-added
tomato paste

⅛ teaspoon salt

⅛ teaspoon pepper

Coat a large nonstick skillet with cooking spray; place over medium-high heat until hot. Add chopped pepper, green onions, and garlic; sauté 7 minutes or until vegetables are crisp-tender. Add water and remaining ingredients; cook mixture 1 minute.

Position knife blade in food processor bowl, and spoon sauce into processor bowl. Process mixture 20 seconds or until chunky. Yield: 1¼ cups (serving size: about 3 tablespoons).

Calories 23 (12% from fat) **Protein** 0.9g **Fat** 0.3g (sat 0.1g) **Carbohydrate** 5.0g **Fiber** 1.2g **Cholesterol** 0mg **Iron** 1.0mg **Sodium** 54mg **Calcium** 10mg

Sweet Potato Casserole

Sweet Potato Casserole

2 egg whites, lightly beaten

3 cups mashed cooked sweet
potato (about 2¼ pounds)

⅓ cup firmly packed brown
sugar

⅓ cup skim milk

2 tablespoons reduced-calorie
margarine, melted

1 teaspoon vanilla extract

½ teaspoon salt

Vegetable cooking spray

½ cup firmly packed brown
sugar

¼ cup all-purpose flour

2 tablespoons chilled
reduced-calorie margarine

⅓ cup chopped pecans

Combine first 7 ingredients in a bowl, and stir well. Spoon sweet potato mixture into an 8-inch square baking dish coated with cooking spray.

Combine ½ cup brown sugar and flour in a bowl, and cut in 2 tablespoons chilled margarine with a pastry blender or 2 knives until mixture is crumbly. Stir in pecans; sprinkle flour mixture over sweet potato mixture. Bake at 350° for 30 minutes. Yield: 8 servings (serving size: ½ cup).

Calories 273 (24% from fat) **Protein** 3.5g **Fat** 7.4g (sat 0.9g) **Carbohydrate** 49.8g **Fiber** 3.3g **Cholesterol** 0mg **Iron** 1.3mg **Sodium** 242mg **Calcium** 56mg

FRIED GREEN TOMATOES WITH LIMA-CORN RELISH

All that's missing from these fried green tomatoes is the deep fat for cooking. We serve them with a zesty relish made of lima beans and corn, a variation on succotash.

1   cup frozen baby lima beans, cooked
1   cup frozen whole-kernel corn, thawed
½   cup diced sweet red pepper
3   tablespoons thinly sliced fresh basil
2   tablespoons hot pepper sauce
1   tablespoon white wine vinegar
1   teaspoon olive oil
2   cloves garlic, crushed
3   tablespoons yellow cornmeal
2   tablespoons grated Parmesan cheese
⅛   teaspoon salt
⅛   teaspoon pepper
8   (¼-inch-thick) green tomato slices
2   teaspoons olive oil
12   (¼-inch-thick) red tomato slices

Combine first 8 ingredients in a large bowl; stir mixture well. Cover and chill 1 hour.

Combine cornmeal and cheese in a small heavy-duty, zip-top plastic bag. Sprinkle salt and ⅛ teaspoon pepper over green tomato slices. Place 1 green tomato slice in cornmeal mixture; seal bag, and shake to coat. Repeat procedure with remaining green tomato slices.

Heat 2 teaspoons oil in a large nonstick skillet over medium-high heat. Add green tomato slices, and cook 3 minutes on each side or until browned.

Arrange lima bean mixture, fried green tomato slices, and red tomato slices on a serving platter. Serve immediately. Yield: 4 servings (serving size: ½ cup bean mixture, 2 fried green tomato slices, and 3 red tomato slices).

Calories 180 (25% from fat) Protein 7.2g Fat 5.0g (sat 1.0g) Carbohydrate 29.0g Fiber 3.4g Cholesterol 2mg Iron 2.2mg Sodium 253mg Calcium 64mg

STEWED TOMATOES AND OKRA

4   cups water
3   cups frozen cut okra
1   teaspoon vegetable oil
½   cup chopped green pepper
¼   cup chopped onion
¼   teaspoon salt
¼   teaspoon pepper
1   (14½-ounce) can no-salt-added whole tomatoes, drained and chopped

Combine water and okra in a medium saucepan; bring to a boil. Reduce heat, and simmer, uncovered, 3 minutes. Drain okra, and set aside.

Heat oil in saucepan over medium heat. Add green pepper and onion; sauté 3 minutes or until tender. Add okra, salt, ¼ teaspoon pepper, and tomatoes; cook until thoroughly heated. Yield: 3 servings (serving size: 1 cup).

Calories 78 (21% from fat) Protein 3.0g Fat 1.8g (sat 0.3g) Carbohydrate 14.2g Fiber 2.2g Cholesterol 0mg Iron 1.5mg Sodium 217mg Calcium 114mg

ROASTED RATATOUILLE

1   (1-pound) eggplant, cut crosswise into ¾-inch slices
2   teaspoons olive oil, divided
Vegetable cooking spray
3   medium zucchini, cut crosswise into ¾-inch slices (about 1 pound)
1½   cups vertically sliced onion
1½   cups (1-inch-square) cut sweet red pepper
1½   cups (1-inch-square) cut green pepper
2   cloves garlic, crushed
2   cups seeded, chopped tomato
2   tablespoons chopped fresh parsley
½   teaspoon dried thyme
¼   teaspoon salt
⅛   teaspoon pepper

Cut each eggplant slice into 4 wedges; place in a bowl. Drizzle with 1 teaspoon oil, and toss well. Arrange eggplant wedges in a single layer on a baking sheet coated with cooking spray. Broil 5½ inches from heat (with electric oven door partially opened) 14 minutes or until browned; place eggplant wedges in a large bowl. Set aside.

Place zucchini in a large bowl. Drizzle with remaining 1 teaspoon oil, and toss well. Arrange zucchini in a single layer on a baking sheet coated with cooking spray. Broil 5½ inches from heat (with electric oven door partially opened) 7 minutes or until browned; add to eggplant, and set aside.

Coat a large nonstick skillet with cooking spray; place over medium heat until hot. Add onion and next 3 ingredients; sauté 10 minutes or until tender. Add tomato; sauté 5 additional minutes.

Add eggplant mixture, parsley, and remaining ingredients to skillet; stir well. Cover, reduce heat, and simmer 15 minutes. Yield: 6 servings (serving size: 1 cup).

Calories 80 (26% from fat) **Protein** 2.8g **Fat** 2.3g (sat 0.3g) **Carbohydrate** 14.7g **Fiber** 3.5g **Cholesterol** 0mg **Iron** 1.6mg **Sodium** 111mg **Calcium** 55mg

ROASTED VEGETABLES WITH SUN-DRIED TOMATO PESTO

3   tablespoons Sun-Dried Tomato Pesto
2   tablespoons balsamic vinegar
1   tablespoon olive oil
⅛   teaspoon salt
Dash of pepper
2   cups (½-inch-thick) sliced red potato (about 10 ounces)
2   cups (½-inch-thick) diagonally sliced zucchini
1½ cups mushroom halves
1   (1-pound) eggplant, cut diagonally into ½-inch slices
Vegetable cooking spray

Prepare Sun-Dried Tomato Pesto; set aside.

Combine vinegar and next 3 ingredients in a large bowl, and stir mixture well. Add potato and next 3 ingredients; toss well to coat. Let stand 3 minutes.

Arrange half of vegetables in a single layer on a jellyroll or shallow roasting pan coated with cooking spray. Bake at 475° for 10 minutes. Turn vegetables, and bake 10 additional minutes or until tender and lightly browned. Repeat procedure with remaining half of vegetables.

Combine vegetables and 3 tablespoons Sun-Dried Tomato Pesto in a bowl; toss gently to coat. Yield: 4 servings (serving size: 1 cup).

Note: Substitute sliced purple onion and sweet red or green peppers for mushrooms and eggplant, if desired.

Calories 147 (28% from fat) **Protein** 4.7g **Fat** 4.5g (sat 0.6g) **Carbohydrate** 24.9g **Fiber** 3.2g **Cholesterol** 0mg **Iron** 1.8mg **Sodium** 173mg **Calcium** 60mg

SUN-DRIED TOMATO PESTO:

6   ounces sun-dried tomatoes, packed without oil
3   cups boiling water
2   tablespoons pine nuts, toasted
2   large cloves garlic
⅔   cup fresh basil leaves
2   tablespoons freshly grated Parmesan cheese
¼   cup fresh flat-leaf parsley leaves
3   tablespoons dry white wine

Combine tomatoes and water; let stand 1 hour or until softened. Drain, reserving ½ cup liquid.

Position knife blade in food processor bowl. Drop nuts and garlic through food chute with processor running; process until minced. Add tomato, basil, cheese, and parsley; process until minced. Add reserved ½ cup liquid and wine through food chute with processor running; process until well blended. Spoon into a zip-top plastic bag; store in refrigerator. Yield: 2 cups (serving size: 1 tablespoon).

Calories 20 (27% from fat) **Protein** 1.1g **Fat** 0.6g (sat 0.1g) **Carbohydrate** 3.2g **Fiber** 0.0g **Cholesterol** 0mg **Iron** 0.1mg **Sodium** 118mg **Calcium** 13mg

QUICK SUCCOTASH

QUICK & EASY

½   cup water
1   (10-ounce) package frozen
    baby lima beans, thawed
1   (10-ounce) package frozen
    whole kernel corn, thawed
¾   cup diced green pepper
½   teaspoon salt
¼   teaspoon dried summer
    savory, crushed
2   cups peeled, seeded, and
    diced tomato

Bring water to a boil in a sauce-pan. Add beans; cook, uncovered, 5 minutes. Add corn and next 3 ingredients; cook 5 minutes, stirring occasionally. Remove from heat, and stir in tomato. Yield: 5 servings (serving size: 1 cup).

Calories 143 (3% from fat) Protein 7.0g Fat 0.5g (sat 0.1g) Carbohydrate 31.0g Fiber 4.0g Cholesterol 0mg Iron 2.4mg Sodium 328mg Calcium 31mg

CORNBREAD DRESSING

Reader Deborah McPherson, a car-diac rehab dietitian, submitted this recipe as part of a low-fat holiday dinner. This heart-healthy side dish was a hit with all her patients in Odessa, Texas.

McPherson Cornbread
2   hard-cooked eggs
1   (12-ounce) can refrigerated
     fluffy buttermilk biscuits
1½   teaspoons rubbed sage
½   teaspoon pepper
5   cups canned low-sodium
     chicken broth, undiluted
⅔   cup chopped celery
⅔   cup chopped onion
2   egg whites, lightly
     beaten
Vegetable cooking spray

Prepare McPherson Cornbread. Set aside.
Slice hard-cooked eggs in half lengthwise, and carefully remove yolks. Chop cooked egg whites, and set aside; reserve egg yolks for another use.
Crumble McPherson Cornbread, and set aside. Bake biscuits accord-ing to package directions; let cool. Tear 8 biscuits into small pieces; reserve remaining 2 biscuits for another use. Combine chopped egg white, crumbled cornbread, torn biscuits, sage, and pepper in a large bowl; set aside.
Bring broth to a boil in a sauce-pan. Add celery and onion; reduce

heat, and simmer, uncovered, 5 minutes. Add broth mixture to cornbread mixture; stir well. Add 2 egg whites, and stir well. Spoon into a 2-quart casserole coated with cooking spray. Bake dressing, uncov-ered, at 400° for 45 minutes. Yield: 12 servings (serving size: ½ cup).

Calories 180 (19% from fat) Protein 7.1g Fat 3.8g (sat 0.9g) Carbohydrate 29.3g Fiber 1.2g Cholesterol 1mg Iron 1.6mg Sodium 391mg Calcium 85mg

MCPHERSON CORNBREAD:

1   cup yellow cornmeal
1   cup all-purpose flour
1   tablespoon baking powder
½   teaspoon salt
1¼   cups skim milk
2   egg whites, lightly beaten
Vegetable cooking spray

Combine cornmeal, flour, baking powder, and salt in a medium bowl, and stir well. Combine milk and egg whites, and add to flour mixture, stirring just until dry ingredients are moistened.
Pour batter into a 9-inch square pan coated with cooking spray. Bake cornbread at 400° for 20 minutes or until a wooden pick inserted in cen-ter of cornbread comes out clean. Remove cornbread from pan; cool completely on a wire rack. Yield: 12 servings (serving size: one 3- x 2¼-inch piece).

Calories 90 (4% from fat) Protein 3.4g Fat 0.4g (sat 0.1g) Carbohydrate 17.7g Fiber 0.9g Cholesterol 1mg Iron 1.0mg Sodium 121mg Calcium 78mg

Polenta with Wild Mushroom Sauce

Don't limit yourself to serving this polenta only with Wild Mushroom Sauce. Polenta can be served with other hearty sauces, too.

1⅓   cups yellow cornmeal
½   teaspoon salt
4   cups water
Vegetable cooking spray
1   tablespoon olive oil
2   cloves garlic, minced
2   thyme sprigs
1   rosemary sprig
6½   cups thinly sliced shiitake mushroom caps (about 1 pound mushrooms)
1   cup canned crushed tomatoes
⅓   cup dry white wine
3   tablespoons balsamic vinegar
⅛   teaspoon salt
⅛   teaspoon pepper
2   tablespoons chopped fresh parsley
3   tablespoons freshly grated Parmesan cheese

Place cornmeal and ½ teaspoon salt in a large saucepan. Gradually add water, stirring constantly with a wire whisk. Bring mixture to a boil, and reduce heat to medium. Cook 15 minutes, stirring often. Spoon polenta into an 8½- x 4½- x 3-inch loafpan coated with cooking spray, spreading evenly. Press heavy-duty plastic wrap onto surface of polenta, and chill 2 hours or until firm.

Heat oil in a large nonstick skillet over medium heat. Add garlic, thyme sprigs, and rosemary sprig; cook 3 minutes or just until garlic begins to brown. Stir in mushrooms and next 5 ingredients; bring to a boil. Cover, reduce heat, and simmer 15 minutes, stirring occasionally. Discard thyme and rosemary sprigs. Add parsley; cook, uncovered, 5 minutes. Remove from heat. Set aside; keep warm.

Invert polenta onto a cutting board; cut crosswise into 12 slices. Place slices on a baking sheet coated with cooking spray. Broil 5½ inches from heat (with electric oven door partially opened) 5 minutes on each side or until golden.

Arrange 2 polenta slices on each of 6 individual serving plates. Top evenly with mushroom sauce and Parmesan cheese. Yield: 6 servings (serving size: 2 polenta slices, ⅓ cup mushroom sauce, and 1½ teaspoons Parmesan cheese).

Calories 178 (21% from fat) **Protein** 6.0g **Fat** 4.2g (sat 1.0g) **Carbohydrate** 30.0g **Fiber** 2.9g **Cholesterol** 2mg **Iron** 2.7mg **Sodium** 359mg **Calcium** 69mg

Asiago Soft Grits

QUICK & EASY

When we invited Birmingham, Alabama chef Frank Stitt to enter our first *Cooking Light* cheese recipe competition for chefs in 1994, he entered this recipe as a side with rabbit. You can also serve it with chicken or pork. Frank suggests using yellow stone-ground grits for variety.

3¾   cups water
2¼   cups canned low-sodium chicken broth, undiluted
¼   teaspoon salt
⅛   teaspoon pepper
3   cloves garlic, chopped
1   cup regular grits, uncooked
½   cup 2% low-fat milk
1½   cups (6 ounces) grated Asiago cheese

Bring first 5 ingredients to a boil in a large saucepan; gradually stir in grits. Cover, reduce heat, and simmer 15 minutes or until thickened, stirring occasionally. Remove from heat, and stir in milk and cheese. Serve warm. Yield: 6 cups (serving size: ½ cup).

Calories 70 (45% from fat) **Protein** 5.3g **Fat** 3.5g (sat 2.1g) **Carbohydrate** 4.2g **Fiber** 0.3g **Cholesterol** 9mg **Iron** 0.5mg **Sodium** 255mg **Calcium** 152mg

NEW ORLEANS DIRTY QUINOA

You'll find the grain quinoa (KEEN-wah) next to the rice at your supermarket.

2   teaspoons Emeril's Creole Seasoning (page 48)
1   tablespoon olive oil
4   ounces chicken livers, finely chopped
1   cup chopped onion
¾   cup diced celery
½   cup diced green pepper
2   tablespoons chopped shallots
½   pound lean Canadian-style bacon, chopped
2   large cloves garlic, minced
1   bay leaf
3   cups quinoa, uncooked
⅓   cup water
1   tablespoon Worcestershire sauce
¼   teaspoon hot sauce
2   (14¼-ounce) cans no-salt-added chicken broth
½   cup sliced green onions

Prepare Emeril's Creole Seasoning. Set aside.

Heat oil in a large saucepan over medium-low heat. Add chicken livers, and sauté 4 minutes or until done. Add onion and next 6 ingredients; sauté 3 minutes or until vegetables are crisp-tender. Add quinoa; cook, stirring constantly, 2 minutes. Add 2 teaspoons Emeril's Creole Seasoning, ⅓ cup water, and next 3 ingredients; bring to a boil. Reduce heat, and simmer, uncovered, 15 minutes or until liquid is absorbed, stirring occasionally. Remove from heat; discard bay leaf, and stir in sliced green onions. Yield: 8 cups (serving size: 1 cup).

Calories 282 (22% from fat) Protein 32.8g Fat 7.0g (sat 1.8g) Carbohydrate 21.5 Fiber 1.3g Cholesterol 105mg Iron 1.8mg Sodium 306mg Calcium 30mg

BARLEY, WILD RICE, AND CURRANT PILAF

QUICK & EASY

½   cup pearl barley, uncooked
¼   cup wild rice, uncooked
1   teaspoon vegetable oil
¾   cup finely chopped onion
⅔   cup finely chopped celery
½   cup finely chopped carrot
1   clove garlic, minced
⅓   cup currants
1   teaspoon rubbed sage
½   teaspoon salt
½   teaspoon dried thyme
¼   teaspoon pepper
2   (10½-ounce) cans low-sodium chicken broth
1   bay leaf

Combine barley and wild rice in a Dutch oven over medium heat. Cook 7 minutes or until lightly browned, stirring often.

Heat oil in a large skillet over medium-high heat. Add onion and next 3 ingredients, and sauté until tender. Add vegetable mixture, currants, and remaining ingredients to mixture in Dutch oven. Bring to a boil; cover, reduce heat, and simmer 50 minutes or until liquid is absorbed, stirring occasionally. Remove and discard bay leaf. Yield: 5 servings (serving size: ¾ cup).

Calories 147 (13% from fat) Protein 5.1g Fat 2.2g (sat 0.5g) Carbohydrate 28.3g Fiber 5.0g Cholesterol 0mg Iron 1.8mg Sodium 296mg Calcium 32mg

WILD RICE-MUSHROOM PILAF

2   cups water
½   cup wild rice, uncooked
Vegetable cooking spray
1   tablespoon olive oil
¾   cup thinly sliced fresh shiitake mushrooms
¾   cup thinly sliced fresh mushrooms
½   cup minced shallots
½   teaspoon salt
¼   teaspoon pepper
⅓   cup Madeira
½   cup julienne-sliced sweet red pepper
¼   cup minced fresh parsley

Combine water and rice in a saucepan; bring to a boil. Cover, reduce heat, and simmer 1 hour or until rice is tender. Drain; set aside.

Coat a nonstick skillet with cooking spray. Add oil, and place over medium-high heat until hot. Add shiitake mushrooms and next 4 ingredients; sauté 2 minutes or until mushrooms are tender. Add wine. Bring to a boil; reduce heat, and simmer, uncovered, 3 minutes or until liquid is absorbed. Combine rice, mushroom mixture, red pepper, and parsley; stir well. Spoon into a 1-quart casserole coated with cooking spray. Bake at 325° for 20 minutes or until heated. Yield: 4 servings (serving size: ¾ cup).

Calories 174 (22% from fat) **Protein** 5.0g **Fat** 4.2g (sat 0.5g) **Carbohydrate** 28.9g **Fiber** 3.0g **Cholesterol** 0mg **Iron** 1.3mg **Sodium** 302mg **Calcium** 18mg

CONFETTI RICE

¾	cup long-grain rice, uncooked
2	tablespoons reduced-calorie margarine
1	cup sliced green onions
1	teaspoon ground cumin
½	teaspoon dried oregano
¼	teaspoon salt
2	cloves garlic, minced
1	medium-size green pepper, seeded and chopped
1	medium-size sweet red pepper, seeded and chopped
¼	cup water
1	(10½-ounce) can low-sodium chicken broth

Place a large nonstick skillet over medium-high heat until hot. Add rice; cook 3 to 4 minutes or until lightly browned. Remove rice from skillet, and set aside.

Melt margarine in skillet over medium-high heat. Add onions and next 6 ingredients; sauté 3 minutes. Add water and broth.

Bring mixture to a boil; cover, reduce heat, and simmer 20 minutes or until liquid is absorbed and rice is tender. Yield: 6 servings (serving size: ¾ cup).

Calories 126 (23% from fat) **Protein** 2.8g **Fat** 3.2g (sat 0.4g) **Carbohydrate** 22.1g **Fiber** 1.1g **Cholesterol** 0mg **Iron** 2.1mg **Sodium** 156mg **Calcium** 27mg

HERBED BASMATI RICE

QUICK & EASY

1	tablespoon margarine
1	large clove garlic, minced
¾	cup basmati rice, uncooked
1½	cups water
½	teaspoon salt
3	tablespoons thinly sliced green onion tops
1	tablespoon minced fresh basil
1½	teaspoons minced fresh thyme
3	tablespoons freshly grated Parmesan cheese

Melt margarine in a small saucepan over medium-high heat. Add garlic, and sauté 1 minute. Add rice; stir well. Add water and salt; bring to a boil. Cover, reduce heat, and simmer 20 minutes or until liquid is absorbed. Stir in onion tops, basil, and thyme, and sprinkle with cheese. Yield: 4 servings (serving size: ¾ cup).

Calories 196 (27% from fat) **Protein** 6.4g **Fat** 5.8g (sat 2.4g) **Carbohydrate** 28.5g **Fiber** 0.5g **Cholesterol** 7mg **Iron** 1.7mg **Sodium** 499mg **Calcium** 142mg

BEYOND WHITE RICE

If you're tired of plain white rice, browse down the rice aisle, and you'll find new ways to serve flavorful rice. Just try selecting a variety that's new to you. Here are some of the varieties you'll find most available:

• **Basmati** rice is the most popular of the aromatic varieties that are valued for their roasted-nut or popcornlike flavor. The aromatic grains separate nicely after cooking and are ideal for pilafs and paellas.

• **Jasmine** offers the same roasted flavor, but it cooks up soft and a bit sticky—just right for chopstick dining.

• **Brown** rices are crunchy and offer more pronounced nutty flavors. In the long and medium grains, brown rice has more bran layers after milling than does white rice.

SPANISH FRIED RICE

QUICK & EASY

1 tablespoon olive oil, divided
4 cups cooked rice (cooked without salt or fat)
⅛ teaspoon saffron powder
½ cup chopped onion
¼ cup chopped celery
¼ cup chopped green pepper
¼ cup chopped sweet red pepper
2 cloves garlic, crushed
¼ cup no-salt-added tomato sauce
1 teaspoon chili powder
½ teaspoon sugar
½ teaspoon salt
Dash of ground red pepper
1 (14½-ounce) can no-salt-added whole tomatoes, drained and chopped

Heat 1½ teaspoons oil in a large nonstick skillet over medium heat. Add rice and saffron; stir-fry 3 minutes. Remove from skillet; set aside.

Heat remaining 1½ teaspoons oil in skillet over medium-high heat. Add onion and next 4 ingredients; stir-fry 2 minutes or until tender. Add tomato sauce and remaining 5 ingredients; cook 2 minutes, stirring often. Return rice to skillet, and stir-fry until thoroughly heated. Yield: 5 servings (serving size: 1 cup).

Calories 232 (12% from fat) **Protein** 4.3g **Fat** 3.1g (sat 0.4g) **Carbohydrate** 46.5g **Fiber** 2.2g **Cholesterol** 0mg **Iron** 2.0mg **Sodium** 255mg **Calcium** 45mg

VIDALIA ONION RISOTTO WITH FETA CHEESE

QUICK & EASY

Sweet Vidalia onions (from Vidalia, Georgia) and Texas Super Sweets are in season in spring and may be hard to get other times of the year. If you don't have sweet onions, you can substitute Bermuda onions or another mild-flavored onion.

2 teaspoons vegetable oil
2 cups chopped Vidalia or other sweet onion
2 large cloves garlic, minced
1½ cups Arborio or other short-grain rice, uncooked
2 (14½-ounce) cans vegetable broth, divided
½ cup (2 ounces) crumbled feta cheese, divided
⅓ cup chopped fresh flat-leaf parsley
¼ cup freshly grated Parmesan cheese
Freshly ground pepper

Heat oil in a saucepan over medium heat. Add onion and garlic, and sauté 1 minute. Stir in rice. Add ½ cup broth; cook, stirring constantly, until liquid is nearly absorbed. Add remaining broth, ½ cup at a time, stirring constantly until each addition is nearly absorbed before adding the next. Remove from heat; stir in ¼ cup feta cheese, parsley, and Parmesan cheese. Spoon rice mixture into a serving bowl; top with remaining ¼ cup feta cheese and pepper. Yield: 5 servings (serving size: 1 cup).

Calories 321 (18% from fat) **Protein** 8.5g **Fat** 6.5g (sat 2.8g) **Carbohydrate** 56.1g **Fiber** 2.3g **Cholesterol** 13mg **Iron** 3.0mg **Sodium** 670mg **Calcium** 135mg

FRESH TOMATO-BASIL RISOTTO WITH MOZZARELLA

QUICK & EASY

1½ cups diced plum tomatoes
2 tablespoons chopped fresh basil
1 tablespoon olive oil
½ teaspoon salt
1 clove garlic, crushed
4 (10½-ounce) cans low-sodium chicken broth
2 teaspoons olive oil
½ cup finely chopped onion
1½ cups Arborio or other short-grain rice, uncooked
⅓ cup dry white wine
½ cup (2 ounces) diced part-skim mozzarella cheese
½ teaspoon freshly ground pepper
2 tablespoons grated Parmesan cheese

Combine first 5 ingredients; stir well, and set aside. Bring broth to a simmer in a medium saucepan (do not boil). Keep warm over low heat.

Heat 2 teaspoons oil in a large saucepan over medium-high heat.

Fresh Tomato-Basil
Risotto With Mozzarella

Add onion; sauté 3 minutes. Add rice; cook, stirring constantly, 1 minute. Add wine; cook, stirring constantly, 1 minute or until liquid is nearly absorbed. Add warm broth, ½ cup at a time, stirring constantly until each addition is absorbed before adding the next (about 20 minutes total). Add tomato mixture; cook, stirring constantly, 2 minutes. Remove from heat, and stir in mozzarella and pepper. Sprinkle each serving with Parmesan cheese. Yield: 6 servings (serving size: 1 cup).

Calories 289 (24% from fat) **Protein** 9.0g **Fat** 7.6g (sat 2.3g) **Carbohydrate** 45.7g **Fiber** 1.6g **Cholesterol** 7mg **Iron** 3.5mg **Sodium** 350mg **Calcium** 101mg

RISOTTO'S RICE

Traditional Italian risottos call for Arborio rice, a short-grain rice high in starch. As the rice cooks, the starch produces a creamy texture instead of the dry, separate grains you get with long-grain rice, or the clumped cooked rice from other short-grain varieties.

Tomato Soup
With Parmesan Cream,
page 183

SOUPS

THESE ARE NOT YOUR MOTHER'S SAME OLD SOUPS. FIRST OF ALL, THEY'RE ALL LOW-FAT. SECOND, WE'VE ADDED A LITTLE SOMETHING TO EACH TO MAKE THEM SPECIAL ENOUGH TO SERVE TO COMPANY. TAKE OUR TOMATO SOUP WITH PARMESAN CREAM, FOR INSTANCE. WE DRIZZLE THE PARMESAN CREAM ONTO THE SURFACE OF THE SOUP IN HEART SHAPES

& STEWS

FOR SPECIAL OCCASIONS. THEN WE DRESS UP PLAIN POTATO SOUP WITH ROASTED GARLIC. AND WHEN WE'RE INTO COMFORT FOOD, OR LOOKING FOR SOMETHING TO TAKE TO MOM WHEN SHE'S SICK, THERE'S NO CONTEST. WE PACK THE SALTINES AND THE CHICKEN NOODLE SOUP.

CHILLED BERRY SOUP

If you prefer a thinner soup, just stir in 1 to 2 tablespoons additional dry red wine.

1½ cups fresh raspberries
1½ cups chopped fresh strawberries
¾ cup water
½ cup dry red wine
3 tablespoons sugar

Rinse raspberries. Combine raspberries, strawberries, and remaining ingredients in a medium saucepan; bring to a boil, stirring constantly. Cover, reduce heat, and simmer 5 minutes. Remove from heat, and cool completely.

Position knife blade in food processor bowl; add berry mixture, and process until smooth. Pour mixture through a wire-mesh strainer into a medium bowl; discard seeds. Cover and chill 8 hours. Yield: 2½ cups (serving size: ½ cup).

Calories 63 (6% from fat) Protein 0.7g Fat 0.4g (sat 0.0g) Carbohydrate 15.6g Fiber 4.1g Cholesterol 0mg Iron 0.5mg Sodium 2mg Calcium 17mg

GAZPACHO

1½ cups no-salt-added tomato juice
3 large tomatoes, quartered and seeded
1 small cucumber, peeled, quartered, and seeded
1 small green pepper, quartered and seeded
1 small onion, quartered
2 tablespoons balsamic vinegar
½ teaspoon salt
¼ teaspoon hot sauce
1 clove garlic, minced
¼ cup sliced cucumber
¼ cup finely chopped green pepper

Position knife blade in food processor bowl; combine first 5 ingredients in bowl. Process until smooth; pour mixture into a large bowl. Stir in vinegar and next 3 ingredients; cover and chill at least 2 hours. Top with cucumber slices and finely chopped green pepper. Serve chilled. Yield: 6 cups (serving size: ½ cup).

Calories 26 (10% from fat) Protein 1.1g Fat 0.3g (sat 0.0g) Carbohydrate 5.9g Fiber 1.2g Cholesterol 0mg Iron 0.5mg Sodium 108mg Calcium 7mg

TECHNIQUE

For Seeding Tomatoes

When you seed and chop the tomatoes for Gazpacho, follow one of these two quick ways to seed the tomatoes:

• Cut the tomato in half horizontally, and scoop out the seeds with a spoon, as pictured.
• Cut the tomato in half horizontally, and hold one half in your hand, skin side toward your palm. Gently squeeze the tomato half to push the seeds out.

Tomato Soup with Parmesan Cream

When we featured this soup in a Valentine's Day article in 1993, we used a wooden pick to fashion the cream into a heart shape on top of the soup, as pictured on page 180.

1   cup peeled, diced baking potato
1   cup water
½   cup chopped onion
2   cloves garlic, halved
1   teaspoon sugar
½   teaspoon dried rosemary, crushed
¼   teaspoon salt
Dash of pepper
2   (14½-ounce) cans no-salt-added whole tomatoes, undrained and coarsely chopped
½   cup 2% low-fat milk
¼   cup plain low-fat yogurt
2   tablespoons freshly grated Parmesan cheese

Combine first 4 ingredients in a large saucepan; bring to a boil. Reduce heat; simmer, uncovered, 10 minutes or until vegetables are tender. Add sugar and next 4 ingredients; bring to a boil. Cover, reduce heat, and simmer 15 minutes.

Place half of tomato mixture in container of an electric blender or food processor; cover and process until smooth. Press pureed mixture through a sieve into a medium saucepan; discard solids. Repeat procedure with remaining mixture.

Add milk to tomato mixture; stir well. Cook over low heat, stirring constantly, until thoroughly heated. Ladle soup into 4 serving bowls.

Combine yogurt and cheese, and stir well; divide evenly among servings, placing ½ teaspoon dollops in a circle on top of each serving. Pull a wooden pick or the tip of a knife continuously through dollops to make heart patterns. Yield: 4 cups (serving size: 1 cup soup and 1 tablespoon Parmesan cream).

Calories 116 (13% from fat) Protein 5.4g Fat 1.7g (sat 1.0g) Carbohydrate 22.2g Fiber 2.5g Cholesterol 5mg Iron 1.2mg Sodium 250mg Calcium 175mg

Roasted Garlic-Potato Soup

This rich soup gets its hearty flavor from bacon and garlic.

5   whole heads garlic
2   bacon slices, diced
1   cup diced onion
1   cup diced carrot
2   cloves garlic, minced
6   cups peeled, diced baking potato (about 2 pounds)
4   cups canned low-sodium chicken broth, undiluted
½   teaspoon salt
¼   teaspoon pepper
1   bay leaf
1   cup 2% low-fat milk
¼   cup chopped fresh parsley

Peel outer skin from each garlic head, and discard skin. Cut off top one-third of each garlic head. Place each garlic head, cut side up, in center of a piece of heavy-duty aluminum foil. Fold foil over garlic, sealing tightly. Bake at 350° for 1 hour or until garlic is soft. Remove from oven, and let cool 10 minutes. Remove and discard papery skin from garlic. Squeeze pulp from each clove to extract ¼ cup pulp; set pulp aside.

Cook bacon in a large saucepan over medium-high heat until crisp. Add onion, carrot, and minced garlic, and sauté 5 minutes. Add potato and next 4 ingredients; bring to a boil. Cover, reduce heat, and simmer 20 minutes or until potato is tender; remove and discard bay leaf.

Combine garlic pulp and 2 cups potato mixture in container of an electric blender or food processor; cover and process until smooth. Return puree to potato mixture in pan; stir in milk, and cook over low heat until thoroughly heated. Remove from heat, and stir in chopped parsley. Yield: 7 cups (serving size: 1 cup).

Calories 199 (14% from fat) Protein 7.8g Fat 3.0g (sat 1.1g) Carbohydrate 38.0g Fiber 3.9g Cholesterol 5mg Iron 2.8mg Sodium 300mg Calcium 150mg

HELPFUL HINTS ABOUT ONIONS

If you cook at all, you probably have a fresh onion in your kitchen. Follow these tips below to pick the right onion for your recipes and to cook with them more easily.

• The season for fresh onions is from April to August. Onions available then usually are sweeter because they have a higher water and sugar content.

• Storage onions are available from August through March. The outer skins are darker and thicker than the fresh onions, and the flavor is stronger, too.

• Fresh onions are more delicate than the heartier storage onions. Refrigerate them, or store them in a cool, dry place. They usually keep about one to two weeks.

• Storage onions will keep for weeks or months without losing vitamins or minerals. Store them in a single layer.

• Onions may be bitter if cooked at high heat, so always sauté them over low or medium heat.

• If your onions seem particularly strong, pour milk or boiling water over onion slices, and let them soak 30 to 40 minutes to make them milder. Then soak the slices briefly in ice water.

• Rub your hands with lemon juice or salt to remove any onion odor.

CHILE-CHEESE SOUP

2   dried pasilla chiles, cut in half lengthwise and seeded
1   cup water
4   large sweet yellow peppers
1   large sweet red pepper
2   teaspoons vegetable oil
1   cup chopped onion
2   cloves garlic, chopped
3   cups canned low-sodium chicken broth, undiluted
2½   cups peeled, diced baking potato (about 1 pound)
1   cup diced carrot
½   teaspoon salt
¼   teaspoon ground white pepper
2   tablespoons plain low-fat yogurt
¼   cup plus 3 tablespoons (1¾ ounces) shredded Monterey Jack cheese

Combine chile halves and water in a saucepan. Bring to a boil; remove from heat. Cover; let stand 1 hour. Drain; finely chop chiles. Set aside.

Cut sweet peppers in half lengthwise; discard seeds and membranes. Place pepper halves, skin side up, on a baking sheet; flatten with palm of hand. Broil 5½ inches from heat (with electric oven door partially opened) 10 minutes or until charred. Place in ice water until cool; peel and discard skins.

Heat oil in a Dutch oven over medium heat. Add onion and garlic; sauté 7 minutes. Stir in yellow pepper, broth, and next 4 ingredients. Bring to a boil; cover, reduce heat, and simmer 35 minutes or until vegetables are tender. Place half of soup in container of an electric blender. Cover; process until smooth. Pour into a bowl. Repeat procedure with remaining soup; stir in chopped chiles. Combine red pepper and yogurt in blender container. Cover; process until smooth.

Ladle soup into bowls; top with red pepper puree and cheese. Yield: 7 servings (serving size: 1 cup soup, 1 tablespoon puree, and 1 tablespoon cheese).

Calories 153 (30% from fat) **Protein** 5.9g **Fat** 5.1g (sat 1.7g) **Carbohydrate** 23.3g **Fiber** 4.5g **Cholesterol** 6mg **Iron** 2.9mg **Sodium** 262mg **Calcium** 87mg

SOUPE À L'OIGNON (FRENCH ONION SOUP)

6   (½-inch) slices French bread baguette
Vegetable cooking spray
1   tablespoon margarine
6   cups thinly sliced onion
½   teaspoon sugar
⅛   teaspoon pepper
3   tablespoons all-purpose flour
4   (14¼-ounce) cans no-salt-added beef broth
1   (10-ounce) can beef consommé, undiluted
½   cup dry white wine
1   tablespoon Worcestershire sauce
6   thin slices (1½ ounces) Gruyère cheese

Place baguette slices on a baking sheet. Bake at 375° for 8 minutes or until lightly browned; set aside.

Coat a Dutch oven with cooking spray; add margarine. Place over medium-low heat until margarine melts. Add onion; sauté 5 minutes. Sprinkle onion with sugar and pepper. Reduce heat to low; cook 20 minutes or until onion is golden, stirring often.

Sprinkle onion with flour; cook, stirring constantly, 2 minutes. Add broth, consommé, and wine; bring to a boil. Reduce heat, and simmer, partially covered, 30 minutes. Remove from heat, and stir in Worcestershire sauce.

Ladle 1½ cups soup into each of 6 ovenproof soup bowls; top each serving with 1 slice bread and 1 slice cheese. Place soup bowls on a large baking sheet, and broil 5½ inches from heat (with electric oven door partially opened) 1 minute or until cheese melts. Yield: 9 cups (serving size: 1½ cups).

Note: Substitute no-salt-added beef broth for the wine in this recipe, if desired.

Calories 204 (23% from fat) **Protein** 8.0g **Fat** 5.1g (sat 1.9g) **Carbohydrate** 28.7g **Fiber** 3.0g **Cholesterol** 8mg **Iron** 1.0mg **Sodium** 522mg **Calcium** 113mg

STEP BY STEP

For Soupe à l'Oignon (French Onion Soup)

1. Sauté the onion for 5 minutes. Add sugar and pepper; then reduce the heat, and cook for 20 minutes or until the onion is golden. Sprinkle the flour over the onion; cook and stir constantly for 2 minutes.

2. Add broth, consommé, and wine; bring to a boil. Reduce the heat, and simmer, partially covered, 30 minutes. Remove Dutch oven from the heat, and stir in Worcestershire sauce.

3. Ladle 1½ cups soup into each of 6 ovenproof soup bowls.

4. Top each serving with a toasted baguette slice and a slice of Gruyère cheese. Place the soup bowls on a large baking sheet, and broil 1 minute or until the cheese melts.

CHUNKY MINESTRONE

Minestrone is the name Italians give hearty vegetable soups with peas, beans, or pasta. You can substitute a small-size uncooked pasta for the rice in this recipe.

2	teaspoons olive oil
1½	cups chopped onion
1	medium carrot, halved lengthwise and sliced (about ¾ cup)
1	clove garlic, minced
½	cup long-grain rice, uncooked
2½	cups water
1	teaspoon dried Italian seasoning
2	(14½-ounce) cans no-salt-added whole tomatoes, undrained and chopped
1	(10½-ounce) can low-sodium chicken broth
1	medium zucchini, halved lengthwise and sliced (about 2 cups)
¼	teaspoon salt
¼	teaspoon pepper
1	(15½-ounce) can cannellini beans, drained
1	(10-ounce) package frozen chopped spinach, thawed and drained
⅔	cup freshly grated Parmesan cheese

Heat oil in a Dutch oven over medium-high heat. Add onion, carrot, and garlic; sauté 3 minutes. Add rice and next 4 ingredients; bring to a boil. Cover, reduce heat, and simmer 20 minutes. Add zucchini and next 4 ingredients, and cook 5 additional minutes. Ladle into individual soup bowls, and sprinkle with cheese. Yield: 10½ cups (serving size: 1½ cups soup and 1½ tablespoons cheese).

Calories 200 (20% from fat) **Protein** 10.6g **Fat** 4.4g (sat 1.8g) **Carbohydrate** 32.0g **Fiber** 4.8g **Cholesterol** 6mg **Iron** 3.6mg **Sodium** 362mg **Calcium** 224mg

Chunky Minestrone

LAMB AND BLACK BEAN CHILI

You can substitute lean ground beef for ground lamb.

1½ pounds lean ground lamb
1 cup chopped onion
2 cloves garlic, minced
2 (14½-ounce) cans no-salt-added whole tomatoes, undrained and chopped
1 cup dry red wine
1 tablespoon chili powder
1½ teaspoons ground cumin
1½ teaspoons dried whole oregano
1 teaspoon sugar
¼ teaspoon salt
3 (15-ounce) cans black beans, drained
¼ teaspoon hot sauce

Combine first 3 ingredients in a Dutch oven. Cook over medium heat until meat is browned, stirring until it crumbles; drain. Wipe drippings from Dutch oven with a paper towel; return mixture to Dutch oven. Add tomatoes and next 6 ingredients; bring to a boil. Cover, reduce heat, and simmer 2 hours, stirring occasionally. Stir in beans and hot sauce. Cover and simmer 30 minutes. Ladle into bowls. Yield: 8 cups (serving size: 1 cup).

Calories 311 (20% from fat) **Protein** 27.9g **Fat** 6.9g (sat 2.3g) **Carbohydrate** 30.8g **Fiber** 5.6g **Cholesterol** 57mg **Iron** 4.5mg **Sodium** 413mg **Calcium** 91mg

VENISON CHILI

2½ pounds venison stew meat
1 tablespoon vegetable oil
2 cups chopped onion
1 cup chopped sweet red pepper
1 cup chopped green pepper
½ cup seeded, chopped poblano chile
6 cloves garlic, minced
1½ teaspoons ground cumin
1 teaspoon fennel seeds
1 teaspoon ground coriander
1 teaspoon paprika
1 teaspoon pepper
½ teaspoon salt
2 tablespoons to ¼ cup chili pepper sauce
1 (14½-ounce) can no-salt-added whole tomatoes, undrained and chopped
1 (12-ounce) can beer

Trim fat from meat; cut meat into ¾-inch cubes. Heat oil in a Dutch oven over medium-high heat. Add meat; cook 5 minutes or until browned. Add onion and next 4 ingredients. Cover; cook 10 minutes, stirring occasionally. Stir in cumin and next 5 ingredients; cook, uncovered, 1 minute. Add pepper sauce, tomatoes, and beer; bring to a boil. Cover, reduce heat, and simmer 1½ hours or until meat is tender. Uncover; cook 10 minutes. Yield: 7 cups (serving size: 1 cup).

Calories 275 (22% from fat) **Protein** 39.4g **Fat** 6.6g (sat 2.0g) **Carbohydrate** 13.8g **Fiber** 2.1g **Cholesterol** 138mg **Iron** 7.1mg **Sodium** 300mg **Calcium** 61mg

TECHNIQUE

For Seeding Chiles

Poblano chiles like the ones used for Venison Chili look like a stretched-out green bell pepper. But the heat they contain can range from mild to wild. Capsaicin, the compound that produces the burn, is found in the seeds and membranes. So when you handle the chiles—poblanos or other hot varieties—wear gloves, or wash your hands thoroughly afterward. Use one of these two techniques to remove the seeds:

Pull out the seeds with your fingertips.

Cut out the seeds with a knife.

BEEF BURGUNDY STEW

For a nonalcoholic version of this stew, use the following to replace the 3 cups red wine: 1 (13½-ounce) can no-salt-added beef broth, ¾ cup nonalcoholic red wine, ⅓ cup water, and ¼ cup red wine vinegar.

1½	pounds lean boneless round steak (½ inch thick)
	Vegetable cooking spray
1	teaspoon vegetable oil
½	teaspoon dried thyme
2	large cloves garlic, minced
2	bay leaves
3	cups Burgundy or other dry red wine
¼	cup tomato paste
½	cup plus 3 tablespoons water, divided
2½	cups quartered fresh mushrooms (about ½ pound)
12	small round red potatoes, quartered (about 1½ pounds)
6	medium carrots, cut into 1-inch pieces (about 1 pound)
2	small onions, quartered (about ½ pound)
2	(10½-ounce) cans low-sodium chicken broth
3	tablespoons cornstarch
¼	cup chopped fresh parsley
1¼	teaspoons salt
¼	teaspoon pepper

Trim fat from steak; cut steak into 1-inch pieces. Coat a Dutch oven with cooking spray; add oil, and place over medium-high heat until hot. Add steak, and cook until browned on all sides, stirring often; drain. Wipe drippings from Dutch oven with a paper towel.

Return steak to Dutch oven, and place over medium heat. Add thyme, garlic, and bay leaves; cook 1 minute. Add wine and tomato paste; bring mixture to a boil. Cover, reduce heat, and simmer 1½ hours or until steak is tender. Add ½ cup water and next 5 ingredients; bring to a boil. Cover, reduce heat, and simmer 40 minutes or until vegetables are tender. Remove and discard bay leaves.

Combine cornstarch and remaining 3 tablespoons water; add to stew. Cook, stirring constantly, 2 minutes or until thickened. Stir in parsley, salt, and pepper. Yield: 12 cups (serving size: 1 cup).

Calories 220 (15% from fat) Protein 16.8g Fat 3.7g (sat 1.1g) Carbohydrate 20.9g Fiber 3.1g Cholesterol 36mg Iron 3.4mg Sodium 312mg Calcium 36mg

Beef Burgundy Stew

CHUNKY CHICKEN CHILI

Vegetable cooking spray
1½ cups chopped onion
1   cup chopped green pepper
3   jalapeño peppers, seeded and chopped
3   cloves garlic, minced
2   tablespoons chili powder
2   teaspoons ground cumin
½   teaspoon dried oregano
2   cups bite-size cooked chicken breast (about 1 pound skinned, boned chicken breasts)
2   cups bite-size cooked chicken thigh (about 1 pound skinned, boned chicken thighs)
1   cup water
1   tablespoon Worcestershire sauce
1   tablespoon Dijon mustard
½   teaspoon ground red pepper
¼   teaspoon black pepper
1   (14½-ounce) can no-salt-added stewed tomatoes
1   (13¾-ounce) can no-salt-added chicken broth
1   (12-ounce) bottle reduced-calorie chili sauce
1   (16-ounce) can Great Northern beans, drained
1¼ cups peeled, diced avocado
1¼ cups chopped purple onion
½   cup plus 2 tablespoons plain nonfat yogurt

Coat a Dutch oven with cooking spray; place over medium heat until hot. Add 1½ cups onion and next 3 ingredients; sauté 5 minutes. Add chili powder, cumin, and oregano; cook 2 minutes. Add cooked chicken breast and next 9 ingredients; boil. Cover, reduce heat, and simmer 20 minutes. Add beans; cook 5 minutes. Ladle into soup bowls; top with avocado, purple onion, and yogurt. Yield: 9 cups (serving size: 1 cup chili and about 2 tablespoons avocado, 2 tablespoons onion, and 1 tablespoon yogurt).

Calories 300 (29% from fat) Protein 27.4g Fat 9.8g (sat 2.2g) Carbohydrate 26.2g Fiber 4.0g Cholesterol 68mg Iron 3.2mg Sodium 289mg Calcium 107mg

CHICKEN NOODLE SOUP

3   quarts plus 1 cup water
1   tablespoon black peppercorns
1   teaspoon dried basil
1   teaspoon dried oregano
3¾ pounds chicken pieces, skinned
3   medium parsnips or carrots, each scraped and quartered
3   cloves garlic, halved
2   medium leeks or onions, each trimmed and quartered
2   stalks celery, each quartered
2   cups sliced carrot
¾   teaspoon salt
⅛   teaspoon pepper
1½ cups fine egg noodles, uncooked

Combine first 9 ingredients in an 8-quart Dutch oven or stockpot; bring to a boil. Reduce heat to medium, and cook, uncovered, 1 hour. Remove from heat.

Remove chicken pieces from broth; place chicken in a bowl, and chill 15 minutes. Strain broth through a sieve into a large bowl; discard solids.

Remove chicken from bones; shred meat into bite-size pieces. Discard bones. Return broth to Dutch oven. Add chicken, sliced carrot, salt, and pepper; bring to a boil. Partially cover, reduce heat to medium, and cook 10 minutes, stirring occasionally. Add noodles; partially cover, and cook 10 additional minutes. Yield: 10½ cups (serving size: 1½ cups).

Note: Make double batches of the broth for this soup, and freeze it for later use.

Calories 227 (18% from fat) Protein 33.3g Fat 4.6g (sat 1.2g) Carbohydrate 11.1g Fiber 1.3g Cholesterol 111mg Iron 1.9mg Sodium 374mg Calcium 31mg

CHICKEN RAGOÛT WITH PUMPKIN DUMPLINGS

1   teaspoon dried thyme
½   teaspoon freshly ground pepper
¾   pound skinned, boned chicken breast halves (about 4 breast halves)
¾   pound skinned, boned chicken thighs (about 7 thighs)
1   tablespoon vegetable oil
1   (1-pound) package frozen small white onions
6   cups sliced shiitake mushroom caps (about 1 pound)
3   cups canned low-sodium chicken broth, undiluted and divided
½   cup dry white wine
2   cloves garlic, minced
¼   cup all-purpose flour
½   teaspoon salt
1   cup all-purpose flour
1   teaspoon baking powder
½   teaspoon baking soda
½   teaspoon salt
1   tablespoon minced fresh parsley
¼   teaspoon freshly ground pepper
1½ tablespoons vegetable shortening
½   cup mashed cooked fresh pumpkin
½   cup low-fat buttermilk
1   cup nonfat sour cream
1   tablespoon minced fresh parsley

Sprinkle thyme and ½ teaspoon pepper over chicken. Heat vegetable oil in a Dutch oven over medium-high heat. Add chicken, and cook 5 minutes on each side or until browned. Remove chicken from Dutch oven, and set aside.

Add onions to Dutch oven, and sauté 5 minutes or until onions are lightly browned. Remove onions, and set aside.

Add mushroom caps and ¼ cup chicken broth to Dutch oven; cook, stirring constantly, 3 minutes or until moisture evaporates. Return chicken and onions to Dutch oven. Add 2½ cups chicken broth, wine, and minced garlic; bring mixture to a boil. Reduce heat, and simmer 1 minute.

Place ¼ cup flour and ½ teaspoon salt in a small bowl. Gradually add remaining ¼ cup chicken broth, stirring with a wire whisk until well blended; add mixture to Dutch oven. Cover and simmer 20 minutes, stirring occasionally.

Combine 1 cup flour and next 5 ingredients in a medium bowl, and cut in shortening with a pastry blender or 2 knives until mixture resembles coarse meal. Add mashed pumpkin and buttermilk to flour mixture, stirring just until dry ingredients are moistened; set dough aside.

Add sour cream to chicken mixture, and stir well. Drop dough onto chicken mixture to form 6 dumplings. Cover and simmer 20 minutes. Remove from heat, and spoon into 6 individual serving bowls. Sprinkle each serving with ½ teaspoon parsley. Yield: 6 servings (serving size: 3 ounces chicken, ¾ cup broth mixture, and 1 dumpling).

Note: Find directions for cooking fresh pumpkin on page 156, or, if desired, substitute the same amount of unsweetened canned pumpkin.

Calories 372 (23% from fat) **Protein** 34.1g **Fat** 9.5g (sat 2.5g) **Carbohydrates** 36.9g **Fiber** 2.0g **Cholesterol** 80mg **Iron** 4.4mg **Sodium** 672mg **Calcium** 106mg

QUICK TIP FOR GARLIC

A head of garlic typically contains 10 to 12 individual cloves. To peel a garlic clove, place a heavy-duty or chef's knife on top of the clove. Hit the flat side of the knife with the palm of your hand; this will slightly smash the clove, separating the peel from the garlic. The peel should then easily slip away from the clove.

Cajun Seafood and Sausage Gumbo

⅓ cup all-purpose flour
1 (12-ounce) container fresh Standard oysters, undrained
Vegetable cooking spray
2 cups frozen cut okra
2 cups chopped onion
1½ cups diced green pepper
1½ cups diced celery
2 cloves garlic, crushed
⅔ cup water
¼ cup chopped fresh parsley
2½ teaspoons paprika
¾ teaspoon dried thyme
½ teaspoon dried oregano
½ teaspoon ground white pepper
½ teaspoon ground red pepper
½ teaspoon black pepper
¼ teaspoon salt
½ pound smoked turkey sausage, cut into ¼-inch slices
2 (8-ounce) bottles clam juice
1 (14½-ounce) can no-salt-added whole tomatoes, undrained and chopped
1 (13¾-ounce) can no-salt-added chicken broth
2 small bay leaves
1 pound unpeeled small fresh shrimp
½ pound fresh lump crabmeat, drained
6 cups hot cooked long-grain rice (cooked without salt or fat)

Place flour in a shallow pan. Bake at 350° for 1 hour or until very brown, stirring every 15 minutes. Set browned flour aside.

Drain oysters, reserving liquid; set both aside.

Coat a Dutch oven with cooking spray; place over medium heat until hot. Add okra and next 4 ingredients; cook 12 minutes or until tender, stirring often. Stir in flour. Add reserved oyster liquid, water, and next 13 ingredients; bring to a boil, stirring constantly. Reduce heat; simmer, uncovered, 1 hour.

Peel and devein shrimp. Add shrimp, oysters, and crabmeat; stir mixture well. Cover and simmer 10 minutes or until shrimp are done and edges of oysters begin to curl. Remove and discard bay leaves. Serve gumbo over rice. Yield: 12 cups (serving size: 1 cup gumbo and ½ cup rice).

Calories 274 (20% from fat) **Protein** 18.1g **Fat** 6.1g (sat 1.3g) **Carbohydrates** 35.6g **Fiber** 2.0g **Cholesterol** 79mg **Iron** 5.1mg **Sodium** 435mg **Calcium** 125mg

Cajun Seafood and Sausage Gumbo

New England Clam Chowder

2 (6½-ounce) cans minced clams, undrained
Vegetable cooking spray
1 cup chopped onion
2 slices turkey bacon
1 clove garlic, minced
3 cups peeled, chopped red potato (about 1¼ pounds)
½ teaspoon dried thyme
2 (8-ounce) bottles clam juice
¼ cup plus 2 tablespoons all-purpose flour
2½ cups 2% low-fat milk
Freshly ground pepper
Chopped fresh parsley (optional)

Drain clams, reserving liquid; set clams and liquid aside.

Coat a Dutch oven with cooking spray; place over medium heat until hot. Add onion, bacon slices, and garlic; sauté 5 minutes. Add reserved clam liquid, potato, thyme, and clam juice; bring mixture to a boil. Cover, reduce heat, and simmer 20 minutes or until potato is tender.

Place 2 cups potato mixture, including bacon, in container of an electric blender; cover and process until smooth. Add potato puree to potato mixture in Dutch oven; stir well. Stir in clams. Combine flour and milk, stirring with a wire whisk until blended; add to chowder. Cook over medium heat, stirring constantly, 10 minutes or until thickened. Sprinkle with pepper.

Garnish with parsley, if desired. Yield: 8 cups (serving size: 1 cup).

Calories 164 (20% from fat) **Protein** 9.7g **Fat** 3.7g (sat 1.5g) **Carbohydrates** 21.9g **Fiber** 1.5g **Cholesterol** 27mg **Iron** 2.5mg **Sodium** 564mg **Calcium** 133mg

Grilled Seafood Cioppino

Cioppino (chuh-PEE-noh) is a traditional Italian fish stew.

¾ pound unpeeled medium-size fresh shrimp
1 tablespoon plus 1 teaspoon olive oil, divided
1 (8-ounce) sourdough baguette, cut crosswise into 12 slices
1½ cups chopped onion
3 cloves garlic, minced
½ cup dry white wine
1 teaspoon dried basil
1 teaspoon dried thyme
½ teaspoon hot sauce
¼ teaspoon salt
¼ teaspoon saffron
2 (14½-ounce) cans stewed tomatoes, undrained
1 (16-ounce) can low-sodium chicken broth
12 small mussels, scrubbed and debearded
¾ pound skinned sea bass, halibut, or snapper fillet, cut into 1-inch pieces
Vegetable cooking spray

Peel and devein shrimp, and set shrimp aside.

Brush 2 teaspoons oil evenly over 1 side of bread slices, and set bread slices aside.

Heat remaining 2 teaspoons oil in a large saucepan over medium heat. Add onion and garlic; sauté 5 minutes or until onion is tender. Add wine and next 7 ingredients; bring to a boil. Reduce heat, and simmer 20 minutes, stirring occasionally.

Add mussels to pan; cover and simmer 5 minutes or until shells open (discard any unopened shells). Remove from heat; set aside, and keep warm.

Thread shrimp and fish alternately onto each of 6 (9-inch) skewers. Coat grill rack with cooking spray; place rack on grill over medium-hot coals (350° to 400°). Place kabobs and bread slices on rack, and grill, uncovered, 6 minutes or until seafood is done and bread is toasted, turning both occasionally.

Ladle soup into 6 individual bowls; top with grilled seafood, and serve with toasted bread. Yield: 6 servings (serving size: 1 cup soup, 2 mussels, 3 ounces shrimp and fish, and 2 bread slices).

Calories 325 (20% from fat) **Protein** 30.9g **Fat** 7.3g (sat 1.7g) **Carbohydrate** 33.6g **Fiber** 2.0g **Cholesterol** 108mg **Iron** 5.0mg **Sodium** 843mg **Calcium** 162mg

OYSTER-ARTICHOKE SOUP

QUICK & EASY

Look for bottled clam juice in supermarkets on aisles with condiments or canned fish.

1	(16-ounce) container Standard oysters, undrained
1	teaspoon margarine
½	cup chopped green onions
3	(8-ounce) bottles clam juice
1	tablespoon chopped fresh parsley
½	teaspoon dried thyme
¼	teaspoon ground red pepper
¼	cup plus 2 tablespoons all-purpose flour
2	cups 2% low-fat milk
1	(14-ounce) can quartered artichoke hearts, drained

Sliced green onions (optional)
Freshly ground black pepper (optional)

Oyster-Artichoke Soup

Drain oysters, reserving ¼ cup juice; set both aside.

Melt margarine in a large saucepan. Add chopped green onions; sauté 3 minutes. Add reserved ¼ cup oyster juice, clam juice, and next 3 ingredients to saucepan; bring mixture to a boil. Reduce heat, and simmer, uncovered, 10 minutes.

Combine flour and milk in a small bowl, stirring with a wire whisk until blended. Add milk mixture to soup. Cook soup over medium heat, stirring constantly, 6 minutes or until thickened. Stir in oysters and artichokes, and cook 3 additional minutes or until edges of oysters curl.

To serve, ladle soup into individual serving bowls; if desired, garnish with sliced green onions and freshly ground black pepper. Yield: 7 cups (serving size: 1 cup).

Calories 127 (26% from fat) Protein 8.9g Fat 3.7g (sat 1.4g) Carbohydrate 14.8g Fiber 0.7g Cholesterol 41mg Iron 5.3mg Sodium 443mg Calcium 149mg

HOW TO BUY OYSTERS

Containers of shucked oysters are labeled "Select," "Standard," or "Stewing." Select are the largest, Standard are average size, and Stewing are the smallest. If you purchase oysters fresh, handle them safely, and keep refrigerated. (It's safe to eat oysters any time of the year when stored properly.)

Italian Cream Cake, page 206

It's time to confess. The staff of *Cooking Light* has a weakness for, um, desserts. In fact, our downfall is such a problem that when we listed all of the recipes we felt we had to include in this book, the list of desserts was embarrassingly long.

DESSERTS

Our favorite of these favorites? Oh, that's a hard one. But we can start by listing all the desserts we've highlighted on our covers over the years. Among them...Streusel Apple Pie...Blueberry-Cherry Crisp...Lemon Macaroon Tartlets...Raspberry Cheesecake Parfaits...Mocha Fudge Pie...Tiramisù...Strawberry Amaretto Cheesecake. And, of course, the recipe voted the staff favorite of all time: Italian Cream Cake. We suggest you make them all.

Streusel Apple Pie

1   (4-inch) vanilla bean, split lengthwise
¼   cup firmly packed brown sugar
1½ tablespoons all-purpose flour
½   teaspoon ground cinnamon
2½ pounds Rome or other cooking apples, peeled, cored, and thinly sliced
1¼ cups all-purpose flour, divided
3   tablespoons ice water
1   teaspoon sugar
¼   teaspoon salt
3   tablespoons vegetable shortening
Vegetable cooking spray
½   cup firmly packed brown sugar
¼   cup regular oats
¼   teaspoon ground cinnamon
3   tablespoons chilled stick margarine

Scrape seeds from vanilla bean into a large bowl; discard bean. Add ¼ cup brown sugar, 1½ tablespoons flour, and ½ teaspoon cinnamon to bowl; stir well. Add apple slices; toss well to coat. Set aside.

Combine ¼ cup flour and ice water, stirring with a wire whisk until well blended; set aside.

Combine ¾ cup flour, 1 teaspoon sugar, and salt in a bowl; cut in shortening with a pastry blender until mixture resembles coarse meal. Add ice water mixture, and toss with a fork until dry ingredients are moistened. Gently press into a 4-inch circle on heavy-duty plastic wrap; cover pastry with additional plastic wrap.

Roll pastry, still covered, into an 11-inch circle. Freeze pastry at least 10 minutes. Remove top sheet of plastic wrap from pastry; invert and fit pastry into a 9-inch pieplate coated with cooking spray. Remove top sheet of plastic wrap. Flute edge of pastry decoratively. Spoon apple mixture into pastry shell. Cover with aluminum foil, and bake at 350° for 45 minutes or until apple mixture is crisp-tender.

Combine remaining ¼ cup flour, ½ cup brown sugar, oats, and ¼ teaspoon cinnamon; cut in margarine until mixture resembles coarse meal. Uncover pie, and sprinkle streusel over apple mixture. Bake, uncovered, 25 additional minutes. Yield: 8 servings (serving size: 1 slice).

Calories 315 (26% from fat) **Protein** 2.7g **Fat** 9.1g (sat 2.2g) **Carbohydrate** 58.2g **Fiber** 4.6g **Cholesterol** 0mg **Iron** 1.6mg **Sodium** 132mg **Calcium** 32mg

Apple Crisp With Macadamia Nuts

QUICK & EASY

¼   cup all-purpose flour
¼   cup sugar
¼   cup firmly packed brown sugar
2   tablespoons chopped macadamia nuts
⅛   teaspoon ground cinnamon
2½ tablespoons chilled stick margarine
5   cups peeled, thinly sliced Rome apple
Vegetable cooking spray
2   tablespoons apricot preserves

Combine first 5 ingredients in a medium bowl; cut in margarine with a pastry blender until mixture resembles coarse meal. Set aside.

Place apple slices in an 8-inch square baking dish coated with cooking spray. Drop preserves by teaspoonfuls onto apple slices; sprinkle evenly with flour mixture. Bake at 375° for 35 minutes or until bubbly and golden. Yield: 6 servings (serving size: ¾ cup).

Calories 216 (30% from fat) **Protein** 0.9g **Fat** 7.3g (sat 1.3g) **Carbohydrate** 39.2g **Fiber** 2.7g **Cholesterol** 0mg **Iron** 0.6mg **Sodium** 62mg **Calcium** 17mg

BLUEBERRY-CHERRY CRISP

Keep blueberries at their freshest by storing them unwashed in the refrigerator. Wash the berries just before you use them.

- ¼ cup low-fat sour cream
- 1 tablespoon plus 1 teaspoon light brown sugar
- 2 cups fresh blueberries
- 2 cups pitted fresh sweet cherries
- ½ cup all-purpose flour
- 2 tablespoons sugar
- 2 tablespoons light brown sugar
- 2 tablespoons margarine, melted

Combine sour cream and 1 tablespoon plus 1 teaspoon brown sugar in a bowl; stir well. Cover and chill at least 30 minutes.

Combine blueberries and cherries in an 8-inch square pan, and toss mixture well.

Combine flour and remaining 3 ingredients in a medium bowl; beat at medium speed of an electric mixer until mixture is crumbly. Sprinkle over blueberry mixture. Bake at 375° for 40 minutes or until lightly browned. Top with sour cream mixture. Yield: 4 servings (serving size: ½ cup fruit crisp and 2 teaspoons topping).

Calories 276 (28% from fat) **Protein** 3.5g **Fat** 8.6g (sat 2.4g) **Carbohydrate** 49.1g **Fiber** 5.7g **Cholesterol** 6mg **Iron** 1.3mg **Sodium** 81mg **Calcium** 42mg

Blueberry-Cherry Crisp

PEACH COBBLER

If fresh peaches are out of season, substitute the same amount of frozen peach slices. Just thaw them before you use them.

2	cups all-purpose flour
1	tablespoon sugar
¼	teaspoon salt
¼	cup plus 2 tablespoons chilled stick margarine, cut into 6 pieces
¼	cup plus 2 tablespoons ice water
	Vegetable cooking spray
6	cups peeled, sliced peaches (about 3¾ pounds)
¾	cup firmly packed brown sugar, divided
2½	tablespoons all-purpose flour
1	tablespoon vanilla extract
1	teaspoon ground cinnamon
¼	cup slivered almonds
1	egg, lightly beaten
1	teaspoon water
1	tablespoon sugar

Position knife blade in food processor bowl; add first 3 ingredients, and pulse 2 or 3 times. Add margarine pieces, and pulse 10 times or until mixture resembles coarse meal. With processor running, slowly add ice water through food chute, processing just until combined (do not form a ball).

Gently press flour mixture into a 4-inch circle on heavy-duty plastic wrap; cover with additional plastic wrap. Roll dough, still covered, into a 15- x 13-inch rectangle. Place dough in freezer 5 minutes or until plastic wrap can easily be removed. Remove top sheet of plastic wrap. Invert and fit dough into a 2-quart baking dish coated with cooking spray, allowing dough to extend over edges of dish; remove top sheet of plastic wrap.

Combine peaches, ½ cup brown sugar, 2½ tablespoons flour, vanilla, and cinnamon in a large bowl; toss gently. Spoon peach mixture into prepared dish; fold edges of dough over peach mixture (it will only partially cover peaches). Sprinkle remaining ¼ cup brown sugar over peach mixture; sprinkle with almonds.

Combine egg and 1 teaspoon water in a small bowl; stir well. Brush egg mixture over dough, and sprinkle with 1 tablespoon sugar. Bake at 375° for 45 minutes or until filling is bubbly and crust is lightly browned. Let cobbler stand 30 minutes before serving. Yield: 10 servings.

Calories 302 (27% from fat) **Protein** 4.5g **Fat** 9.2g (sat 1.6g) **Carbohydrate** 51.5g **Fiber** 2.8g **Cholesterol** 11mg **Iron** 1.9mg **Sodium** 149mg **Calcium** 39mg

LEMON MACAROON TARTLETS

The tartlet crusts are actually chewy macaroon "cups" filled with a lightened lemon curd.

Macaroon Tart Shells

¾	cup sugar
1	tablespoon plus 2 teaspoons cornstarch
½	teaspoon grated lemon rind
⅓	cup water
⅓	cup fresh lemon juice
1	egg, lightly beaten
2	drops yellow food coloring (optional)
½	cup frozen reduced-calorie whipped topping, thawed
2	tablespoons flaked sweetened coconut, toasted

Prepare Macaroon Tart Shells, and set aside.

Combine sugar, cornstarch, and lemon rind in a saucepan, and stir well. Gradually add water and lemon juice; stir with a wire whisk until blended. Bring to a boil over medium heat, and cook, stirring constantly, 1 minute. Gradually stir one-fourth of hot lemon mixture into egg; add to remaining lemon mixture, stirring constantly. Cook over medium heat, stirring constantly, 1 minute or until thickened. Pour mixture into a bowl; stir in food coloring, if desired. Place plastic wrap on surface, and chill.

Spoon 1 tablespoon plus 1 teaspoon lemon mixture into each

prepared shell. Top evenly with whipped topping and coconut. Yield: 1 dozen (serving size: 1 tartlet).

Calories 204 (32% from fat) **Protein** 2.1g **Fat** 7.2g (sat 6.0g) **Carbohydrate** 34.1g **Fiber** 1.1g **Cholesterol** 18mg **Iron** 0.6mg **Sodium** 66mg **Calcium** 9mg

MACAROON TART SHELLS:

To keep the shells from being tough, spoon the flour into the measuring cup instead of packing it. Use large eggs, and spread the mixture thinly into the muffin cups. Baked shells may be frozen for later use.

2 cups flaked sweetened coconut
½ cup sugar
¼ cup plus 2 tablespoons all-purpose flour
1 teaspoon vanilla extract
2 egg whites
Vegetable cooking spray

Combine first 5 ingredients in a bowl; stir well. Spoon mixture evenly into 12 muffin cups coated with cooking spray, pressing mixture into bottom and up sides of muffin cups. Bake at 400° for 15 minutes or until edges are browned. (Do not overbake.) Cool 2 minutes in pan on a wire rack. Remove from pan; cool completely on wire rack. Yield: 1 dozen (serving size: 1 shell).

Calories 133 (40% from fat) **Protein** 1.4g **Fat** 6.0g (sat 5.3g) **Carbohydrate** 19.2g **Fiber** 1.0g **Cholesterol** 0mg **Iron** 0.5mg **Sodium** 53mg **Calcium** 3mg

PEAR CHARLOTTE

A charlotte is any fruit or custard dessert that's molded into a container lined with ladyfingers, sponge cake, or bread. This version couldn't be simpler. All you do is trim white bread slices to fit the sides and bottom of the dish. Then pour in the sweet pear filling, and bake.

Vegetable cooking spray
1 Bartlett or Anjou pear
8 (½-ounce) slices very thin white bread
3½ pounds very ripe Bartlett or Anjou pears
2 teaspoons margarine
⅓ cup firmly packed dark brown sugar
1½ tablespoons lemon juice
¼ teaspoon ground cinnamon
¾ cup vanilla nonfat frozen yogurt, softened

Coat a 1-quart glass soufflé dish with cooking spray; line bottom of dish with wax paper.

Cut 1 pear in half lengthwise. Cut a ⅛-inch-thick slice from a pear half. Center pear slice in bottom of prepared dish.

Trim crusts from bread; discard crusts. Cut 1 bread slice into small cubes; set cubes aside. Cut 5 bread slices in half lengthwise. Standing bread slices vertically in dish, line sides with 10 bread halves. Place 1 bread slice in bottom of dish; arrange bread cubes tightly around whole bread slice.

Peel and core 3½ pounds pears; cut lengthwise into slices to equal 8 cups, and set aside.

Melt margarine in a large skillet over medium heat. Stir in sugar, lemon juice, and cinnamon. Add pear slices; stir gently. Cover and cook pear mixture 15 minutes, stirring occasionally. Uncover and cook 15 additional minutes. Drain pear slices, reserving liquid.

Spoon pear slices into dish; press firmly with the back of a spoon. With scissors, trim tops of bread halves even with pear slices; reserve trimmed bread tops. Dip remaining whole bread slice and reserved trimmed bread tops in reserved pear liquid; arrange in center of dish over pear slices. Cover bread completely with aluminum foil, and cut 6 (1-inch) slits in foil. Bake at 350° for 50 minutes or until lightly browned. Uncover and cool in dish 1 hour on a wire rack.

To serve, loosen edges of charlotte with a knife; invert charlotte onto a serving plate, and peel off wax paper. Combine yogurt and ¼ cup plus 2 tablespoons reserved pear cooking liquid; stir well. Serve with charlotte. Yield: 6 servings (serving size: 1 wedge charlotte and 3 tablespoons yogurt sauce).

Calories 262 (10% from fat) **Protein** 3.5g **Fat** 2.9g (sat 0.4g) **Carbohydrate** 59.9g **Fiber** 6.1g **Cholesterol** 1mg **Iron** 1.5mg **Sodium** 131mg **Calcium** 86mg

CARAMEL-PINEAPPLE UPSIDE-DOWN CAKE

1 (15¼-ounce) can unsweetened pineapple slices, undrained
½ cup granulated sugar
2½ tablespoons water
¼ cup margarine, divided
Vegetable cooking spray
9 maraschino cherry halves
½ cup firmly packed brown sugar
1 egg
1 egg white
1¼ cups all-purpose flour
½ teaspoon baking soda
½ teaspoon baking powder
¼ teaspoon salt
½ cup nonfat buttermilk
½ teaspoon vanilla extract

Drain pineapple slices, reserving ¼ cup pineapple juice. Set aside 5 pineapple slices, reserving remaining slices for another use.

Combine granulated sugar and water in a small heavy saucepan. Place over medium-low heat, and cook 6 minutes or until sugar dissolves. (Do not stir.) Cover, increase heat to medium, and cook 1 minute. Uncover and cook 5 additional minutes or until sugar mixture is amber or golden.

Remove from heat, and let stand 1 minute. Add 1 tablespoon margarine, stirring until margarine melts. Gradually add reserved ¼ cup pineapple juice, stirring constantly. (The caramelized sugar will harden and stick to spoon.) Place over medium heat, and cook, stirring constantly, 3 minutes or until caramel melts and mixture is smooth.

Pour caramel mixture into a 9-inch round cakepan coated with cooking spray. Position 1 pineapple slice in center of pan; cut remaining 4 pineapple slices in half, and arrange slices spoke-fashion around whole slice in center. Place a cherry half in center of each pineapple slice; set aside.

Beat remaining 3 tablespoons margarine at medium speed of an electric mixer until creamy, and gradually add brown sugar, beating well (about 5 minutes). Add egg and egg white, and beat well.

Combine flour and next 3 ingredients in a bowl. Add flour mixture to margarine mixture alternately with buttermilk, beginning and ending with flour mixture. Beat at low speed after each addition until blended. Stir in vanilla.

Pour batter evenly over pineapple. Bake at 350° for 30 minutes or until a wooden pick inserted in center comes out clean. Cool in pan 5 minutes; invert cake onto a serving plate. Serve warm. Yield: 10 servings (serving size: 1 slice).

Calories 210 (23% from fat) Protein 3.1g Fat 5.3g (sat 1.1g) Carbohydrate 37.8g Fiber 0.4g Cholesterol 22mg Iron 1.1mg Sodium 199mg Calcium 51mg

STRAWBERRY SHORTCAKE

Large, amber-colored turbinado sugar crystals have a slight molasses flavor. Find them in specialty food shops and in some supermarkets.

Strawberry Topping
2 cups all-purpose flour
2 teaspoons baking powder
¼ teaspoon baking soda
¼ teaspoon salt
¼ cup sugar
3 tablespoons plus 1 teaspoon chilled stick margarine, cut into small pieces
¾ cup 1% nonfat buttermilk
1 egg white, lightly beaten
1½ teaspoons turbinado or granulated sugar
½ cup frozen reduced-calorie whipped topping, thawed
Fresh strawberries (optional)

Prepare Strawberry Topping; cover and chill.

Combine flour and next 4 ingredients; cut in margarine with a pastry blender until mixture resembles coarse meal. Add buttermilk; stir just until dry ingredients are moistened.

Turn dough out onto a floured surface. Knead dough 5 or 6 times. Roll dough to ½-inch thickness; cut with a 3-inch biscuit cutter. Place rounds on a baking sheet, and brush with egg white; sprinkle with turbinado sugar.

Bake at 450° for 10 minutes or until golden. Split biscuits, and place bottom halves of biscuits on

Strawberry Shortcake

individual serving plates. Top each with ⅔ cup Strawberry Topping and top half of biscuit. Spoon whipped topping evenly over each shortcake. Garnish with fresh strawberries, if desired. Yield: 6 servings (serving size: 1 shortcake and ⅔ cup strawberry topping).

Calories 350 (20% from fat) **Protein** 7.1g **Fat** 7.8g (sat 1.4g) **Carbohydrate** 64.1g **Fiber** 3.5g **Cholesterol** 1mg **Iron** 2.6mg **Sodium** 274mg **Calcium** 152mg

STRAWBERRY TOPPING:

4   **cups sliced fresh strawberries**
1   **tablespoon sugar**
¼   **cup red currant jelly**
2   **tablespoons water**

Combine strawberries and sugar; let stand 30 minutes.

Combine jelly and water in a small saucepan; place over low heat. Cook, stirring until jelly melts.

Remove from heat, and stir into strawberry mixture. Spoon topping into a bowl; cover and chill. Yield: 4 cups (serving size: ⅔ cup).

Calories 67 (4% from fat) **Protein** 0.6g **Fat** 0.3g (sat 0.0g) **Carbohydrate** 16.9g **Fiber** 2.3g **Cholesterol** 0mg **Iron** 0.3mg **Sodium** 5mg **Calcium** 13mg

MOCHA PUDDING CAKE

QUICK & EASY

1   cup all-purpose flour
2   teaspoons baking powder
¼   teaspoon salt
1   cup sugar, divided
¼   cup plus 2 tablespoons
    unsweetened cocoa, divided
1½ tablespoons instant coffee
    granules
½   cup 1% low-fat milk
3   tablespoons vegetable oil
1   teaspoon vanilla extract
Vegetable cooking spray
1   cup boiling water
2¼ cups low-fat vanilla ice
    cream

Combine flour, baking powder, salt, ⅔ cup sugar, ¼ cup cocoa, and coffee granules in a large bowl. Combine milk, oil, and vanilla; add to dry ingredients, stirring well. Spoon batter into an 8-inch square pan coated with cooking spray.

Combine remaining ⅓ cup sugar and 2 tablespoons cocoa. Sprinkle over batter. Pour boiling water over batter. (Do not stir.) Bake at 350° for 30 minutes or until cake springs back when lightly touched in center. Serve warm, topped with ice cream. Yield: 9 servings (serving size: one 3- x 3-inch piece and ¼ cup low-fat ice cream).

Calories 247 (25% from fat) **Protein** 4.2g **Fat** 6.8g (sat 2.1g) **Carbohydrate** 43.0g **Fiber** 0.4g **Cholesterol** 5mg **Iron** 1.4mg **Sodium** 102mg **Calcium** 131mg

Mocha
Pudding Cake

SOUR CREAM POUND CAKE

The original unlightened version of this cake belonged to the grandmother of staff member Polly Linthicum. In the November/December 1993 issue of *Cooking Light*, we made it healthier so Polly and her family could keep tradition each holiday and keep their waistlines, too.

¾   cup margarine, softened
3   cups sugar
1⅓   cups fat-free egg substitute
1½   cups low-fat sour cream
1   teaspoon baking soda
4½   cups sifted cake flour
¼   teaspoon salt
2   teaspoons vanilla extract
Vegetable cooking spray

Beat margarine at medium speed of an electric mixer until creamy; gradually add sugar, beating well. Gradually add egg substitute to creamed mixture, beating well.

Combine sour cream and baking soda, and stir well. Combine flour and salt. With mixer running at low speed, add flour mixture to margarine mixture alternately with sour cream mixture, beginning and ending with flour mixture. Stir in vanilla.

Spoon batter into a 10-inch tube pan coated with cooking spray. Bake at 325° for 1 hour and 35 minutes or until a wooden pick inserted in center of cake comes out clean.

Cool in pan 10 minutes. Remove cake from pan, and cool on a wire rack. Yield: 24 servings (serving size: 1 slice).

Note: Substitute 8 egg whites for 1⅓ cups egg substitute, if desired. Add egg whites, one at a time, to batter.

Calories 250 (28% from fat) **Protein** 3.5g **Fat** 7.7g (sat 2.3g) **Carbohydrate** 42.0g **Fiber** 0.0g **Cholesterol** 6mg **Iron** 1.8mg **Sodium** 152mg **Calcium** 33mg

THE WAY TO PERFECT POUND CAKES

Just follow these tips for picture-perfect pound cakes:

• Use the type of flour specified in the recipe. Light cakes often call for sifted cake flour. If you don't sift the flour, or if you substitute all-purpose, then you may add too much flour to the batter and cause the cake to be dry.

• Be sure to measure flour accurately. Use a measuring cup for dry ingredients, and lightly spoon the flour into the cup; then level it with the flat part of a knife or spatula. Do not pack or shake the flour in the measuring cup.

• Let margarine and milk reach room temperature before mixing.

• Beat the margarine and sugar mixture well at the beginning of the mixing process. If you don't mix it well enough at this stage, the cake texture may be coarse.

BASIC SPONGE CAKE

Here's a basic sponge cake recipe that allows you to make three different desserts: this simple cake, Sugared Almond-Topped Cake, and Triple-Berry Trifle.

1   cup sifted cake flour
1   teaspoon baking powder
¼   teaspoon salt
3   eggs, separated
1   cup sugar, divided
2   teaspoons vanilla extract
¼   cup water
2   egg whites

Combine first 3 ingredients; stir well, and set aside. Beat 3 egg yolks in a large mixing bowl at high speed of an electric mixer 1 minute. Gradually add ¾ cup sugar, beating constantly until egg yolks are thick and pale (about 5 minutes). Add vanilla and ¼ cup water, beating at low speed until blended. Add flour mixture to egg yolk mixture, beating at low speed until blended; set mixture aside.

Beat 5 egg whites at high speed of mixer until foamy. Gradually add remaining ¼ cup sugar, 1 tablespoon at a time, beating until stiff peaks form. Gently stir one-fourth of egg white mixture into batter. Gently fold in remaining egg white mixture.

Pour batter into an ungreased 10-inch tube pan. Bake at 350° for 35 minutes or until cake springs back when touched lightly in center. Invert pan; cool 45 minutes.

Loosen cake from sides of pan, using a narrow metal spatula; remove cake from pan. Yield: 10 servings (serving size: 1 slice).

Calories 141 (10% from fat) Protein 3.4g Fat 1.6g (sat 0.5g) Carbohydrate 28.0g Fiber 0.0g Cholesterol 64mg Iron 0.9mg Sodium 119mg Calcium 28mg

SUGARED ALMOND-TOPPED CAKE

If you want stronger almond flavor in this cake, substitute 1 teaspoon almond extract for the 2 teaspoons vanilla in the recipe for Basic Sponge Cake.

Basic Sponge Cake batter (at left)
⅓   cup firmly packed brown sugar
2   tablespoons all-purpose flour
¼   teaspoon ground cinnamon
2   tablespoons margarine
1   tablespoon plus 1 teaspoon skim milk
⅓   cup sliced almonds

Pour Basic Sponge Cake batter into an ungreased 10-inch springform pan, spreading batter evenly. Bake at 350° for 25 minutes or until cake springs back when touched lightly in center. Remove cake from oven, and set aside.

Combine sugar, flour, and cinnamon; stir well. Melt margarine in a small saucepan over medium heat; add sugar mixture, stirring well. Gradually add milk, stirring with a wire whisk. Cook, stirring constantly, 2 minutes. Remove from heat; stir in almonds. Spread almond mixture over warm cake. Broil cake 3 inches from heat (with electric oven door partially opened) 1 minute or until bubbly. Using a sharp knife, cut into wedges. Serve warm or at room temperature. Yield: 10 servings (serving size: 1 slice).

Calories 214 (24% from fat) Protein 4.2g Fat 5.6g (sat 1.1g) Carbohydrate 37.0g Fiber 0.4g Cholesterol 64mg Iron 1.4mg Sodium 149mg Calcium 47mg

TRIPLE-BERRY TRIFLE

Vegetable cooking spray
Basic Sponge Cake batter (at left)
3   (8-ounce) cartons vanilla low-fat yogurt
¼   cup sugar
1   (10-ounce) package frozen raspberries in light syrup, thawed and undrained
2   cups frozen blueberries, thawed
3   cups halved fresh strawberries
3   tablespoons cream sherry
3   fresh strawberry halves

Coat a 15- x 10- x 1-inch jellyroll pan with cooking spray, and line with wax paper. Coat wax paper with cooking spray. Spread Basic Sponge Cake batter evenly into prepared pan. Bake at 350° for 15 minutes or until cake springs back when touched lightly in center.

Immediately loosen cake from sides of pan, and invert onto a wire rack. Peel off wax paper, and cool completely. Cut cake into ¾-inch cubes; set cubes aside.

Place a colander in a 2-quart glass measure or medium bowl. Line colander with 4 layers of cheesecloth, allowing cheesecloth to extend over edges. Spoon yogurt into colander; cover loosely with plastic wrap, and chill 1 hour. Spoon yogurt cheese into a bowl; discard liquid. Add sugar; stir well. Cover and chill.

Position knife blade in food processor bowl, and add raspberries to bowl. Process until smooth. Pour into a bowl; stir in blueberries and 3 cups strawberries. Set aside.

Line bottom of a 2-quart trifle bowl with one-third of cake cubes; drizzle with 1 tablespoon sherry. Spoon half of berry mixture over cake cube layer; spoon one-third of yogurt mixture over berry layer. Repeat layers. Place remaining cake cubes over yogurt mixture. Drizzle remaining 1 tablespoon sherry over cake cubes. Spoon remaining yogurt mixture over top. Cover and chill up to 4 hours. Arrange 3 strawberry halves on top of trifle. Yield: 15 servings (serving size: ½ cup).

Calories 176 (11% from fat) **Protein** 4.5g **Fat** 2.1g (sat 0.8g) **Carbohydrate** 34.6g **Fiber** 2.8g **Cholesterol** 44mg **Iron** 0.9mg **Sodium** 96mg **Calcium** 76mg

CARROT CAKE WITH CREAM CHEESE ICING

We suggest using freshly grated carrots rather than packaged preshredded carrots for the best flavor in this cake.

1¾   cups all-purpose flour
⅔   cup whole wheat flour
2   teaspoons baking soda
⅛   teaspoon salt
1   teaspoon ground cinnamon
¾   teaspoon ground allspice
¼   teaspoon ground nutmeg
¾   cup firmly packed brown sugar
3   tablespoons vegetable oil
2   eggs
3   cups coarsely shredded carrot (about 1 pound)
½   cup raisins
⅔   cup nonfat buttermilk
2   teaspoons vanilla extract
1   (8-ounce) can crushed pineapple in juice, drained
Vegetable cooking spray
Cream Cheese Icing

Combine first 7 ingredients in a medium bowl; stir well.

Combine sugar and oil in a large bowl; stir well. Add eggs, one at a time, beating well with a wire whisk after each addition. Stir in carrot, raisins, buttermilk, vanilla, and pineapple. Add flour mixture, and stir well.

Spoon batter into a 13- x 9- x 2-inch pan coated with cooking spray. Bake at 350° for 30 minutes or until a wooden pick inserted in center comes out clean. Cool completely in pan on a wire rack.

Prepare Cream Cheese Icing while cake cools. Spread Cream Cheese Icing over top of cooled cake. Yield: 18 servings (serving size: one 3- x 2-inch piece).

Calories 274 (18% from fat) **Protein** 3.9g **Fat** 5.6g (sat 2.2g) **Carbohydrate** 53.3g **Fiber** 1.6g **Cholesterol** 33mg **Iron** 1.3mg **Sodium** 212mg **Calcium** 31mg

CREAM CHEESE ICING:

2   teaspoons light butter (do not soften)
6   ounces Neufchâtel cheese (do not soften)
3¾   cups sifted powdered sugar
¾   teaspoon vanilla extract

Beat butter and cheese at high speed of an electric mixer until fluffy. Gradually add sugar; beat at low speed until well blended. Add vanilla; beat well. Yield: 1¾ cups (analysis per 1 tablespoon).

Calories 80 (18% from fat) **Protein** 0.6g **Fat** 1.6g (sat 1.0g) **Carbohydrate** 16.2g **Fiber** 0.0g **Cholesterol** 5mg **Iron** 0.0mg **Sodium** 26mg **Calcium** 5mg

"This cake tastes so rich, it's hard to believe it's light. I made it about 15 times for photography when we featured it on a cover, and it traveled great when I froze it overnight. Now, at our house, it's the traditional cake for birthdays, holidays, and company."

——Kellie Kelley,
Test Kitchens Staff

TIPS FOR A WINNING CAKE

This is it! We voted Italian Cream Cake to be our staff's favorite of all time. Follow these tips for making the icing, especially if it's a hot, humid day.

• Chill a glass or metal mixing bowl before you make the icing.
• Use chilled butter and cream cheese (not softened) straight from the refrigerator. Do not soften them ahead of time, or the icing will not have the proper consistency.
• Mix the icing only until the sugar is incorporated. Do *not* beat it. Excessive beating "warms up" the cream cheese and allows it to become too soft.
• If it's an exceptionally hot, humid day, set the bowl of cream cheese icing into a larger bowl of ice water to keep it from melting while you frost the cake.

ITALIAN CREAM CAKE

Cream Cheese Icing
Vegetable cooking spray
½   cup light butter, softened
2   cups sugar
2   egg yolks
2   cups all-purpose flour
1   teaspoon baking soda
1   cup low-fat buttermilk
½   cup chopped pecans
1   teaspoon butter extract
1   teaspoon coconut extract
1   teaspoon vanilla extract
6   egg whites
Lemon rind strips (optional)

Prepare Cream Cheese Icing; cover and chill.

Coat bottoms of 3 (9-inch) round cakepans with cooking spray (do not coat sides of pans); line bottoms of cakepans with wax paper. Coat wax paper with cooking spray, and dust with flour; set aside.

Beat butter at medium speed of an electric mixer until butter is creamy; gradually add sugar, beating well. Add egg yolks, one at a time, beating well after each addition.

Combine 2 cups flour and baking soda; stir well. Add flour mixture to butter mixture alternately with buttermilk, beginning and ending with flour mixture. Stir in pecans and next 3 ingredients.

Beat egg whites at high speed of mixer until stiff peaks form (do not overbeat). Fold egg whites into batter; pour batter into prepared pans. Bake at 350° for 23 minutes. Cool in pans 5 minutes on wire racks.

Loosen cake layers from sides of pans using a narrow metal spatula, and turn out onto wire racks. Peel off wax paper, and cool completely.

Place 1 cake layer on a serving plate, and spread with ⅔ cup Cream Cheese Icing; top with second cake layer. Repeat with ⅔ cup icing and third cake layer. Spread remaining icing over cake. Garnish with lemon rind strips, if desired. Yield: 20 servings (serving size: 1 slice).

Calories 300 (24% from fat) **Protein** 4.5g **Fat** 8.0g (sat 3.7g) **Carbohydrate** 53.8g **Fiber** 0.5g **Cholesterol** 39mg **Iron** 0.7mg **Sodium** 166mg **Calcium** 28mg

CREAM CHEESE ICING:

1   tablespoon light butter (do not soften)
1   (8-ounce) package Neufchâtel cheese (do not soften)
1   (1-pound) package powdered sugar, sifted
1   teaspoon vanilla extract

Beat butter and cheese at high speed of an electric mixer until fluffy. Gradually add sugar, and beat at low speed until blended. Add vanilla; beat well. Yield: 2⅔ cups (analysis per 1 tablespoon).

Calories 58 (22% from fat) **Protein** 0.5g **Fat** 1.4g (sat 0.9g) **Carbohydrate** 10.9g **Fiber** 0.0g **Cholesterol** 5mg **Iron** 0.0mg **Sodium** 23mg **Calcium** 4mg

STRAWBERRY-AMARETTO CHEESECAKE

You can find almond-flavored amaretto cookies in well-stocked supermarkets or specialty shops. Cookie size varies with the brand, so crumble just enough to measure the ¼ cup you need for the crust. You can substitute vanilla wafers.

Vegetable cooking spray
¼   cup amaretto cookie crumbs
1   (24-ounce) carton 1% low-fat cottage cheese
2   (8-ounce) cartons light process cream cheese
1   cup sugar, divided
2   tablespoons amaretto (almond-flavored liqueur)
2   eggs
2   egg whites
⅛   teaspoon cream of tartar
2¾   cups halved fresh strawberries, divided
1   tablespoon sugar
1   fresh mint sprig (optional)

Coat bottom of a 10-inch springform pan with cooking spray, and sprinkle with crumbs. Set aside.

Position knife blade in food processor bowl; add cottage cheese and cream cheese, and process 1 minute or until smooth, scraping sides of processor bowl once. Add ¾ cup plus 2 tablespoons sugar, amaretto, and 2 eggs; process until smooth. Pour into a large bowl.

Beat egg whites and cream of tartar at high speed of an electric mixer until foamy. Gradually add remaining 2 tablespoons sugar, 1 tablespoon at a time, beating until stiff peaks form. Gently stir one-fourth of egg white mixture into cheese mixture. Gently fold in remaining egg white mixture.

Pour batter into prepared pan. Bake at 300° for 45 to 50 minutes or until almost set (center will be soft but will become firm when chilled). Remove from oven; cool on a wire rack. Cover; chill 8 hours.

Combine ¾ cup strawberries and 1 tablespoon sugar in container of an electric blender; cover and process until smooth.

Stir in remaining 2 cups strawberries. Spoon sauce evenly over cheesecake. Garnish with mint sprig, if desired. Yield: 14 servings (serving size: 1 slice).

Calories 231 (30% from fat) **Protein** 11.4g **Fat** 8.5g (sat 3.8g) **Carbohydrate** 26.2g **Fiber** 0.7g **Cholesterol** 52mg **Iron** 0.5mg **Sodium** 431mg **Calcium** 84mg

CHEESECAKE CRACK CONTROL

If you've never baked a cheesecake that developed a crater across the top, then you're unusual. Cheesecakes have a tendency to crack as they bake or cool, and it's a real disappointment when the cake is for company. Over the years, we've been on a mission to eliminate cracks altogether. We haven't solved the problem completely, but we have discovered that the cakes are less likely to crack when we use the following techniques. You may want to try these on some of your favorite cheesecake recipes.

• Don't overbeat the cream cheese mixture. The more air you incorporate, the more likely it is that the cake will crack. That's why we instruct you to combine cream cheese, sugar, eggs, and other ingredients all together to beat. The standard method of beating the cream cheese first, then gradually adding other ingredients, allows too much air to get into the mixture.

• Bake cheesecakes at a low temperature. Around 300° is good. This allows the filling to heat and cook slowly.

• Abrupt changes in temperature tend to make the cheesecake crack. We recommend that you turn off the oven when the cheesecake is done and then leave it in the oven to cool for an hour.

• How do you know when it's done? Here's the test we use: The cake should be set around the edges, but the center portion should wiggle slightly when you shake the pan. A knife stuck into this center section will not come out clean, but the cake will be too dry if you continue to bake until the center is set.

COFFEE CHEESECAKE

Vegetable cooking spray

¾ cup graham cracker crumbs

2 tablespoons sugar

2 tablespoons reduced-calorie stick margarine, melted

1 tablespoon unsweetened cocoa

⅔ cup sugar

⅓ cup all-purpose flour

1 tablespoon cornstarch

1 teaspoon vanilla extract

1 (8-ounce) package Neufchâtel cheese

1 (8-ounce) carton nonfat cream cheese

2 eggs

½ cup skim milk

2½ tablespoons instant coffee granules

⅓ cup nonfat sour cream

3 egg whites

¼ cup sugar

Coat a 9-inch springform pan with cooking spray. Combine graham cracker crumbs and next 3 ingredients, and stir well. Firmly press crumb mixture into bottom and 2 inches up sides of pan; set pan aside.

Combine ⅔ cup sugar and next 6 ingredients in a large bowl; beat at high speed of an electric mixer until blended. Combine milk and coffee granules; stir well. Add milk mixture and sour cream to cream cheese mixture; beat until smooth.

Beat egg whites at high speed of mixer until soft peaks form.

Gradually add ¼ cup sugar, 1 tablespoon at a time, beating until stiff peaks form. Gently fold egg white mixture into cheese mixture.

Pour batter into prepared pan. Bake at 300° for 1 hour or until almost set. Turn oven off; loosen cheesecake from sides of pan, using a narrow metal spatula or knife. Let cheesecake stand in oven with door slightly open for 1 hour. Remove cheesecake from oven; cover and chill 8 hours. Yield: 12 servings (serving size: 1 slice).

Calories 211 (30% from fat) Protein 8.2g Fat 7.0g (sat 3.4g) Carbohydrate 27.8g Fiber 0.1g Cholesterol 53mg Iron 0.7mg Sodium 286mg Calcium 90mg

TIRAMISÙ

⅔ cup sifted powdered sugar

1 (8-ounce) carton low-fat cream cheese

1½ cups frozen reduced-calorie whipped topping, thawed and divided

½ cup sugar

¼ cup water

3 egg whites

½ cup hot water

1 tablespoon sugar

1 tablespoon instant espresso coffee granules

2 tablespoons Kahlúa or other coffee-flavored liqueur

20 ladyfingers

½ teaspoon unsweetened cocoa

Combine powdered sugar and cream cheese in a large bowl, and beat at high speed of an electric mixer until mixture is well blended. Gently fold 1 cup whipped topping into cheese mixture.

Combine ½ cup sugar, ¼ cup water, and egg whites in top of a double boiler; place over simmering water. Beat mixture at high speed of mixer until stiff peaks form. Gently stir one-fourth of egg white mixture into cheese mixture. Gently fold in remaining egg white mixture, and set aside.

Combine ½ cup hot water, 1 tablespoon sugar, coffee granules, and liqueur. Stir mixture well.

Split ladyfingers in half lengthwise. Arrange 20 ladyfinger halves, cut sides up, in bottom of an 8-inch square baking dish. Drizzle half of espresso mixture over ladyfinger layer. Spread half of cheese mixture over ladyfinger halves; repeat procedure with remaining ladyfinger halves, espresso mixture, and cheese mixture. Spread remaining ½ cup whipped topping evenly over cheese mixture; sprinkle with cocoa.

Place a wooden pick in each corner of dish and in center of Tiramisù to keep plastic wrap from sticking to whipped topping; cover with plastic wrap. Chill 2 hours. Yield: 8 servings (serving size: one 4- x 2-inch piece).

Note: If you freeze the dessert two hours before serving, it will cut more cleanly.

Calories 226 (28% from fat) Protein 4.7g Fat 7.0g (sat 4.1g) Carbohydrate 30.0g Fiber 0.0g Cholesterol 41mg Iron 0.1mg Sodium 199mg Calcium 49mg

RASPBERRY CHEESECAKE PARFAITS

¼   cup lite ricotta cheese
¼   cup nonfat process cream
     cheese
2   tablespoons sugar
2   tablespoons no-sugar-added
     all-fruit seedless raspberry
     spread, melted
1   cup fresh raspberries
¼   cup plus 2 tablespoons
     vanilla wafer cookie crumbs
     (about 10 cookies)
2   tablespoons frozen
     reduced-calorie whipped
     topping, thawed

Position knife blade in food
processor bowl; add first 3 ingredients. Process until smooth, scraping
sides of processor bowl once; set
mixture aside.

Combine raspberry spread and
raspberries, and stir gently. Spoon
¼ cup raspberry mixture into each
of 2 (8-ounce) parfait glasses. Top
each with 2 tablespoons ricotta mixture, 3 tablespoons cookie crumbs,
2 tablespoons ricotta mixture, ¼
cup raspberry mixture, and 1 tablespoon whipped topping. Chill parfaits at least 2 hours before serving.
Yield: 2 servings.

Calories 244 (22% from fat) **Protein** 8.6g
Fat 5.9g (sat 2.1g) **Carbohydrate** 40.2g
Fiber 4.6g **Cholesterol** 9mg **Iron** 0.7mg
Sodium 269mg **Calcium** 138mg

Raspberry
Cheesecake
Parfaits

CHOCOLATE PUDDING

QUICK & EASY

⅔ cup sugar

⅓ cup unsweetened cocoa

¼ cup cornstarch

1 tablespoon all-purpose flour

⅛ teaspoon salt

3 cups 1% low-fat milk

1 tablespoon margarine

1 teaspoon vanilla extract

¼ cup plus 2 tablespoons frozen reduced-calorie whipped topping, thawed

Combine first 5 ingredients in a saucepan; stir well. Gradually add milk, stirring with a wire whisk until well blended. Bring to a boil over medium heat; cook, stirring constantly, 1 minute. Remove from heat; stir in margarine and vanilla.

Spoon ½ cup pudding into each of 6 individual dessert dishes. Cover with plastic wrap; cool to room temperature. Chill at least 3 hours. Remove plastic wrap from dessert dishes; top each serving with 1 tablespoon whipped topping. Yield: 6 servings (serving size: ½ cup).

Calories 211 (19% from fat) Protein 5.7g Fat 4.4g (sat 1.9g) Carbohydrate 37.4g Fiber 0.1g Cholesterol 5mg Iron 1.0mg Sodium 138mg Calcium 162mg

BOSTON CREAM PIE

Vanilla Pastry Cream
Vegetable cooking spray

3½ tablespoons margarine, softened

½ cup sugar

1 egg yolk

1½ cups sifted cake flour

1½ teaspoons baking powder

⅛ teaspoon salt

½ cup skim milk

1 teaspoon vanilla extract

2 egg whites

3 tablespoons sugar

Chocolate Glaze

Prepare Vanilla Pastry Cream; cover and chill.

Coat a 9-inch round cakepan with cooking spray; line bottom of pan with wax paper. Set aside.

Beat margarine at medium speed of an electric mixer until creamy; gradually add ½ cup sugar, beating well. Add egg yolk; beat well. Combine flour, baking powder, and salt; add to margarine mixture alternately with milk, beginning and ending with flour mixture. Mix at low speed until blended after each addition. Stir in vanilla.

Beat egg whites at high speed of mixer until foamy. Gradually add 3 tablespoons sugar, 1 tablespoon at a time, beating until stiff peaks form. Gently stir one-fourth of egg white mixture into batter. Gently fold in remaining egg white mixture. Pour into prepared pan. Bake at 350° for 35 minutes or until cake springs back when touched in center. Cool

in pan 5 minutes on a wire rack, and remove from pan. Peel off wax paper; cool completely on wire rack.

Prepare Chocolate Glaze; set aside.

Using a serrated knife, split cake in half horizontally. Place bottom layer, cut side up, on a serving plate. Spread Vanilla Pastry Cream over bottom cake layer; top with remaining cake layer. Spread Chocolate Glaze over top of cake. Chill 1 hour or until glaze is set. Yield: 10 servings (serving size: 1 slice).

Calories 281 (27% from fat) Protein 4.6g Fat 8.4g (sat 2.8g) Carbohydrate 47.9g Fiber 0.1g Cholesterol 46mg Iron 1.6mg Sodium 126mg Calcium 99mg

VANILLA PASTRY CREAM:

⅓ cup sugar

2½ tablespoons cornstarch

1¼ cups 2% low-fat milk

⅓ cup maple syrup

1 egg, lightly beaten

1 teaspoon margarine

1 teaspoon vanilla extract

Combine sugar and cornstarch in a saucepan; stir well. Gradually add milk and maple syrup; stir with a wire whisk until blended. Bring to a boil over medium heat, and cook, stirring constantly, 1 minute. Remove from heat. Gradually stir one-fourth of hot milk mixture into egg; add to remaining milk mixture, stirring constantly. Cook over medium heat, stirring constantly, 1 minute or until thickened. Remove from heat; stir in margarine and vanilla. Pour mixture into a bowl; place plastic wrap on surface of pastry cream, and chill.

CHOCOLATE GLAZE:

1   tablespoon maple syrup
2   tablespoons water
1   teaspoon margarine
2   (1-ounce) squares semisweet chocolate

Combine all ingredients in top of a double boiler; bring water to a boil. Reduce heat to low; cook until chocolate melts, stirring often.

BUTTERSCOTCH CREAM PIE

1   cup all-purpose flour
⅛   teaspoon salt
3   tablespoons vegetable shortening
3   tablespoons plus 2 teaspoons ice water
Vegetable cooking spray
⅔   cup firmly packed dark brown sugar
⅔   cup all-purpose flour
⅛   teaspoon salt
2   cups 1% low-fat milk
1   egg yolk
2   teaspoons margarine
1½   teaspoons vanilla extract
½   cup frozen reduced-calorie whipped topping, thawed
2   teaspoons dark brown sugar

Combine 1 cup flour and ⅛ teaspoon salt; cut in shortening with a pastry blender until mixture resembles coarse meal. Sprinkle ice water, 1 tablespoon at a time, over surface of flour mixture; toss with a fork until dry ingredients are moistened. Gently press dough into a 4-inch circle on heavy-duty plastic wrap; cover with additional plastic wrap. Roll dough, still covered, into an 11-inch circle. Place dough in freezer 5 minutes or until plastic wrap can be easily removed.

Remove top sheet of plastic wrap from dough; invert and fit dough into a 9-inch pieplate coated with cooking spray. Remove top sheet of plastic wrap. Fold edges of dough under, and flute. Prick bottom and sides of dough with a fork. Bake at 425° for 15 minutes or until lightly browned; cool crust completely on a wire rack.

Combine ⅔ cup sugar, ⅔ cup flour, and ⅛ teaspoon salt in a medium saucepan. Gradually add milk and egg yolk, stirring with a wire whisk until well blended. Place over medium heat, and cook, stirring constantly, 16 minutes or until thickened and bubbly. Remove from heat; stir in margarine and vanilla. Pour mixture into prepared crust; cover with plastic wrap. Chill 4 hours or until set.

Remove plastic wrap. Dollop whipped topping over filling, and sprinkle dollops evenly with 2 teaspoons brown sugar. Yield: 8 servings (serving size: 1 slice).

Calories 250 (26% from fat) **Protein** 5.0g
Fat 7.1g (sat 2.3g) **Carbohydrate** 41.3g
Fiber 0.7g **Cholesterol** 30mg **Iron** 1.9mg
Sodium 122mg **Calcium** 102mg

MERINGUE ALERT

Over the past few years, you may have heard warnings about the health risks of eating uncooked eggs. The latest recommendation from the United States Department of Agriculture (USDA) is that all eggs be thoroughly cooked. We've modified our recipe for meringues to make sure that they are safe to eat.

We now recommend that you bake any pie with a meringue at 325° for 25 minutes, as in our recipe for Coconut Cream Pie on page 212. You can use the same procedure in this recipe for any of your own meringue pies.

For a quick no-bake pie topping, use reduced-calorie whipped topping, as we did for Butterscotch Cream Pie (at left).

Coconut Cream Pie

1   cup vanilla wafer crumbs
     (26 wafers)
2   tablespoons reduced-calorie
     margarine, melted
Vegetable cooking spray
⅓   cup plus 1 tablespoon sugar
3   tablespoons cornstarch
¼   teaspoon salt
2½   cups skim milk
2   egg yolks, lightly beaten
½   cup plus 1 tablespoon flaked
     coconut, divided
1   teaspoon vanilla extract
½   teaspoon imitation coconut
     extract
3   egg whites
3   tablespoons sugar

Combine crumbs and margarine
in a bowl, and stir well. Press into
bottom and up sides of a 9-inch
pieplate coated with cooking spray.
Bake at 350° for 10 minutes; cool
on a wire rack.

Combine ⅓ cup plus 1 tablespoon
sugar, cornstarch, and salt in a
heavy saucepan; gradually stir in
milk. Cook over medium heat, stirring constantly with a wire whisk,
until mixture comes to a boil. Cook
mixture 1 additional minute, and
remove from heat.

Gradually stir one-fourth of hot
mixture into yolks, and add to
remaining hot mixture. Cook over
medium heat, stirring constantly, 2
minutes or until mixture thickens.
Remove from heat, and stir in ½
cup coconut, vanilla, and coconut
extract. Cover with plastic wrap,
and set aside.

Beat egg whites at high speed of an
electric mixer until foamy. Gradually add 3 tablespoons sugar, 1
tablespoon at a time, beating until
stiff peaks form and sugar dissolves
(2 to 4 minutes).

Pour hot filling into prepared
crust. Spread egg white mixture over
hot filling, sealing to edge of crust.
Sprinkle with remaining 1 tablespoon coconut. Bake at 325° for 25
minutes or until golden. Cool completely on a wire rack. Yield: 9 servings (serving size: 1 slice).

Calories 220 (36% from fat) **Protein** 4.9g
Fat 8.8g (sat 3.5g) **Carbohydrate** 29.9g
Fiber 0.3g **Cholesterol** 50mg **Iron** 0.5mg
Sodium 219mg **Calcium** 97mg

EDITOR'S CHOICE

*"I first made Mocha
Fudge Pie for my
wife's birthday, and
now we serve it at other special
occasions, too. Every soul who has
tasted it has raved about it—
including me."*

——Doug Crichton, Editor

*"This is my favorite
because it's chocolate,
quick, easy, impressive,
and delicious. I especially like
Mocha Fudge Pie because it uses
convenience products that save me
time, yet it doesn't taste like it
came out of a box."*

——Leigh Fran Jones,
Test Kitchens Staff

Mocha Fudge Pie

QUICK & EASY

⅓   cup hot water
4   teaspoons instant coffee
     granules, divided
½   (19.85-ounce) box light
     fudge brownie mix (about
     2 cups)
2   teaspoons vanilla extract,
     divided
2   egg whites
Vegetable cooking spray
¾   cup 1% low-fat milk
3   tablespoons Kahlúa or other
     coffee-flavored liqueur,
     divided
1   (3.9-ounce) package
     chocolate-flavored instant
     pudding-and-pie filling mix
3   cups frozen reduced-calorie
     whipped topping, thawed
     and divided
Chocolate curls (optional)

Combine hot water and 2 teaspoons coffee granules in a medium
bowl; stir well. Add brownie mix, 1
teaspoon vanilla, and egg whites;
stir until well blended. Pour mixture
into a 9-inch pieplate coated with
cooking spray. Bake at 325° for 22
minutes. Let crust cool completely.

Combine milk, 2 tablespoons
Kahlúa, 1 teaspoon coffee granules,
remaining 1 teaspoon vanilla, and
pudding mix in a bowl; beat at
medium speed of an electric mixer
1 minute. Gently fold in 1½ cups
whipped topping. Spread pudding
mixture evenly over brownie crust.

Mocha Fudge Pie

Combine remaining 1 teaspoon coffee granules and remaining 1 tablespoon Kahlúa in a bowl; stir well. Gently fold in remaining 1½ cups whipped topping. Spread whipped topping mixture over pudding mixture. Garnish with chocolate curls, if desired. Serve immediately, or store loosely covered in refrigerator. Yield: 8 servings (serving size: 1 slice).

Nonalcoholic Mocha Version: When making the pudding mixture, substitute 2 tablespoons 1% low-fat milk for the Kahlúa. In the topping, omit the Kahlúa, and dissolve the instant coffee granules in 1 tablespoon water.

Calories 292 (22% from fat) **Protein** 4.4g **Fat** 7.0g (sat 5.3g) **Carbohydrate** 51.5g **Fiber** 0.0g **Cholesterol** 1mg **Iron** 0.8mg **Sodium** 345mg **Calcium** 47mg

Note: Store remaining brownie mix in a heavy-duty, zip-top plastic bag in refrigerator; use mix to make another pie or a small pan of brownies. To make brownies, combine about 2 cups mix, ¼ cup water, and 1 lightly beaten egg white in a bowl. Stir just until combined. Spread in an 8-inch square pan coated with cooking spray. Bake at 350° for 23 to 25 minutes.

HONEY-GRAPEFRUIT GRANITA

1⅓ cups Basic Sugar Syrup
4   cups fresh pink grapefruit juice (about 10 large grapefruit)
⅓   cup honey

Prepare Basic Sugar Syrup. Combine 1⅓ cups syrup and juice in a large bowl, and stir well. Set mixture aside.

Place honey in a small bowl. Microwave at HIGH 30 seconds or until warm. Add to juice mixture; stir well. Pour mixture into a 13- x 9- x 2-inch dish; cover and freeze at least 8 hours or until firm.

Remove mixture from freezer, and scrape entire mixture with the tines of a fork until fluffy. Spoon into a freezer-safe container; cover and freeze up to 1 month. Yield: 6 cups (serving size: 1 cup).

Calories 248 (1% from fat) **Protein** 0.9g **Fat** 0.2g (sat 0.0g) **Carbohydrate** 63.7g **Fiber** 0.0g **Cholesterol** 0mg **Iron** 3.4mg **Sodium** 2mg **Calcium** 13mg

BASIC SUGAR SYRUP:

2¼ cups sugar
2   cups water

Combine sugar and water in a large saucepan, and stir well. Bring sugar mixture to a boil, and cook, stirring constantly, 1 minute or until sugar dissolves. Store sugar syrup in an airtight container in the refrigerator. Yield: 3 cups.

Fresh Orange Sorbet

FRESH ORANGE SORBET

To get fresh juice for this sorbet, you'll need about 10 medium-size oranges and 2 medium-size lemons.

2½ cups water
1 cup sugar
Orange rind strips from 2
   oranges
2⅔ cups fresh orange juice
⅓ cup fresh lemon juice
Orange rind curls (optional)

Combine water and sugar in a small saucepan, and bring mixture to a boil. Add orange rind strips; reduce heat, and simmer 5 minutes. Remove and discard orange rind strips. Remove liquid from heat, and let cool completely. Stir in orange juice and lemon juice.

Pour mixture into freezer container of a 4-quart hand-turned or electric freezer. Freeze according to manufacturer's instructions. Pack freezer with additional ice and rock salt; let mixture stand in freezer 1 hour before serving.

Scoop sorbet into individual bowls. Garnish with orange rind curls, if desired. Serve immediately. Yield: 6 cups (serving size: ¾ cup).

Calories 182 (0% from fat) **Protein** 0.8g
Fat 0.1g (sat 0.0g) **Carbohydrate** 46.4g
Fiber 0.2g **Cholesterol** 0mg **Iron** 0.1mg
Sodium 11mg **Calcium** 4mg

NECTARINE-DAIQUIRI SORBET

1 cup sugar
2 cups water
4 cups sliced unpeeled fresh
   nectarines (about 1½
   pounds)
½ cup fresh lime juice
½ cup light rum

Combine sugar and water in a saucepan. Cook over medium heat, stirring until sugar dissolves. Remove from heat, and cool. Set mixture aside.

Position knife blade in food processor bowl. Add nectarines, lime juice, and rum, and process until smooth. Spoon nectarine mixture into a bowl; add sugar mixture, and stir well.

Pour mixture into freezer container of a 4-quart hand-turned or electric freezer; freeze according to manufacturer's instructions. Pack freezer with additional ice and rock salt. Let sorbet stand 1 hour before serving. Yield: 16 servings (serving size: ½ cup).

Calories 83 (2% from fat) **Protein** 0.3g
Fat 0.2g (sat 0.0g) **Carbohydrate** 17.2g
Fiber 0.8g **Cholesterol** 0mg **Iron** 0.1mg
Sodium 0mg **Calcium** 2mg

HEAVENLY LEMON SHERBET

When removing the yellow rind, be careful not to remove any of the white pith underneath, or your sherbet will taste bitter.

1 lemon
1 cup sugar
3 cups 2% low-fat milk
½ cup fresh lemon juice
½ cup water
⅛ teaspoon salt

Using a vegetable peeler, carefully remove rind from lemon.

Position knife blade in food processor bowl, and add rind and sugar; process until rind is minced. Spoon sugar mixture into a bowl. Add milk and remaining 3 ingredients; stir well.

Pour lemon mixture into freezer container of a 4-quart hand-turned or electric freezer, and freeze according to manufacturer's instructions. Pack freezer with additional ice and rock salt; let stand 1 hour before serving. Yield: 5½ cups (serving size: ½ cup).

Calories 108 (11% from fat) **Protein** 2.4g
Fat 1.3g (sat 0.8g) **Carbohydrate** 23.4g
Fiber 0.0g **Cholesterol** 5mg **Iron** 0.1mg
Sodium 60mg **Calcium** 88mg

Chocolate Chip Bars

¼ cup plus 2 tablespoons
  margarine, softened
⅓ cup sugar
¾ cup firmly packed dark
  brown sugar
2 egg whites
2 teaspoons vanilla extract
2½ cups all-purpose flour
½ teaspoon baking soda
⅛ teaspoon salt
½ cup semisweet chocolate
  mini-morsels
Vegetable cooking spray

Beat margarine at medium speed of an electric mixer until creamy. Gradually add sugars, beating well. Add egg whites, one at a time, beating mixture well after each addition. Stir in vanilla.

Combine flour, baking soda, and salt; gradually add to margarine mixture, beating well. Stir in chocolate morsels.

Press dough into bottom of a 13- x 9- x 2-inch pan coated with cooking spray. Bake at 375° for 10 minutes. Cool in pan. Yield: 4 dozen (serving size: 1 bar).

Calories 67 (30% from fat) **Protein** 0.9g **Fat** 2.2g (sat 0.7g) **Carbohydrate** 11.0g **Fiber** 0.2g **Cholesterol** 0mg **Iron** 0.4mg **Sodium** 35mg **Calcium** 7mg

Fudgy Mint Brownies

¼ cup margarine, softened
¾ cup sugar
2 tablespoons water
2 teaspoons vanilla extract
1 egg
¾ cup all-purpose flour
¼ teaspoon baking powder
⅛ teaspoon salt
⅓ cup unsweetened cocoa
8 hard round peppermint
  candy pieces, finely crushed
1 egg white
Vegetable cooking spray

Beat margarine at medium speed of an electric mixer until creamy; gradually add sugar, beating mixture well. Add water, vanilla, and egg, and beat well.

Combine flour and next 4 ingredients; add to margarine mixture, stirring just until dry ingredients are moistened. Set aside.

Beat egg white at high speed of mixer until stiff peaks form; gently fold into cocoa mixture.

Pour into an 8-inch square pan coated with cooking spray. Bake at 350° for 25 minutes. Cool in pan on a wire rack. Yield: 12 brownies (serving size: one 2½- x 2-inch bar).

Calories 144 (30% from fat) **Protein** 2.4g **Fat** 4.8g (sat 1.1g) **Carbohydrate** 23.0g **Fiber** 0.2g **Cholesterol** 19mg **Iron** 0.9mg **Sodium** 87mg **Calcium** 14mg

Ginger Cookies

¼ cup plus 2 tablespoons
  margarine, softened
⅔ cup plus 3 tablespoons
  sugar, divided
¼ cup molasses
1 egg
2 cups all-purpose flour
2 teaspoons baking soda
1 teaspoon ground ginger
1 teaspoon ground cinnamon
½ teaspoon ground mace
Vegetable cooking spray

Beat margarine at medium speed of an electric mixer until creamy; gradually add ⅔ cup sugar, beating mixture well. Add molasses and egg, and beat well.

Combine flour, baking soda, ginger, cinnamon, and mace. Gradually add flour mixture to margarine mixture, stirring until well blended. Divide dough in half; wrap each portion of dough in plastic wrap. Freeze dough 30 minutes.

Shape each portion of dough into 26 (1-inch) balls. Roll balls in remaining 3 tablespoons sugar. Place 2 inches apart on cookie sheets coated with cooking spray. Bake at 350° for 12 minutes or until cookies are lightly browned. Remove from cookie sheets; cool on wire racks. Store cookies in an airtight container. Yield: 52 cookies (serving size: 1 cookie).

Calories 46 (29% from fat) **Protein** 0.6g **Fat** 1.5g (sat 0.3g) **Carbohydrate** 7.7g **Fiber** 0.1g **Cholesterol** 4mg **Iron** 0.3mg **Sodium** 49mg **Calcium** 13mg

It's 5 P.M. Do you know what you're cooking for dinner tonight? Believe it or not, we know the feeling. That's why we thought you'd appreciate the following planned quick and easy menus.

EASY MENUS

For a sweet ending to any menu, try one of these no-cook dessert ideas:

• Dollop fresh blueberries with lemon low-fat yogurt. • Drizzle fresh peaches, cantaloupe or honeydew melon with honey, lime juice, and grated lime rind. • Pile fresh strawberries into large, stemmed glasses, and add a generous splash of champagne.

• Serve a scoop of frozen vanilla nonfat yogurt topped with maple syrup, a dash of cinnamon, and toasted chopped walnuts.

• Combine fresh raspberries with blueberries, and serve over pineapple sherbet.

SIMPLE SPAGHETTI SUPPER

Serves 4
Calories per serving: 440
(Calories from fat: 25%)

•Greek Spaghetti With Tomatoes and Feta
(page 92)

•Creamy Cucumber Dressing
(page 135) with mixed greens
(1½ cups serving greens and 1½ tablespoons dressing)

French hard rolls
(1 each)
Toss torn curly leaf lettuce with Creamy Cucumber
Dressing. If desired, add other vegetables like red
onions or green pepper rings to your salad.

EASY GRILLED SUPPER

Serves 4
Calories per serving: 527
(Calories from fat: 25%)

•Hawaiian Chicken
(page 104)

Yellow rice
(¾ cup serving)

Steamed broccoli with lemon slices
(½ cup serving)

Trim 1 pound broccoli; remove tough ends. Cut into
spears. Arrange in a vegetable steamer over boiling
water. Cover; steam 5 to 8 minutes or until crisp-tender.

IT'S A CHILI KIND OF DAY

Serves 8
Calories per serving: 395
(Calories from fat: 19%)

•Chili Mac
(page 95)

•Chile Corn Sticks
(page 35)

QUICK SKILLET DINNER

Serves 4
Calories per serving: 547
(Calories from fat: 12%)

•Three-Pepper Pork Cutlets
(page 85)

Steamed fresh green beans with fresh lemon juice
(1 cup serving)

Hot cooked wild rice
(½ cup serving)

Trim ends of green beans. Arrange 1 pound green beans in a vegetable steamer over boiling water. Cover and steam 3 minutes.

EASY & IMPRESSIVE DINNER

Serves 2
Calories per serving: 571
(Calories from fat: 20%)

•Chicken Cutlets With Peppers and Mushrooms
(page 109)

•Herbed Basmati Rice
(page 177)

Hoagie rolls
(1 each)

EASY, FRESH & FIT FOR COMPANY

Serves 4
Calories per serving: 503
(Calories from fat: 12%)

•Glazed Mahimahi
(page 49)

•Fresh Tomato-Squash Salad
(page 126)

Hot cooked orzo
(¾ cup serving)

QUICK & HEARTY
SALAD MEAL

Serves 4
Calories per serving: 433
(Calories from fat: 14%)

•Southwestern Turkey and Black Bean Salad
(page 131)

Flour tortillas
(1 each)

FAST & FANCY
SUMMER BRUNCH

Serves 6
Calories per serving: 257
(Calories from fat: 26%)

•Fresh Tomato and Basil Quiche
(page 61)

Fresh fruit

For a fresh fruit side, slice 1 medium cantaloupe into 18 slices, and serve with mixed berries. We suggest strawberries and blackberries.

HOW TO
LIGHTEN UP

Here's your chance to learn the most important secrets from the *Cooking Light* test kitchens. Over the years, we've experimented with cooking techniques, new products, special equipment, and flavor combinations to create the delicious, satisfying, and healthy recipes you've come to expect. We hope you'll try out these ideas on your own favorite recipes to make them healthier, but still great tasting.

USE BIG, BOLD FLAVORS ▶

It's true. Fat has flavor. So when you take out the fat, it's only natural that you need to add some flavor back. Here are some ways we do it:

•**Splash on high-flavored ingredients** like infused vinegars and oils (a little goes a long way).

•**Cook with low-fat, flavor-packed fresh herbs,** pungent spices, tart citrus, and hot chiles.

•**Add extra flavor** to rice by cooking it in broth, or by cooking it in orange juice and water.

•**Sauté vegetables in a little broth,** wine, or fruit juice for a flavor boost.

•**Spread on flavor with mustards,** salsas, or low-fat salad dressings.

REMEMBER THAT LESS IS MORE ▶

By using just a little of some products, you can get more flavor, more fat savings, and a recipe that's better for you.

•**Use a small amount of "real" ingredients** richest in flavor, like freshly grated Parmesan cheese or pecans on top of breads, rolls, or loaves.

•**Use less salt** to allow the natural flavors of food to come through. Or, add fresh herbs or spices instead of salt.

•**Eat no more than 6 ounces of cooked lean meat,** fish, or poultry a day. In fact, you might consider meat a side dish and grains or vegetables as the main dish once each week.

•**Spray pans with vegetable cooking spray** instead of greasing them with oil, shortening, butter, or lard.

USE LOW-FAT INGREDIENTS ▶

•**Make your own low-fat chips,** bagels or tortillas, and save fat grams. (See page 13 for directions.)

•**Substitute low-fat or nonfat products for regular products.** Try a variety of low-fat and nonfat products to see which ones you like. (See the low-fat substitution chart inside the back cover.)

•**Use applesauce or prune puree** as a replacement for some of the fat in bread or desserts.

•**Remove skin** from chicken or turkey either before or after cooking it.

LEARN THE TECHNIQUES ▶

Here are some techniques that have become standard practice in the *Cooking Light* test kitchens:

•**Toast spices, nuts, and seeds** to bring out a more pronounced flavor. Stir dried spices or seeds for a few minutes in a hot skillet (with or without oil). To toast nuts, spread them in a shallow pan, and bake at 350° for 10 to 15 minutes, stirring occasionally.

•**Bake, broil, roast, grill, poach, or microwave** whenever possible. Use a meat rack to allow fat to drip away.

•**Use scented chips** when grilling. Just make sure to soak the chips at least 30 minutes so they will smoke and not burn. (See the step-by-step technique on page 52.)

•**Marinate meats** in a heavy-duty, zip-top plastic bag. The bag takes little space in the refrigerator, and it's convenient to turn the bag over to make sure all of the food takes on the flavor.

•**Roast peppers and other vegetables** in your oven to bring out a rich, roasted flavor. (See the step-by-step technique on page 167.)

HAVE THE RIGHT EQUIPMENT ▶

•**Use the following equipment to make light cooking easier:** grill basket, nonstick skillet or wok, roasting pan, fat skimmer, steamer basket, pressure cooker, smoker, and microwave.

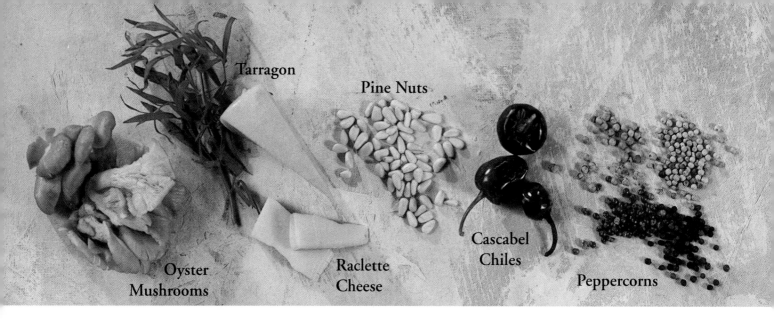

Tarragon

Pine Nuts

Cascabel
Chiles

Oyster
Mushrooms

Raclette
Cheese

Peppercorns

PICTORIAL

•**Annatto seeds,** or achiote seeds, are used more for the yellow color they add to foods rather than their flavor. They're available whole or ground in Indian or Spanish specialty stores.

•**Asiago** is a semifirm to hard Italian cheese with a nutty, sharp flavor and a light yellow interior with holes.

•**Bulgur** is a nutty wheat product made when whole wheat kernels are soaked, cooked, and dried. After some of the bran is removed, the kernel is cracked into small pieces.

•**Cardamom seeds** are aromatic seeds that provide a spicy-sweet flavor. Ground cardamom is one of the most expensive spices in the world and can be found in most spice sections.

•**Cascabel chiles** are dried chiles with a rich, smoky, woodsy flavor. They often are used in salsas and stews.

•**Cilantro** is the green, feathery leaf of the coriander herb. It looks like parsley and has a strong, lemony flavor.

•**Couscous** is a bead-shaped pasta that's a culinary specialty of North Africa. A flour coating keeps the grains separate when cooked.

•**Crimini mushrooms** have a robust, earthy flavor and look like a dark version of button mushrooms.

•**Currants** are tiny seedless raisins. Dried currants can be found next to the raisins in your supermarket.

•**Gingerroot** is a knobby, brown root that adds a spicy-hot flavor to food.

The freshest are thick and unshriveled and can be found in produce sections of supermarkets and in Asian stores.

•**Goat cheese** is a soft creamy white cheese with a distinct, slightly sour taste. It is found in gourmet cheese sections of supermarkets.

•**Gouda** is a semisoft to hard cheese that is smooth with small holes. Flavor ranges from mild and nutty when young to sharp when aged.

•**Gruyère (groo-YEHR)** is a nutty, firm cheese with small holes. It's similar to Swiss cheese. It's good for shredding, slicing, snacking, or cooking.

•**Habanero chiles** are small, bright chiles considered to be the hottest in the world. They're interchangeable

Cardamom
Seeds

Gouda Cheese

Asiago Cheese

Shallots

Annatto Seeds

Portobello
Mushrooms

Gingerroot

Couscous

Shiitake Mushrooms

Gruyère Cheese

Serrano Chiles

GLOSSARY

with Scotch bonnet chiles. Use rubber gloves when handling.

•**Oyster mushrooms** have a peppery, robust flavor. This Asian mushroom is pale cream to gray and has a large, flowerlike cap and a short, fat stem.

•**Pearl barley** is barley with the hull removed. It is the most popular form for cooking and adds a nutty flavor and chewy texture to soups and casseroles. Use ¾ cup uncooked pearl barley to yield 3 cups cooked barley.

•**Peppercorns** are berries that grow in grapelike clusters on a pepper plant native to India. The most common types are black, white, green, and pink. They are usually sold in jars on the spice shelf in large supermarkets.

•**Pine nuts**, or pignolia, are small, oblong nuts gathered from pine trees. They are expensive and high in fat, but their strong flavor makes a little go a long way. Pine nuts can be eaten raw or toasted.

•**Portobello mushrooms** are large mushrooms with a meaty texture and a full-bodied flavor that makes them ideal for meatless main dishes.

•**Raclette cheese** gets its name from the French word *racler*, which means "to scrape." When heated, this nutty, mellow cheese melts to make a good spread for bread or boiled potatoes.

•**Serrano chiles** are tiny, slightly pointed, green to yellow chiles. These fiery-hot chiles are available fresh in

most supermarkets and are easily interchanged with jalapeños.

•**Shallots** are tiny, delicate-flavored onions, which are often used in French cooking. They are considered the backbone of many French sauces.

•**Shiitake (she-TAHK-ee) mushrooms** taste almost like steak. They are sometimes called forest mushrooms or Chinese black mushrooms. To use dried ones, cut off the tough stems, rehydrate the caps in hot water, and chop. Look for them in produce or ethnic food sections of supermarkets and in Asian groceries.

•**Tarragon** is an aromatic, slender-leafed herb that tastes like licorice. It's used often to make flavored vinegars.

Bulgur

Habanero Chiles

Pearl Barley

Goat Cheese

Crimini Mushrooms

Currants

Cilantro

VEGETABLE COOKING CHART

VEGETABLE	SERVINGS	PREPARATION	COOKING INSTRUCTIONS (Add salt, if desired)
Asparagus	3 to 4 per pound	Snap off tough ends. Remove scales, if desired.	To boil: cook, covered, in small amount of boiling water 6 to 8 minutes or until crisp-tender. To steam: cook, covered, on a rack above boiling water 8 to 12 minutes.
Beans, dried (also peas, dried)	6 to 8 per pound	Sort and wash beans. Cover with water 2 inches above beans; soak overnight. Drain.	Cover soaked beans with water. Bring to a boil; cover, reduce heat, and simmer 1½ to 2 hours or until tender.
Beans, green	4 per pound	Wash; trim ends, and remove strings. Cut into 1½-inch pieces.	Cook, covered, in small amount of boiling water 12 to 15 minutes.
Beets	3 to 4 per pound	Leave root and 1 inch of stem; scrub with vegetable brush.	Cook, covered, in boiling water 35 to 40 minutes. Remove peel.
Broccoli	3 to 4 per pound	Remove outer leaves and tough ends of lower stalks. Wash; cut into spears.	To boil: cook, covered, in small amount of boiling water 10 to 15 minutes. To steam: cook, covered, on a rack above boiling water 15 to 20 minutes.
Brussels Sprouts	4 per pound	Wash; remove discolored leaves. Cut off stem ends; slash bottom with an X.	Cook, covered, in small amount of boiling water 8 to 10 minutes.
Cabbage	4 per pound	Remove outer leaves; wash. Shred or cut into wedges.	Cook, covered, in small amount of boiling water 5 to 7 minutes (shredded) or 10 to 15 minutes (wedges).
Carrots	4 per pound	Scrape; remove ends, and rinse. Leave tiny carrots whole; slice large carrots, or cut into strips.	Cook, covered, in small amount of boiling water 8 to 10 minutes (slices) or 12 to 15 minutes (strips).
Cauliflower	4 per medium head	Remove outer leaves and stalk. Wash. Leave whole, or break into flowerets.	Cook, covered, in small amount of boiling water 10 to 12 minutes (whole) or 8 to 10 minutes (flowerets).
Corn	4 per 4 large ears	Remove husks and silks. Leave corn on the cob, or cut off tips of kernels, and scrape cob with dull edge of knife.	Cook, covered, in boiling water to cover 10 minutes (on cob) or in small amount boiling water 8 to 10 minutes (cut).
Eggplant	2 to 3 per pound	Wash and peel. Cut into cubes, or cut crosswise into slices.	To boil: cook, covered, in small amount of boiling water 8 to 10 minutes. To sauté: cook in small amount of margarine or vegetable oil 5 to 8 minutes.
Greens	3 to 4 per pound	Remove stems; wash thoroughly. Tear into bite-size pieces.	Cook, covered, in 1 to 1½-inch boiling water 5 to 8 minutes (spinach), 10 to 20 minutes (Swiss chard), 30 to 45 minutes (collards, turnip greens, mustard, kale).
Okra	4 per pound	Wash and pat dry. Trim ends.	Cook, covered, in small amount of boiling water 5 to 10 minutes

VEGETABLE COOKING CHART

VEGETABLE	SERVINGS	PREPARATION	COOKING INSTRUCTIONS (Add salt, if desired)
Onions	4 per pound	Peel; cut large onions into quarters or slices, or leave small onions whole.	Cook, covered, in small amount of boiling water 15 minutes or until tender. Or sauté slices in margarine 3 to 5 minutes.
Peas, snow	4 per pound	Wash; trim ends, and remove tough strings.	Cook, covered, in small amount of boiling water 3 to 5 minutes, or sauté in vegetable oil or margarine 3 to 5 minutes.
Peppers, green	1 per medium pepper	Cut off top, and remove seeds. Leave whole to stuff and bake; cut into thin slices or strips to sauté.	To bake: cook, covered, in boiling water 5 minutes; stuff and bake at 350° for 15 to 25 minutes. To sauté: cook in small amount of margarine or vegetable oil 3 to 5 minutes.
Potatoes, all-purpose or small red	3 to 4 per pound	Scrub potatoes; peel, if desired. Leave whole, or slice or cut into chunks.	To cook: cook, covered, in small amount of boiling water 30 to 40 minutes (whole) or 15 to 20 minutes (slices or chunks). To bake: bake at 400° for 1 hour or until done.
Potatoes, sweet	2 to 3 per pound	Scrub potatoes; leave whole to bake, or slice or cut into chunks to boil.	To bake: bake at 375° for 1 hour or until done. To boil: cook in boiling water to cover for 20 to 30 minutes.
Pumpkin	4½ to 5 cups cooked, mashed pumpkin per one 5-pound pumpkin	Slice in half crosswise. Remove seeds.	Place, cut side down, on baking pan. Add water to a depth of ½ inch. Bake at 325° for 45 minutes or until tender. Cool; peel and mash.
Squash, summer	3 to 4 per pound	Wash; trim ends. Leave whole, slice, or dice.	To boil: cook, covered, in small amount of boiling water 8 to 10 minutes (slices) or 15 minutes (whole). To steam: cook, covered, on a rack over boiling water 10 to 12 minutes (sliced or diced).
Squash, winter (*including acorn, butternut, hubbard, spaghetti*)	2 per pound	Rinse; cut in half, and remove seeds.	To boil: cook, covered, in boiling water 20 to 25 minutes. To bake: place, cut side down, in shallow baking dish; add ½ inch water. Bake, uncovered, at 375° for 30 minutes. Turn and season or fill; bake 20 to 30 minutes or until tender.
Tomatoes	4 per pound (*2 large tomatoes*)	Wash; peel, if desired. Slice or cut into quarters.	Generally served raw or used as ingredient in cooked dishes.
Turnips	3 per pound	Wash; peel, and slice or cube.	Cook, covered, in boiling water to cover 15 to 20 minutes or until tender.

The recipes that appear in this cookbook use the standard United States method for measuring liquid and dry or solid ingredients (teaspoons, tablespoons, and cups). The information in the following charts is provided to help cooks outside the U.S. successfully use these recipes. All equivalents are approximate.

Metric Equivalents for Different Types of Ingredients

A standard cup measure of a dry or solid ingredient will vary in weight depending on the type of ingredient. A standard cup of liquid is the same volume for any type of liquid. Use the following chart when converting standard cup measures to grams (weight) or milliliters (volume).

Standard Cup	Fine Powder (ex. flour)	Grain (ex. rice)	Granular (ex. sugar)	Liquid Solids (ex. butter)	Liquid (ex. milk)
1	140 g	150 g	190 g	200 g	240 ml
¾	105 g	113 g	143 g	150 g	180 ml
⅔	93 g	100 g	125 g	133 g	160 ml
½	70 g	75 g	95 g	100 g	120 ml
⅓	47 g	50 g	63 g	67 g	80 ml
¼	35 g	38 g	48 g	50 g	60 ml
⅛	18 g	19 g	24 g	25 g	30 ml

Useful Equivalents for Dry Ingredients by Weight

(To convert ounces to grams, multiply the number of ounces by 30)

1 oz	=	¹⁄₁₆ lb	=	30 g
4 oz	=	¼ lb	=	120 g
8 oz	=	½ lb	=	240 g
12 oz	=	¾ lb	=	360 g
16 oz	=	1 lb	=	480 g

Useful Equivalents for Length

(To convert inches to centimeters, multiply the number of inches by 2.5)

1 in				=	2.5 cm	
6 in	=	½ ft		=	15 cm	
12 in	=	1 ft		=	30 cm	
36 in	=	3 ft	= 1 yd	=	90 cm	
40 in				=	100 cm	= 1 m

Useful Equivalents for Liquid Ingredients by Volume

¼ tsp						=	1 ml	
½ tsp						=	2 ml	
1 tsp						=	5 ml	
3 tsp	=	1 tbls			=	½ fl oz	=	15 ml
		2 tbls	=	⅛ cup	=	1 fl oz	=	30 ml
		4 tbls	=	¼ cup	=	2 fl oz	=	60 ml
		5⅓ tbls	=	⅓ cup	=	3 fl oz	=	80 ml
		8 tbls	=	½ cup	=	4 fl oz	=	120 ml
		10⅔ tbls	=	⅔ cup	=	5 fl oz	=	160 ml
		12 tbls	=	¾ cup	=	6 fl oz	=	180 ml
		16 tbls	=	1 cup	=	8 fl oz	=	240 ml
		1 pt	=	2 cups	=	16 fl oz	=	480 ml
		1 qt	=	4 cups	=	32 fl oz	=	960 ml
						33 fl oz	=	1000 ml = 1 l

Useful Equivalents for Cooking/Oven Temperatures

	Fahrenheit	Celsius	Gas Mark
Freeze Water	32° F	0° C	
Room Temperature	68° F	20° C	
Boil Water	212° F	100° C	
Bake	325° F	160° C	3
	350° F	180° C	4
	375° F	190° C	5
	400° F	200° C	6
	425° F	220° C	7
	450° F	230° C	8
Broil			Grill

EQUIVALENT WEIGHTS & MEASURES

FOOD	WEIGHT OR COUNT	MEASURE OR YIELD
Apples	1 pound (3 medium)	3 cups sliced
Bananas	1 pound (3 medium)	2½ cups sliced or about 2 cups mashed
Bread	1 pound	12 to 16 slices
	about 1½ slices	1 cup soft crumbs
Cabbage	1 pound head	4½ cups shredded
Carrots	1 pound	3 cups shredded
Cottage cheese	1 pound	2 cups
Chocolate morsels	6-ounce package	1 cup
Coffee	1 pound	80 tablespoons (40 cups perked)
Corn	2 medium ears	1 cup kernels
Cornmeal	1 pound	3 cups
Crackers, graham crackers	14 squares	1 cup fine crumbs
saltine crackers	28 crackers	1 cup finely crushed
vanilla wafers	22 wafers	1 cup finely crushed
Flour, all-purpose or whole wheat	1 pound	3½ cups unsifted
Green pepper	1 large	1 cup diced
Lemon	1 medium	2 to 3 tablespoons juice; 2 teaspoons grated rind
Lettuce	1 pound head	6¼ cups torn
Macaroni	4 ounces dry (1 cup)	2½ cups cooked
Mushrooms	3 cups raw (8 ounces)	1 cup sliced cooked
Nuts, pecans	1 pound	2¼ cups nutmeats
walnuts	1 pound	1⅔ cups nutmeats
Oats, quick cooking	1 cup	1¾ cups cooked
Onion	1 medium	½ cup chopped
Orange	1 medium	⅓ cup juice; 2 tablespoons grated rind
Peaches or Pears	2 medium	1 cup sliced
Potatoes, white	3 medium	2 cups cubed cooked or 1¾ cups mashed
sweet	3 medium	3 cups sliced
Raisins, seedless	1 pound	3 cups
Rice, long-grain	1 cup	3 cups cooked
precooked	1 cup	2 cups cooked
Shrimp, raw in shell	1½ pounds	2 cups (¾ pound) cleaned, cooked
Spaghetti	8 ounces dry	4 to 5 cups cooked
Strawberries	1 quart	4 cups sliced
Sugar, brown	1 pound	2⅓ cups firmly packed
powdered	1 pound	3½ cups unsifted
Tomato	2½ pounds	3 cups seeded, chopped, and drained

NUTRIENT ANALYSIS

The nutritional information at the end of each recipe helps you fit these dishes into your daily eating plan.

HOW TO USE IT, AND WHY

Glance at the end of our recipes, and you'll see how committed we are to helping you make the best of today's light cooking. Using the registered dietitians and foods professionals of *Cooking Light* and Oxmoor House, along with a computer system that analyzes every ingredient used in each recipe, we give you authoritative nutritional information.

We go to such lengths so you can see how *Cooking Light* recipes fit into your healthy eating plan. If you are trying to lose weight, the calorie and fat figures will help you the most. And if you are keeping a close eye on the sodium and cholesterol in your diet, we provide these numbers, too. Since many women don't get enough iron or calcium, we can help you there as well. Finally, there's a fiber analysis to help those of us—which is most of us—who don't get the roughage we need.

WHAT IT MEANS, AND HOW WE GET THERE

Besides the calories and nutrients we list at the end of each recipe, there are a few things we abbreviate for space.

> *g* for gram
> *mg* for milligram
> *sat* for saturated fat

Keep in mind that some alcohol calories evaporate when the food is heated, and our calculations for the nutrient grid reflect that adjustment. Also, only the amount of a marinade that is actually absorbed by the food is calculated.

When we give a range for an ingredient (3 to 3½ cups flour, for instance), we calculate the lesser amount.

Your calorie requirements will vary according to your size, weight, and level of physical activity. The chart at the bottom of this page is a general guide for most people. Pregnant and breast-feeding women need more protein and calories.

UNDERSTANDING PERCENTAGE OF CALORIES FROM FAT

Our recipes also list the percentage of calories derived from fat, because current dietary recommendations encourage eating no more than 30% of total calories from fat. This recommendation applies to the total diet, however—not to individual recipes. Most *Cooking Light* recipes contain no more than 30% of calories from fat; those recipes that do exceed that figure are carefully evaluated by our team of registered dietitians to trim the fat as much as possible, without sacrificing flavor and texture.

YOUR DAILY NUTRITION GUIDE			
	Women ages 25 to 50	Women over 50	Men over 24
Calories	2,000	2,000 or less	2,700
Protein	50g	50g or less	63g
Fat	67g or less	67g or less	90g or less
Carbohydrates	299g	299g	405g
Fiber	25g to 35g	25g to 35g	25g to 35g
Cholesterol	300mg or less	300mg or less	300mg or less
Iron	15mg	10mg	10mg
Sodium	2,400mg or less	2,400mg or less	2,400mg or less
Calcium	800mg	800mg	800mg

The nutritional values used in our calculations either come from a computer program produced by Computrition Inc., or are provided by food manufacturers.

GENERAL RECIPE INDEX

Recipe Title Index

All recipes in red are Quick & Easy.

✯ ✯ ✯ ✯ ✯
EDITOR'S CHOICE RECIPES

TIPS & TECHNIQUES

Turn the page to find low-fat and handy substitution charts.